Crossing Law's Border

Law and Society Series
W. Wesley Pue, Founding Editor

We pay tribute to the late Wes Pue, under whose broad vision, extraordinary leadership, and unwavering commitment to sociolegal studies our Law and Society Series was established and rose to prominence.

The Law and Society Series explores law as a socially embedded phenomenon. It is premised on the understanding that the conventional division of law from society creates false dichotomies in thinking, scholarship, educational practice, and social life. Books in the series treat law and society as mutually constitutive and seek to bridge scholarship emerging from interdisciplinary engagement of law with disciplines such as politics, social theory, history, political economy, and gender studies.

Recent books in the series include:

L. Jane McMillan, *Truth and Conviction: Donald Marshall Jr. and the Mi'kmaw Quest for Justice* (2018)

Sarah Grace Marsden, *Enforcing Exclusion: Precarious Migrants and the Law in Canada* (2018)

Jasminka Kalajdzic, *Class Actions in Canada: The Promise and Reality of Access to Justice* (2018)

David Moffette, *Governing Irregular Migration: Bordering Culture, Labour, and Security in Spain* (2018)

Constance Backhouse, *Claire L'Heureux-Dubé: A Life* (2017)

Christopher P. Manfredi and Antonia Maioni, *Health Care and the Charter: Legal Mobilization and Policy Change in Canada* (2017)

Julie Macfarlane, *The New Lawyer: How Clients Are Transforming the Practice of Law*, 2nd ed. (2017)

Annie Bunting and Joel Quirk, eds., *Contemporary Slavery: Popular Rhetoric and Political Practice* (2017)

Larry Savage and Charles W. Smith, *Unions in Court: Organized Labour and the Charter of Rights and Freedoms* (2017)

Allyson M. Lunny, *Debating Hate Crime: Language, Legislatures, and the Law in Canada* (2017)

For a complete list of the titles in the series, see the UBC Press website, www.ubcpress.ca.

Crossing Law's Border
Canada's Refugee Resettlement Program

SHAUNA LABMAN

UBCPress · Vancouver · Toronto

© UBC Press 2019
All rights reserved. No part of this publication may be reproduced, stored in a retrieval system, or transmitted, in any form or by any means, without prior written permission of the publisher, or, in Canada, in the case of photocopying or other reprographic copying, a licence from Access Copyright, www.accesscopyright.ca.

28 27 26 25 24 23 22 21 20 19   5 4 3 2 1

Printed in Canada on FSC-certified ancient-forest-free paper
(100% post-consumer recycled) that is processed chlorine- and acid-free.

ISBN 978-0-7748-6217-2 (hardcover)
ISBN 978-07748-6218-9 (pbk.)
ISBN 978-0-7748-6219-6 (PDF)
ISBN 978-0-7748-6220-2 (EPUB)
ISBN 978-0-7748-6221-9 (Kindle)

Cataloguing-in-publication data for this book is available
from Library and Archives Canada.

Canadä

UBC Press gratefully acknowledges the financial support for our publishing program of the Government of Canada (through the Canada Book Fund), the Canada Council for the Arts, and the British Columbia Arts Council.

This book has been published with the help of a grant from the Canadian Federation for the Humanities and Social Sciences, through the Awards to Scholarly Publications Program, using funds provided by the Social Sciences and Humanities Research Council of Canada, and with the help of the University of British Columbia through the K.D. Srivastava Fund.

Printed and bound in Canada by Friesens
Set in Zurich, Univers, and Minion by Apex CoVantage, LLC
Copy editor: Stacy Belden
Proofreader: Dallas Harrison
Indexer: Cheryl Lemmens
Cover designer: David Drummond

UBC Press
The University of British Columbia
2029 West Mall
Vancouver, BC V6T 1Z2
www.ubcpress.ca

This work is dedicated to my grandparents, Bill and Margaret Skinner, and Lillian and Nathan Labman. Great people who came, or whose parents came, to Canada from diverse parts of the world and made this home.

Contents

List of Tables / viii

Acknowledgments / ix

List of Abbreviations / xii

1 Law's Role in Resettlement / 1

2 Movement / 17

3 History, Humanitarianism, and Law / 32

4 Numbers, Access, and Rights / 56

5 Privatized Protection / 81

6 The State of Sponsorship / 110

7 Beyond the Convention / 125

8 Unsettling Refugee Resettlement / 154

Appendix: Federal Court of Canada Resettlement Cases / 170

Notes / 179

Index / 240

Tables

1 UNHCR resettlement data, 2010–17 / 6
2 *Refugee Convention* state parties, 1951–2018 / 37
3 Government-assisted/private sponsorship ranges and landings, 2001–21 / 57
4 Private sponsorship ranges and landings, 1979–2021 / 96
5 Designated source countries by year, 1997–2011 / 128
6 Humanitarian and compassionate applications outside Canada, 2002–10 / 135

Acknowledgments

At its beginning, this book was simply a kernel of inspiration and a fair amount of passion. Developing the former and maintaining the latter were only achieved through the support of many people. Catherine Dauvergne has been invaluable as my supervisor, mentor, collaborator, and friend. Words are not adequate for my gratitude. Donald Galloway, Daniel Hiebert, and Jennifer Hyndman likewise provided continual insight and ideas throughout the doctoral project and beyond. A conversation with Wes Pue at a difficult time for me is what brought me into the PhD program, and I would not be here today without his guidance. Randy Schmidt at UBC Press has been patiently confident as I rethought and revamped portions of this work and paused for parenthood. Ann Macklem, Stacy Belden, and David Drummond acted with what seemed like swift magic to clarify and illustrate my vision.

To the anonymous reviewers, thank you for your careful reading and excellent suggestions to improve the manuscript. For financial and institutional support, many thanks to the University of British Columbia, the University of Manitoba, the Social Sciences and Humanities Research Council, the Liu Institute for Global Issues, the Pierre Elliott Trudeau Foundation, and the Legal Research Institute at the University of Manitoba. As legislative and policy change, legal challenges, political promises, and refugee rhetoric swelled over recent years, Robson Hall research assistants helped me keep pace. It has been a pleasure to work with Tisha Alam, Segen Andemariam, Jonathan Andrews, Erika Day, Alicia Dueck-Read, Nora Fien, Madison Pearlman, and Anna Tourtchaninova.

I am indebted to those who provided candour, historical reminiscences, critical insight, and valued connections throughout the project. In particular, my sincere thanks go out to Howard Adelman, Rivka Augenfeld, Michael Casasola, François Crépeau, Janet Dench, Tom Denton, Brian Dyck, Chris Friesen, David Matas, Francisco Rico Martinez, Mike Molloy, and Peter Showler for taking the time to discuss my research with me over the years. Debra Pressé's commitment to refugees and Canada's resettlement program was always evident. Her willingness to share her immense knowledge is much appreciated and now sadly missed.

The energy, compassion, and commitment of the staff of the United Nations High Commissioner for Refugees with whom I worked in New Delhi has stayed with me through the years. In Manitoba, I have likewise found a dedicated community working tirelessly to support refugees at organizations including the Immigrant and Refugee Community Organization of Manitoba, Welcome Place, and Hospitality House. My best days are those spent working with Shereen Denetto, Dorota Blumczynska, Abdikheir Ahmed, Noelle Depape, and Louise Simbandumwe to myth-bust and educate.

As an academic, you work to create community, and I feel fortunate to be surrounded by amazing scholars always ready to motivate or distract as is required and often over coffee. In particular, Laura Madokoro, Sarah Zell, Jamie Liew, Orly Linovski, Sarah Ciurysek, Asha Kaushal, Efrat Arbel, Erin Tolley, Geoffrey Cameron, Christina Cook, Brenda Gunn, Debra Parkes, Lori Wilkinson, Jerome Cranston, Audrey Macklin, Karen Busby, Lorna Turnbull, and Thom Bargen give me strength. The Migration Law Research Cluster that I co-founded with Gerald Heckman and Amar Khoday at Robson Hall has been a great means of connecting community and academia in a continual discussion on refugee protection.

Memories of the first refugee families I worked with as they moved towards their resettlement have propelled my research. In Winnipeg, my family has now privately sponsored a refugee family, and I thank the families that worked with us on this endeavour, which opened my eyes to aspects of the program I had never thought through before. Sara, Lorena, Natalia, and Jhocelyne, it is a joy to watch you thrive. The act of resettlement is one of creating a new home. I am mindful that I was able to return to my hometown to commence my career and complete this work. For too long, I was far away from my family, and being home is an immense and unexpected gift. I am forever thankful to my parents Jean and Cyril for their love and support, which ranges from proofreading to weekly sleep-overs with their grandchildren. My sisters Raphaelle and Jessica challenge me as only sisters can and will jump on a plane on a moment's notice when needed. My extended Beauvilain family offers inquisitive curiosity and long nights of discussion. My partner Chris has been by my side from the beginning with constant encouragement, support, absolute faith in my abilities, uncharacteristic patience, and the most delectable meals imaginable. Thank you.

Finally, my children Hugo and Yael remind me daily that life is precious and home is strength. It is for them and with them that I hope to make the world better.

Abbreviations

AWR	women at risk
BRRA	*Balanced Refugee Reform Act*
BVOR	blended visa office–referred
CBSA	Canadian Border Services Agency
CCCRR	Canadian Christian Council for the Resettlement of Refugees
CPJ	Citizens for Public Justice
DCO	designated countries of origin
DFN	designated foreign national
EU	European Union
GAR	government-assisted refugee
GRSI	Global Refugee Sponsorship Initiative
ICRC	International Committee of the Red Cross
IDP	internally displaced person
IFHP	Interim Federal Health Program
IGCR	Intergovernmental Committee on Refugees
ILO	International Labour Organization
IRO	International Refugee Organization
IRPA	*Immigration and Refugee Protection Act*
IRPR	*Immigration and Refugee Protection Regulations*
ISSBC	Immigrant Services Society of British Columbia
JAS	joint assistance sponsorship
JIAS	Jewish Immigrant Aid Services
MFU	*Multilateral Framework of Understandings on Resettlement*
MIIC	Manitoba Interfaith Immigration Council

NGO	non-governmental organization
PCISA	*Protecting Canada's Immigration System Act*
PRRA	pre-removal risk assessment
PSR	private sponsorship of refugees
RAD	Refugee Appeal Division
RSTP	Refugee Sponsorship Training Program
SAH	sponsorship agreement holder
UNGA	United Nations General Assembly
UNHCR	United Nations High Commissioner for Refugees
UNRRA	United Nations Relief and Rehabilitation Agency
UPP	urgent protection program

1

Law's Role in Resettlement

In the fall of 2015, a new reality hit Canada. Refugees were the topic of conversation – at dinner tables, at schools, in the media, and by politicians in the lead up to a federal election. Not only were they discussed; refugees were present in these spaces. They were invited in, welcomed, and the promises of the politicians swirled around how many to admit. In many ways, this newfound space for welcome was triggered by the now iconic image of a drowned Syrian boy, Alan Kurdi, and the world's sudden recognition that more needed to be done. In Canada, which was far from the refugee flows, that "more" translated into more resettlement.

With his election on 19 October 2015, the new Canadian Prime Minister Justin Trudeau set to make his campaign promise of resettling 25,000 government-assisted Syrian refugees to Canada a reality. The number – 25,000 – was a massive increase from government resettlement that in recent years had averaged 7,500. The large resettlement number also drew comparisons to the origins and heyday of Canadian resettlement during the Indochinese crisis of the 1970s. Humanitarianism was palpable as the government acted on resettlement promises and individuals came together to do the same through private sponsorship. The work of this book is coming to a close in 2017 as the Syrian resettlement momentum continues in Canada and increasingly draws the interest of other states as the war in Syria and crises in other regions relentlessly carry on. It is impossible to give a starting or final word on a shifting and evolving resettlement program. This book is framed, however, by the Indochinese and Syrian resettlements to Canada and all that happened in between.

Refugees and Resettlement

Refugees flee. They fear persecution, and they escape. Where they escape to depends on where they begin, the immediacy of their need for escape, their means and access, and their own physical abilities. Some barely get across an international border. Some get across the world. The reality of the disproportionate distribution of refugees results in a dual system of protection. By international agreement, many countries have recognized that if refugees arrive on their territories they will not be sent back. This is the principle of *non-refoulement* set out in Article 33 of the 1951 *Convention Relating to the Status of Refugees (Refugee Convention)*.[1] Other countries have not become a party to the *Refugee Convention* or simply have an overwhelming and unmanageable number of refugees entering their territories. As a result, some countries that are far from the refugee flows have agreed to voluntarily bring refugees, who have fled elsewhere but who have not received adequate protection, to their territories. This is the act of third country resettlement, commonly referred to simply as resettlement or refugee resettlement.

Resettlement is defined by the United Nations High Commissioner for Refugees (UNHCR) as "the selection and transfer of refugees from a State in which they have sought protection to a third State which has agreed to admit them – as refugees – with permanent residence status."[2] The decision to resettle a refugee is only made in the absence of local integration or voluntary repatriation. This statement belies the complexity of resettlement decisions that are explored in the substance of this book. Resettlement is regarded by the UNHCR as serving two further functions: working not only as a solution but also as a tool of protection and the expression of international burden sharing.[3] Possibly as a result of its multiple purposes, and due to its voluntary nature, resettlement's usage has been ad hoc, intermittent, and sometimes manipulative, all with incredibly low numbers even in moments of celebratory resettlement highs.

This book explores the intersection of rights, responsibility, and obligation in the absence of a legal scheme for refugee resettlement. By examining the Canadian resettlement program, I ask how law influences the voluntary act of resettlement and, conversely, how resettlement contorts the law of asylum. The chapters show that the core concept of refugee protection – *non-refoulement* – is often compromised by resettlement, both by the resettlement selection process and by the influence of resettlement practices on in-country asylum. Nonetheless, resettlement provides a positive complementary addition to in-country asylum claims. Refugees come to Canada and are welcomed. My intent with this book, at a moment when the world is looking to Canada as a model of resettlement success, is to assess the current programs and practices of resettlement so as to promote the use of resettlement in a way that not only encourages resettlement but also maintains a commitment to the notion of refugee protection.

Beyond this, the book is about the relationship between refugees and the law. I demonstrate that law plays an influential role even in the voluntary, non-legal act of resettlement. Within a sovereign nation-state, law is clear. It is based on a formal or written constitution that establishes general law-making and law enforcement powers. In the international realm, by contrast, law is based on consensus and lacks a centralized, hierarchical structure. The refugee travels from a home state to the international realm and, ideally although not ultimately, back to a state, be it her return to her home state or her acceptance in a new state. During this journey, law weaves in and out. Both the individual states' domestic laws and the consensus-based international laws influence the refugee's journey.

The central law that applies to refugees is the international legal obligation of *non-refoulement*. *Non-refoulement* grants the refugee protection against return to the country where she fears persecution. It does so by preventing the state bound by the *Refugee Convention* from expelling a refugee from its territory. States that have become party to the *Refugee Convention* have thus taken on the responsibility for refugees who arrive in their territories. In total, 145 states are party to the *Refugee Convention*.[4] The concept of *non-refoulement* can be found in other international and regional documents,[5] and some scholars assert that it has reached the status of customary international law, binding even those states that are not party to the *Refugee Convention*.[6] In non-convention states or in states where refugee recognition processes are not in place, the UNHCR is often permitted to grant mandate refugee status under the *Statute of the United Nations High Commissioner for Refugees (UNHCR Statute)*.[7]

A refugee's fate is determined by where she claims protection. If the refugee reaches a state that is party to the *Refugee Convention*, *non-refoulement* triggers a domestic legal system that, in theory, will process the claim and accord the refugee a bundle of rights set out in the *Refugee Convention* but linked to the entitlement rights of citizens in the new state. If the refugee claims asylum in a state in which the UNHCR is granting "mandate status," she will be recognized as a refugee but still lack the solution of a state.[8] Despite the UNHCR's grant of refugee status, the refugee will not be permitted necessarily to remain in the state. The consequence is a massive refugee population in limbo, having fled one state but not finding a solution in another.

Refugees in states that have either not joined, or are not living up to their obligations under, the *Refugee Convention* encounter the conceptual failure of both universal human rights and refugee protection. In the realm between persecuting and protecting states, refugees lack anywhere to assert their rights or find protection. The global refugee population under the UNHCR's mandate was 19.9 million at the end of 2017.[9] At that time, 13.4 million refugees were considered to be in protracted situations, living in forty host countries.[10] Under the UNHCR's framework, there are two aspects to a refugee's journey: protection and solution. The *UNHCR Statute* begins thus:

> The United Nations High Commissioner for Refugees, acting under the authority of the General Assembly, shall assume the function of providing *international protection*, under the auspices of the United Nations, to refugees who fall within the scope of the present Statute and of seeking *permanent solutions* for the problem of refugees by assisting Governments and, subject to the approval of the Governments concerned, private organizations to facilitate the voluntary repatriation of such refugees, or their assimilation within new national communities.[11]

While the "international protection" responsibilities of asylum are supported by a strong legal basis, "permanent solutions" depend on voluntary burden sharing. The recognition of refugee status thus triggers protection, but it does not necessarily offer a solution. Three solutions are possible: local integration, voluntary repatriation, or third country resettlement. Essentially, the refugee may stay where she is, if so welcomed; go home, if it is safe; or go to another country, if that country is willing to take her. There are many "ifs" on the solution side. While the international community has imposed the legal obligation of *non-refoulement* to ensure protection, solutions have been left as voluntary decisions by individual states.[12]

The Legal Periphery

Refugee protection is about law; refugee solutions are not. And, yet, the law is there on the periphery of refugee solutions. Resting on the edge, the law does interesting things to both solutions and protection. This juxtaposition of protection and solution is most acute with the solution of third country resettlement. Resettlement offers a solution, but it is also conceived of as protection in and of itself and as representative of international burden sharing. In the less globalized world of the early twentieth century, resettlement was in fact the dominant response to refugees. Travel was more difficult, and states therefore appeared farther apart. *Non-refoulement* was practically irrelevant in much of the global North where access to asylum was difficult to reach. Increasing refugee flows following the Second World War were significant enough to demand and achieve an international response in the consequent *Refugee Convention*. The convention legalized *non-refoulement* on an individuated case-by-case basis, but resettlement was left to continue on a voluntary basis. The lack of law attached to resettlement was a purposeful absence. The international community recognized the importance of burden sharing and prominently placed it in the preamble to the *Refugee Convention,* but burden sharing was not made into a binding legal obligation.[13]

From the state perspective, however, resettlement tends to fit into a legal framework. Resettlement resembles immigration in the application and selection of individuals from abroad for citizenship in the new state. To facilitate this process, a domestic legal framework is placed on the voluntary act of protection and international burden sharing. Resettlement requires a government to decide on its approach to the selection and integration of refugees and how to fund the program. In Canada, this entails that regulations frame the resettlement process. The law is thus both present and absent in refugee resettlement. The underlying question is what to make of this legal positioning? What does the law do for resettlement? What does the absence of law entail? How does the legally framed, but voluntary, act of resettlement influence the non-voluntary legal arm of refugee protection? By answering these questions, law is brought into the story of resettlement. Resettlement is revealed in the previously unaddressed light of the law. Resettlement is not simply a voluntary act that states may or may not do at their leisure. It is also an act of international protection and burden sharing that is influenced by law and that, through its voluntary nature, influences the international refugee law of *non-refoulement*.

Canada at the Forefront

Three states have traditionally been the leaders in resettlement: Canada, Australia, and the United States. Combined, they have tended to receive approximately 90 percent of the UNHCR's resettlement referrals. In the 2017 calendar year, the United States resettled 33,400 refugees, while Canada resettled 26,600 refugees, and Australia resettled 15,100 refugees.[14] They are all Western states far removed from refugee flows. In-country claims of asylum triggering *non-refoulement* occur in these three states but never in the numeric masses encountered by the refugee-receiving countries that neighbour the refugee-producing countries, which are generally in the global South. Large-scale resettlement programs recognize these geographic realities and contribute to international refugee burden sharing. In total, and as illustrated in Table 1, over thirty states now offer resettle-

TABLE 1
UNHCR resettlement data, 2010–17

Year	Submissions	Departures	Countries of resettlement
2010	108,042	72,914	28
2011	91,843	61,649	22
2012	74,840	69,252	26
2013	92,915	71,449	25
2014	103,890	73,608	30
2015	134,044	81,893	30
2016	162,575	125,835	37
2017	75,200	65,100	35

Source: Based on data from UNHCR, "UNHCR Projected Global Resettlement Needs 2015, 2016, 2017, and 2018," UNHCR Resettlement, online: <https://www.unhcr.org/resettlement.html>; "Global Trends: Forced Displacement in 2017," online: *UNHCR* <www.unhcr.org/5b27be547.pdf>.

ment programs with yearly resettlement numbers ranging from the tens of thousands to single digits.[15]

In 2012, Belgium and Switzerland established formal resettlement programs.[16] That same year, Germany, Hungary, and Spain received the first arrivals under their newly established regular resettlement programs.[17] Japan shifted from a pilot to a regular resettlement program starting in 2015.[18] Italy also began its regular resettlement program in 2015.[19] Due to the large refugee influx into Europe in 2015, the region has been developing several resettlement-related initiatives.[20] In July 2015, the Council of the European Union Conclusions on Resettlement was adopted, which made available 22,500 resettlement places for 2015–17 by twenty-seven member states as well as Iceland, Liechtenstein, Norway, and Switzerland.[21] As a result of this adoption, countries like Bulgaria, Croatia, Cyprus, Estonia, Greece, Latvia, Lithuania, Malta, Poland, Slovakia, and Slovenia began implementing formal resettlement programs for the first time.[22] The European Union (EU) Commission adopted a recommendation in September 2017 calling on EU member states to offer resettlement places to 50,000 refugees by October 2019. Furthermore, negotiations are ongoing regarding the creation of a permanent EU resettlement framework.[23] As of October 2018, 18,400 people have been resettled so far as part of the EU resettlement scheme launched in July 2015.[24] Meanwhile, US resettlement numbers decreased 65 percent between 2016 and 2017.[25]

The focus in this book is on Canadian resettlement. The Canadian program offers diverse and creative resettlement models. It is also a program that has undergone a recent period of political and legal flux. As such, the Canadian program offers a wide range of resettlement insight that is of comparative benefit and helpful to an international examination of resettlement in a moment of international curiosity and interest. This book consists of eight chapters. Following this chapter, Chapter 2, "Movement," situates resettlement in its international context as a durable solution and addresses resettlement's connection to asylum access and border control. Chapter 3, "History, Humanitarianism, and Law," examines Canada's immigration history from ad hoc refugee protection to the creation and reform of a legalized regime. Chapters 4–7 follow the Canadian resettlement models. Resettlement in Canada occurs through either a government program, citizen-supported private sponsorship, or a blend of the two. Within these two main models, the program permits resettlement of a specific group of refugees sharing the same ethnicity, language, and/or culture to one location, thereby creating immediate social networks and previously permitted source country resettlement from specifically identified countries. Chapter 4, "Numbers, Access, and Rights," examines Canada's government-assisted resettlement program. It sets out the distinction between resettlement and refugee law and the juxtapositioning of the two in refugee protection. Chapter 5, "Privatized Protection," looks at the introduction of a complementary scheme of private sponsorship in Canada and how the addition of private citizens into resettlement affects the approach to, and selection of, refugees for resettlement. Chapter 6, "The State of Sponsorship," follows the evolution of private sponsorship into the creation of the Blended Visa Office–Referred program and the government's global promotion of sponsorship to other states at the height of an asylum crisis. Chapter 7, "Beyond the Convention," probes the programs within these programs – group sponsorship and source country sponsorship – and what these selection processes reveal about the shifting focus of Canadian resettlement. With this examination of the full context of the Canadian resettlement program, Chapter 8, "Unsettling Refugee Resettlement," argues that Canada's excitement about resettlement, and, particularly, with private sponsorship, is moving the program in a precarious direction that risks both its own sustainability and respect for the principle of *non-refoulement*. The book ends with the argument that Canada must reclaim its resettlement program as a positive complement to asylum and provides recommendations to achieve this rebalancing.

Bringing Law into Resettlement

Resettlement's international status as the most-favoured or least-favoured solution to the refugee "problem" fluctuates over time. What remains constant is that it is a necessary, albeit modest, solution to and component of refugee protection and burden sharing. Arguably because of its given, but limited, role and use by only a select number of states, resettlement receives minimal consideration but increasing interest. It is attached to burden-sharing proposals with little elaboration beyond its stated presence in the plan[26] and unproblematically presumed in human rights agendas.[27] Alternative resettlement models such as group resettlement, in-country processing, and private sponsorship receive limited and specific examination disconnected from an all-encompassing approach to resettlement or the relationship between resettlement and asylum. The aim here is to remedy this absence and provide a singular and thorough analysis of resettlement as a whole.

Establishing a comprehensive picture of Canadian resettlement allows for the question of law to be introduced and identifies a hitherto unaddressed linkage between law and resettlement. At law's border, resettlement is ultimately unsettled from the unquestioned cursory role it usually plays in refugee discourse. As a voluntary endeavour taken on by willing states, resettlement is ad hoc with terms, conditions, and approaches that vary between states and understandings of intentions that vary between individuals. A succinct and straightforward understanding of how resettlement operates is impossible. The greatest obstacle in pursuing this project was achieving a clear picture of a scattered program with a variety of players, conflicting interests, and fluctuating policy. In particular, government rhetoric can often cover or blur unstated intentions, which was particularly the case during this project as the research period spanned the significant legislative reform of Canadian refugee law.[28]

Many in the Canadian resettlement community, particularly among private sponsorship groups and those in government, were resistant to the book's premise that law and resettlement are linked. That resettlement is a voluntary scheme seemed to close off any openness to the possibility of law's relevance. Furthermore, resettlement sits in a vulnerable position by the very absence of a legal obligation. Critiquing a voluntary government program requires delicacy. Research for Chapter 5's discussion of the expansion of private sponsorship into a tool for family reunification predicted a 2012 announcement by the Canadian government to place significant limits on the program to curtail this tendency towards family reunification. Concerns that Canada's source country class resettlement required reform led, instead, to the removal of the class, as is discussed in Chapter 7.

Refugee advocacy tends to focus on Canada's meeting of its international obligations to refugees. Resettlement is often sidelined in an unstated, but apparent, "be-grateful-for-what-we-have" mentality or, conversely, so celebratory of increases that the corresponding asylum commitments get forgotten. I encountered significant hesitancy in interviews and casual conversations with those working in resettlement in

Canada to express any criticisms of the program's operation beyond the desire for more freedom for more resettlement.[29] By putting resettlement at the forefront of a critical examination, this project sought to provide an accurate assessment of the program free from concerns about the consequences of criticism. Nevertheless, the research arises out of my sincere belief in the importance and continuance of the resettlement of refugees as a voluntary activity.

Beyond Traditional Concepts of Law

It is necessary to pause for a moment to state my conception of the term "law." The fluidity of law – from the tenuous grounding of international law to the firm foundation of domestic law – and the peripheral presence of law even in the voluntary scheme of refugee resettlement have already been reviewed. This is not an examination of doctrinal law in either its domestic or its international form. Rather, law is embraced in both forms and in all of their nuances to explore its hidden influences and consequences. To situate my understanding of law for this purpose, I took as my starting point Desmond Manderson's notion of "apocryphal jurisprudence," by which he means work that "focuses on what is missing from a certain conception of law, about the resources that yet remain within it to speak of these absences and failures, and about drawing our attention to how and where the law gives out."[30] In this way, one can move away from the specificity of legal rules and concern with the definition of law to broader explanations of law's purpose, its interest, and its power.[31] The idea of the apocrypha moves me likewise outside of traditional approaches to, and understandings of, the law. The hope is that with such a temperament the project can move beyond the traditional conception of refugee law to see the multitude of legal influences in both refugee law and policy in domestic and international spheres.

This book seeks to explore refugee law not at the border or at the point of an asylum claim but, rather, further afield in the operation of the non-legal act of resettlement. The reluctance by some to even contemplate the possibility of a law-based discussion on the legally lacking voluntary scheme of resettlement illustrates the apocryphal nature of the project that appears by definition incomprehensible. I am interested in how refugees are influenced by the law and from outside of the law and what this does to their access to protection and to their rights. Manderson speaks of the apocrypha's interest in "the marginal, in voices excluded by normative law, and by the complex layers of that exclusion."[32] Refugees waiting in a state of legal limbo at both actual and metaphorical borders are the clear manifestation of these marginal excluded voices.[33]

Law's influence outside of its application has been previously examined in other manners as well. Robert Mnookin and Lewis Kornhauser present an argument on how the legal system surrounding divorce affects the bargaining process between separating couples that occurs outside of this system.[34] This is an approachable analogy to the task at hand. They suggest that the interactions between separating couples occur "in the shadow of the law," by which they mean that bargaining is influenced by a knowledge of the legal outcomes if the legal process were to be invoked.[35] In essence, it is not the law but, rather, an awareness of the law that is relevant – law's shadow.[36] While this project does not address the individual bargaining between parties that these authors consider, it does pursue the basic premise that law affects outcomes outside of its direct application.

The rejection of traditional legal theory is further supported by Margaret Davies in her work *Asking the Law Question*.[37] While the substance of Davies's text examines the various theories of and approaches to law that constitute the legal canon, it is her introduction that sets out her own understanding of law that is most relevant to my interests. Davies presents the basic understanding of law as a means of ordering society. The suggestion is that law is a "huge system of categorization."[38] This is evident in the refugee context where categorizations of legality and illegality dominate. But, just as Manderson urges us to turn to other sources to understand law, the reality for Davies is that law cannot be separated out: "[W]e cannot dissociate our understanding of law from our conventional environments – our language, our social existence, and the institutions which structure our lives."[39] Seeking an answer to her own query of what the law is, she notes that "[l]imiting jurisprudence to the idea of law in a legal system is therefore only reinforcing the artificial distinction between law and non-law."[40] Again, this is the fault of defining law against politics and morality and all that is not law because it is all "always there *in* law."[41] Moreover, as Davies points out, "*legal* definitions are never separated from popular ones."[42] Law expands outward from its basic function. The legal/illegal categorizations break down in a realm where various laws interweave. These intersections are at the crux of this project.

The further difficulty in situating this work in anything other than apocryphal theory is the failure of traditional legal theory to envision such a fluidity of law. Legal theorists tend to think only in national units. Often this is linked to the objective of seeking legitimacy for law's authority within a legal system.[43] Catherine Dauvergne refers to this as "law's traditional tie to the nation."[44] It reverberates throughout modern legal philosophy and serves almost as a precondition of any attempt to explain law.[45] Even the concept of international law, which is only a component of the discussion that follows, struggles to locate itself in a discipline of law based in domestic legal systems. Jutta Brunnée and Stephen Toope address this challenge of international law. These authors grapple with the perception of international law, by social scientists as well as by traditional legal theorists and lawyers, that is trapped in "the distorting optic of the domestic law analogy."[46] While it is unnecessary to explore in depth their attempt to set international law in a theoretical framework that is understandable by both social scientists and legal scholars, their recognition of the need for a language of law that can stand up to interdisciplinary work is insightful as much for the challenges they set out as for the solutions they put forward. Brunnée and Toope note: "In looking for such interdisciplinary insights, scholars have often adopted reductionist definitions of the 'other' discipline because they have not been actively involved in the constitutive internal disciplinary debates and processes that lead to healthy uncertainty and nuance."[47] In the case of law, they point out that outsiders can easily grasp a basic appropriation of the positivist view of law as sovereign enforcement.[48] Again, this is the basic idea of the categorization of law and non-law that is set out by Davies. The difficulty for Brunnée and Toope is that international law fails to fit within this theoretical framework.[49]

The task here is to search for where law is absent and to look differently at the law that is present. It serves not only to give law a greater presence but also to provide a warning to be wary of its greater influence. Law as an academic pursuit remains relatively young. In 1887, the first law journal, the *Harvard Law Review*, commenced as an effort to legitimize the law school's place in a university setting. Examining the historical development of the now ubiquitous law review, Bernard Hibbitts notes: "As the patron of a 'learned' journal ... [a law school] could at last make common academic cause with other progressive departments and professional schools on its campus ... [and] more fundamentally ... demonstrate that the law was amenable to 'scientific' study."[50] And, yet, over a century later, law remains an outsider in academia, markedly distinct from the social sciences and humanities and not so easily amenable to scientific study.[51] Law's outsider status is a consequence of its inherent presence inside. It cannot be extracted for analysis. And, so, while this project is about law and an effort to extract and analyze the unique instances of law that arise in resettlement, it is also, inevitably, about much more.

My research intention is to map and assemble existing resettlement scholarship and models into a singular and thorough analysis of what resettlement is. Establishing this picture of resettlement allows for the question of law to be introduced. An unrecognized linkage between law and resettlement is identified, analyzed, and assessed. At law's border, resettlement is ultimately unsettled from the unquestioned cursory role it usually plays in refugee discourse. The novelty of the question of law's role in resettlement, combined with the scarcity of academic literature considering resettlement, necessitated a multi-pronged research design and methodological approach to the work. A variety of sources of information is required in each chapter to define, clarify, and analyze the research question. That said, the methodology is grounded in the legal discipline. Statutory and judicial authority frame and define resettlement. International law and Canadian and other states' statutory laws, regulations, court decisions, and policies have been collected and interpreted. The *Refugee Convention,* and Canada's *Immigration and Refugee Protection Act* (*IRPA*) and *Immigration and Refugee Protection Regulations,* as well as predecessor legislation, are at the forefront of this analysis.[52] Chapter 4 devotes particular attention to judicial review of visa officer decision-making on resettlement cases in the Canadian Federal Court. Legislative review and Standing Committee reports are examined in Chapters 4–7 to reveal the considerations underlying law's movement, and particular attention is paid to the nuanced shifts that have occurred from the previous *Immigration Act* to the *IRPA*.[53] Two access-to-information requests were also made to Citizenship and Immigration Canada, which is now called Immigration, Refugees and Citizenship Canada, to gain statistics on humanitarian and compassionate grounds applications made under the *IRPA* and a breakdown of permanent resident visas issued under the vulnerable/urgent need exception in the *IRPA*.[54] How these layers of law, both domestic and international, interact and conflict with each other demonstrates law's relevance to resettlement.

Other primary texts, including Canadian government documents and those produced by the UNHCR, are examined and critiqued. Library-based traditional legal research of secondary sources supports the interpretation of primary texts. There is also a necessary historical context to the analysis. To understand how states and Canada, in particular, engage with refugees requires a long-term view of the creation and development of laws and policies in the twentieth century. The historical component of the project was achieved through the review of primary and secondary sources. Chapter 5's discussion of the origins of private sponsorship in Canada predating the Indochinese boat people relied on documents from the Jewish Immigrant Aid Society found in the Canadian Jewish Congress Charities Committee National Archives. Interviews were further conducted with representative players from both the public and the private sector involved in the creation of Canada's private sponsorship scheme.[55]

Media coverage from Canada's national and provincial newspapers and government news releases were broadly surveyed through Factiva searches of relevant terms to provide insight into government positioning and public perspectives on specific events and policies. Interviews in Canada were conducted with representatives from the UNHCR, Citizenship and Immigration Canada, the Immigrant Services Society of British Columbia, Immigrant Settlement and Integration Services Nova Scotia (now Immigrant Services Association of Nova Scotia), the Manitoba Interfaith Immigration Council, and the City of Winnipeg Wellness and Diversity Coordinator. The interviews and conversations sought to address knowledge gaps, clarify and confirm policies and procedures, expose any outstanding issues, redundancies, or contradictions in resettlement policies, test tentative conclusions, and explore options for reform.

I also represented the Canadian Council for Refugees as a delegate on a fact-finding mission to Colombia in November 2010.[56] The objective of the delegation was to gather information on the human rights situation within the country in the face of declining acceptance rates of Colombian refugees at the Immigration and Refugee Board of Canada as well as significantly reduced source country class resettlement from Colombia to Canada.[57] Interviews were conducted with twelve organizations in Bogota.[58] Through the assistance of the Jesuit Refugee Service, we visited an internally displaced persons (IDP) camp in Soacha, south of Bogota, and met with several IDPs. The purpose of my participation was twofold. First, participation on the delegation enabled first-person interviews and insights on the largest source country resettlement program offered by Canada to inform Chapter 7's examination of this resettlement class. This involvement was crucial to my understanding of the program at a time of program flux. It preceded the Canadian government's announced repeal of the source country class by four months.[59] Second, my participation enabled a working relationship with the Canadian Council for Refugees, which granted me access to a wide range of involved participants in refugee resettlement for informal interview purposes. These conversations shaped my insight and understanding of the program from a wide array of perspectives across Canada.

The book therefore represents the gathering together and mapping of existing resettlement scholarship, historical documents, primary policy and legislative material, government and United Nations reports, documents, posted data, and statistical reports. While the information itself is not new, it has not previously been brought together into a singular examination, nor has there been an overlay of legal analysis onto the data as is achieved here. The project is not primarily empirical in the narrow meaning of analysis of a gathered data set, but it is nonetheless based on observation and analysis. The gathered information sets out a picture of Canada's resettlement models, policies, and intentions, the UNHCR's interactions, and, to an extent, the attitudes and approaches to resettlement in both Canada and among UNHCR officials. The creation of such a comprehensive picture establishes the schematic basis of the book and enables comparative textual analysis of scholarly and primary sources and an understanding of the intersection of the theoretical with the practical application of the models. Ultimately, as a book about law, one point of the project was to make a persuasive argument.[60] The methodology is structured around gathering the factual evidence to evaluate this argument. The analytical work on the place of law within resettlement will permit the argument to be made that resettlement is more legally influenced by and influential to the legal scheme than assumed. Canada's resettlement program requires attentive restructuring to ensure refugee protection is forefront.

My research into resettlement commenced with a graduate thesis entitled *The Invisibles: An Examination of Refugee Resettlement*.[61] That project, following from work I had done with the UNHCR in New Delhi, argued that refugees who fail to make it to the frontiers of safe states are simply not seen, with attention focused on asylum claimants. It is interesting to reflect back on that work's focus on invisibility since this book shows how the intervening years have brought resettlement refugees to the forefront of visibility with the assertion that they are, in fact, the only "real" refugees. With new initiatives in Canada to reduce human smuggling, promote resettlement, and reduce refugee processing in Canada, this book reveals how refugees waiting in camps are now much more commonly noted in government news releases, opinion pieces, and, arguably, public consciousness than they were a decade ago. Yet there is a danger in getting what you wish for. With the assertion that resettlement is the right way to achieve refugee protection, those refugees waiting in camps with practically no chance of resettlement remain as invisible as they were before. At the same time, refugees validly claiming asylum are losing legitimacy and visibility in the juxtaposition of resettlement and asylum. This book seeks to call out this imbalance and force a more critical assessment of humanitarian efforts and refugee protection. Complementarity between asylum and resettlement must be the central axis.

2

Movement

There was a time when the refugee "problem" was thought to be solvable. While the movement of people has always occurred, and the Old Testament speaks of welcoming the stranger,[1] the twentieth century marked the first modern attempts by the international community to act together to address refugee flows. These first attempts were reactive to individual events and offered specified solutions for particular refugees. Even the scope of the *Convention Relating to the Status of Refugees (Refugee Convention)* was originally limited to persons who became refugees as a result of events occurring in Europe before 1 January 1951.[2] The 1967 *Protocol Relating to the Status of Refugees (1967 Protocol)* confronted the reality that refugee crises are chronic and worldwide, and it expanded the *Refugee Convention*'s temporal and geographic coverage, but it still did not acknowledge the permanence of the problem.[3] In fact, the continuation of the Office of the United Nations High Commissioner for Refugees (UNHCR) was originally only for three years.[4] The office was renewed by the United Nations General Assembly (UNGA) every five years thereafter. This temporal limitation on the UNHCR's continuation repeated until December 2003.[5] At that time, the UNGA removed the limitation and created a permanent framework for refugee protection. While stating that the UNHCR would now continue "until the refugee problem is solved," the removal of the temporal limitation speaks to the recognition of the increasing unlikelihood of such a resolution.[6]

Access to Asylum

A refugee, by international definition, is an individual who has been forced to flee his or her homeland for fear of persecution on account of race, religion, nationality, membership in a particular social group, or political opinion.[7] While the refugee definition applies equally to all who are found to meet it, the protection attached to refugee status can differ greatly. Protection ranges from new citizenship to crowded camps. The determining factor is where the refugee status is claimed. The *Refugee Convention* obliges state parties to not send back *("refoule")* refugees who have arrived within the state's territory.[8] While state parties are expected to grant refugee status and, sometimes, a route to citizenship to the refugees who reach their shores, other states, often overwhelmed by refugees and determined to discourage further flows, have not become party to the *Refugee Convention* or do not live up to their convention obligations.

The conundrum is that protection requires reaching a state party to the *Refugee Convention*, and the states closest to the refugee flows, as a result of their proximity, have often not become parties.[9] Those countries that are state parties are often far away and difficult to access. While access is a question of geography and ease of travel – by foot, car, raft, container ship, or airplane, with variable conditions on all – legitimate and questionable border control measures influence access. Interdictions at sea, visa requirements, and both the offshoring and the outsourcing of migration control all work to deny access.[10] The majority of refugees find themselves inadequately protected, often in camps grudgingly set up in the neighbouring countries from which they have fled.[11]

The unequal distribution of refugees, through both policies and proximity – what Matthew Gibney dubs the "tyranny of geography"[12] – also means that no state wants to be the state with the softest policies drawing asylum seekers to its shores. And states are learning from each other. How they position themselves and interpret their responsibilities and obligations affects how other states see them and how they in turn choose to address similar issues. While the origins of each state's policies may differ – foreign policy, controlled access, or humanitarianism – states are now operating with an underlying fear of the foreigner and a desire to regain greater border control. Canada's former minister of citizenship and immigration made clear that Canada was not "the world's doormat."[13] And what has been the result? Legally mandated protection is too often inaccessible.

Seeking Solutions

In non-party states and states without their own refugee protection structures, the UNHCR may grant mandate refugee status to identify asylum seekers meeting the criteria for refugee protection. A recognized mandate refugee receives protection from the UNHCR despite being in a country that is not party to the *Refugee Convention* or regardless of whether the host county recognizes her as a refugee. The UNHCR then seeks "durable solutions" for these refugees. Durable solutions comprise local integration in the receiving country, voluntary repatriation to the country of origin where the situation has changed so as to make this a possibility, or resettlement to a third country.[14] The UNHCR's movement from protection to durable solutions therefore requires a shift from one arm to the other. The impossibility of this task is evident in the numerical realities of refugee numbers, camps, and protraction. While, theoretically, the two arms of protection and solution embrace the refugee "problem," the reality is that the majority of the world's refugees slip through the fingers of this embrace and wait in limbo for resolution. Interestingly, the visual capturing of the UNHCR's challenge can be seen in the agency's logo, which has two hands cupping over a person in a house-like shape. While the image is meant to convey protection, one can also easily picture the refugee either trapped or falling through the space between the hands.

While voluntary repatriation and local integration require negotiation with origin and host states, individual states concerned with refugee protection and the problems of protraction can independently and voluntarily decide to take on resettlement at any numerical level they determine to be appropriate. Resettlement is thus the solution controlled by the states seeking solutions. If willing, these states could solve the refugee problem through the resettlement of all refugees in cases where local integration or repatriation proves impossible. Over the years, various proposals have been posited to share or distribute the responsibility for refugees. Founded in 1919, pursuant to the Treaty of Versailles, the League of Nations was the first international organization to address refugee issues.[15]

In response to an appeal from the International Committee of the Red Cross, the League of Nations appointed a high commissioner for refugees in 1921. The first high commissioner for refugees, Fridtjof Nansen, was tasked with resolving the specific problem of the Russian refugees created by civil war and famine in the Soviet Union.[16] His solution for the Russian and subsequent Armenian, Assyrian, and other Christian refugees following the fall of the Ottoman Empire was a travel document. The "Nansen passport" gave refugees a legal identity and enabled them to travel internationally. Refugees were perceived through a redistributive lens. Rather than a promise not to turn refugees away, the passport assisted in the movement of refugees – their "egress" and "ingress" – in an "equitable" manner to willing states.[17] Nansen's 1922 high commissioner's report refers to the passport in international burden-sharing language as "a great step towards a more equitable distribution of Russian refugees."[18]

In 1924, the League of Nations entered into an arrangement with the International Labour Organization (ILO) in which the ILO matched refugees with countries and employers in need of workers. Once the refugee commissioner had identified the refugees, the ILO coordinated the refugees' job placements and emigration.[19] Between 1925 and 1929, the ILO coordinated employment placements for approximately 50,000 refugees.[20] The ILO model highlights the challenge of resettlement in the merger of refugee protection and immigration incentives. The upcoming chapters will elaborate this tension.

Following Nansen's death in 1930, the League of Nations opted to create the Nansen International Office, which was charged with the protection of refugees under the league's mandate.[21] The Nazi rise to power in 1933 triggered an outpouring of new refugees, mostly Jews from Germany, and the League of Nations was forced to address the issue. By the 1930s, the *refoulement* of refugees was commonplace,[22] but the inclusion in the 1933 League of Nations' *Convention Relating to the International Status of Refugees* that state parties were obliged not to expel authorized refugees from their territories and to avoid "non-admittance [of refugees] at the frontier" received little support.[23] The League of Nations also appointed an independent high commissioner for refugees coming from Germany.[24] James G. McDonald, the American professor who first held the post from 1933 to 1935, resettled approximately two-thirds of the 80,000 refugees who left Germany during his tenure.[25] The concept of *refoulement* is not even mentioned in either the 1936 *Provisional Arrangement Concerning the Status of Refugees Coming from Germany* or the consequent 1938

Convention Concerning the Status of Refugees Coming from Germany.[26] The 1938 convention, however, did specifically address resettlement.[27]

The year 1938 also saw the merging of the League of Nations' Nansen International Office, which was scheduled to terminate, with the office of the high commissioner for refugees coming from Germany. The resulting high commissioner was assigned the responsibility to oversee the application of the 1933 and 1938 conventions, assist governments, and "coordinate in general humanitarian assistance along with resettlement and other solutions."[28] A separate organization, the Intergovernmental Committee on Refugees (IGCR), was also created at the League of Nations conference in Evian, France, which was convened in July 1938 to address the growing refugee crisis.[29] The two organizations were essentially amalgamated in February 1939 when the High Commissioner Sir Herbert Emerson concurrently became director of the IGCR.[30] The United Nations Relief and Rehabilitation Agency (UNRRA) was created by the allied powers in 1943 in preparation for the liberation of Europe. The UNRRA was not a refugee agency but, rather, was focused on the repatriation of displaced persons. It was during this period that the reality shifted from an individual's inability to return home to his or her unwillingness to return home. Tensions arose between Eastern and Western states on the freedom to refuse return.[31]

The League of Nations' inability to prevent the Second World War signalled its downfall, and it dissolved as the war drew to a close. At the conclusion of the war, the world's leaders sought to form a new international forum for world opinion. The United Nations was established on 24 October 1945. The League of Nations' dissolution caused the high commissioner's office to close on 31 December 1946.[32] That same year, the International Refugee Organization (IRO) was established by a resolution of the UNGA.[33] The IRO was designed to assist those persons who could not be repatriated or who "in complete freedom and after receiving full knowledge of the facts ... expressed valid objections to returning to [their countries of origin.]"[34] The IRO was strongly supported by the United States, and its resettlement mandate was intentionally to counter the UNRRA's repatriation focus, which was supported by the Soviet bloc.[35]

By mid-1947, the IRO had assumed the responsibilities of the UNRRA, the IGCR, and, indirectly, the League of Nations' high commissioner for refugees.[36] The IRO oversaw the resettlement of displaced Europeans to countries such as the United States, Canada, and Australia. Between 1947 and 1951, the IRO resettled close to one million refugees, including 329,000 in the United States, 182,000 in Australia, 132,000 in Israel, 123,000 in Canada, and 170,000 in various European states.[37] During this same period, a mere 54,000 people were repatriated to Eastern and Central Europe.[38] The IRO was a specialized agency of limited duration, closing in 1951. With the Second World War creating a continued flow of refugees, the United Nations was again forced to revisit the refugee issue, leading to the creation of the UNHCR and the *Refugee Convention*. By resolution on 3 December 1949, the UNGA decided to establish a High Commissioner's Office for Refugees.[39] The *Statute of the Office of the United Nations High Commissioner for Refugees (UNHCR Statute)* was adopted by the UNGA on 14 December 1950.[40] The UNHCR began its work on 1 January 1951 with thirty-three staff and a budget of $30,000.[41] The *Refugee Convention* was adopted on 28 July 1951 and came into force on 22 April 1954.[42] On 4 December 1952, Denmark became the first state to ratify the *Refugee Convention*.

Given the early-twentieth-century tendency to resolve refugee crises through the movement and transfer of refugees overseas, it is not surprising that the UNHCR commenced as a reactionary organization with an "exilic" orientation.[43] Unlike its predecessors, however, the *Refugee Convention* successfully garnered state support to address asylum through the concept of *non-refoulement*. One explanation for this reorientation is that, with the IRO's mandate ending, a core of refugee rights was necessary to maintain the willingness of states to offer resettlement as a viable alternative.[44] Resettlement would therefore continue as a protection mechanism when refugee rights could not be attained. While resettlement is indeed part of some countries' current refugee schemes, the difference between these programs and the earlier agendas of the IGCR and the IRO is that resettlement is now state-centred rather than flowing from the international refugee agency.[45] The *Refugee Convention* thus established the dichotomous protection relationship between resettlement and *non-refoulement* that is traced throughout this book.

The South Asian boat people crisis of the 1970s and early 1980s, examined later in this book, brought a resurgence in resettlement enthusiasm with 1.2 million Indochinese resettled by the UNHCR between 1976 and 1989. By the late 1970s, the UNHCR was involved in the resettlement of

200,000 persons per year, and, at one point in 1979, a UNHCR representative reported that "resettlement was viewed as the only viable solution for 1 in 20 of the global refugee population under the responsibility of UNHCR."[46] Beginning in the late 1980s, however, with refugee flows still increasing from Indochina and state resettlement quotas diminishing, resettlement came to be viewed by the UNHCR as the least preferred durable solution. By 1991, the UNHCR's Executive Committee had issued a conclusion emphasizing that resettlement be pursued "only as a last resort, when neither voluntary repatriation nor local integration is possible."[47] Concerns that large-scale resettlement was leading to the abandonment of asylum in first countries of asylum and serving as a pull factor for individuals to leave home for social and economic reasons, combined with an increased emphasis on voluntary repatriation, limited enthusiasm for resettlement. At the same time, there was a numerical explosion of refugees from Third World countries as the revolution of transportation opened access to the West and the end of the Cold War removed ideological protection incentives.[48] The realities of resettlement fatigue and the fear of enticing mixed migration flows and ostensibly offering an immigration program through resettlement had therefore hit by the early 1990s. By 1996, the UNHCR was resettling only 1 in every 400 individuals of the global refugee population under its care.[49] The new century has seen a revival of resettlement yet again. However, before examining resettlement in the twenty-first century, it is necessary to probe the underlying justifications for resettlement's pendulum-like position in the regime.

Exile and Containment

Both the mechanism of resettlement and the principle of *non-refoulement* contemplate a solution that is outside of a return to the home state. This has been negatively labelled as the "exilic bias" of both the *Refugee Convention* and the *UNHCR Statute*.[50] Gervase Coles suggests that the "thrust was directed almost exclusively to separation and alienation."[51] In addition, as the regime developed in the Cold War era, an exile orientation was perceived to be within states' interests. It expressed a "Eurocentric humanitarianism" that reflected the earlier tension between the UNRRA and the IRO and idealized settlement in the civilized West and garnered "ideological points" for taking in refugees from the East.[52]

The critique of the exilic focus centres on the concern over the accepted detachment from the home country. It has been challenged as a violation of human rights[53] and, more recently, as facilitating the interests of those driving the refugees out and as serving to counter the interests of peace building.[54] By the 1990s, there was a general consensus that a paradigm shift had occurred in the refugee regime that was tied to an ostensible concern with human rights and humanitarianism. Turning to the foundational conceptualizations of refugee issues in human rights terms, the reorientation offered a focused concern for refugees as human beings rather than a state-based focus on borders.[55] This shift thus signalled a new focus on countries of origin, repatriation, and human rights monitoring. The move was couched in the language of a "repatriation turn"[56] and "preventative protection."[57] The focus was on preventing and resolving the causes of refugee flows. A major project was jointly undertaken by the ILO and the UNHCR in 1992 to investigate the capacity of foreign aid to minimize unwanted migration.[58] With respect to refugees, it was argued that the two "Rs" of relief and resettlement needed to expand to four "Rs" through the inclusion of repatriation and the reduction of root causes.[59] The early 1990s also saw the UNHCR undergo a comprehensive management review, resulting in a "care and maintenance" sector that prioritized assistance over protection.[60] The suggestion was that a "full-belly" theory – "the idea that rights and legal protection were pointless for 'starving' refugees" – guided this move.[61]

While ideologically legitimate, this geopolitical shift was regarded by many as merely a shift in terminology but not in underlying interests. Accusations pointed to "engineered regionalism"[62] and the "demise of protection,"[63] with the move clearly pointed towards containment and encampment.[64] Humanitarianism was merely the "ideological guise."[65] The actual shift was then seen to be about shifting state interests from an "exilic bias" to a "source control bias." Alexander Aleinikoff concisely presents the dilemma:

> Rather than a paradigm shift, then, we may well be witnessing the troubling use of humanitarian discourse to mask a reaffirmation of state-centeredness ... If this analysis is correct, then the story of change is not about the melding of refugee law into human rights law; rather, it

is the exchange of an exilic basis for policies of containment – detention of asylum seekers, visa requirements, closing opportunities for resettlement, pushbacks and return.[66]

Interestingly, the second half of the 1990s also marked a period of budget shortfalls for the UNHCR and the reduction of humanitarian and development assistance.[67] Western states were able to deter refugee flows and avoid their legal obligations to refugees while maintaining a rhetoric of concern. Refugees, meanwhile, often lacked either protection or a "full belly."

Another layer of analysis contends that the shifting of state interest was tied to a change in the composition of the refugee flow. B.S. Chimni argues that the paradigm shift was achieved through the creation of the "myth of difference":

[T]he nature and character of refugee flows in the Third World were represented as being radically different from refugee flows in Europe since the end of the First World War. Thereby, an image of a "normal" refugee was constructed – white, male and anti-communist – which clashed sharply with individuals fleeing the Third World.[68]

Founded on a myth that demonstrated dissimilarities in volume, nature, and cause between European and Third World refugees, Chimni shows how this approach "articulated a set of policy proposals which justified restrictive measures. The proposals included the rejection of the exilic bias of international refugee law; a nearly sole reliance on the solution of voluntary repatriation; and an emphasis on the responsibility of the state of physical origin."[69] Whereas Western states wished to embrace the ideological notion of the Cold War exile, there was the potential with the "new" Third World refugees to resolve the flight-causing political conflicts and return home. Exile no longer made sense. Chimni therefore suggests that the "repatriation turn" in refugee policy was "the outcome of a marriage between convenient theory, untested assumptions and the interests of states."[70]

The validity of these arguments is difficult to deny in the face of a regime that seemingly turned to human rights but, instead, created a reality that has fallen deeper into protraction where rights are glaringly lacking. A socio-legal analysis of compliance with international human rights law and refugee law in Kenya and Uganda deplores the reality that "as a matter of fact *no refugee* enjoyed his or her rights when confined to a camp/settlement."[71] In Jennifer Hyndman's study of camps along the Somali-Kenyan border, she observes: "Legal arguments of protection and assistance are navigated, and in some cases avoided, through the introduction of a more politicized and exigent set of humanitarian practices."[72] In Hyndman's analysis, "[h]umanitarian assistance at the end of the millennium is synonymous with neither protection, in the legal sense, nor solutions to displacement," a fact tied to the realities of refugee camps that "remove evidence of human displacement from view and contain 'the problem' without resolution, as noncommunities of the excluded."[73] Matthew Gibney similarly concludes: "Western states seemed, by the end of the 1990s, to have foiled the globalization of asylum, at least temporarily."[74] Refugees remained contained far from the Western world.

For many, the events of the 1990s served to teach an important lesson in advocacy. Advocates recognized their potential complicity in state evasion of protection through the promotion of humanitarian assistance and repatriation. Aleinikoff wearily warns of the risk of becoming "unwitting allies in reinforcing the state-centered paradigm they seek to overthrow."[75] He suggests: "[R]efugee scholars and advocates would do well to stay off the repatriation bandwagon until there are far stronger reasons to believe that the international regime stands ready and able to keep its human rights commitments to returnees or other victims of persecution."[76] James Hathaway likewise recognizes the potential subversion of the idealized theory: "There is, however, a very real risk that governments will seize on the Coles framework [critiquing the exilic bias] in order to divert attention from their failure to provide meaningful protection to refugees."[77] Bandwagons, the rhetoric of "least preferred," and critiques of varying solutions as being misdirected risk the corruption of a regime designed to be holistic and multi-pronged. Protection and solution sit as the central components of the refugee regime. Their achievement requires support for each aspect: protection as well as all three forms of solution. Sacrificing any one for the promotion of the other strengthens neither protection nor solution but, rather, creates more cracks for refugees to slip through into protraction.

The onset of the twenty-first century returned resettlement to the foreground of protection attention. Resettlement was at the forefront of the UNHCR's initiatives such as the "Convention Plus" approach in 2002, which articulated the strategic use of resettlement,[78] the rewriting of the resettlement handbook in 2011,[79] and the more recent culminations of the 2016 *New York Declaration for Refugees and Migrants* and the 2018 *Global Compact for Refugees*, with promises of more equitable sharing of the responsibility to host and support refugees.[80] This action aligned with a renewed interest in resettlement by states. As Hyndman notes, "[p]ublic opinion and government planning cycles are more likely to favour refugee resettlement in which eligible, screened refugees in need of protection can be brought to Canada in controlled numbers for settlement."[81] Moreover, the securitized paradigm shift triggered by the 2001 terrorist attacks[82] arguably contributed to a renewed interest in resettlement.[83] As the body of the book reveals, the control and order inherent in resettlement offer states a protection measure counter to the unpredictable nature, and, by necessity, often illegal/irregular, entrance of asylum seekers.

Resettlement's most recent resurgence must be understood in the context of shifting protection paradigms that may be mere restatements of state interest. While the promotion of increases in resettlement numbers is urged, the willingness of states to comply with this call must be cautiously approached. The reasons behind the willingness are crucial to an assessment of whether resettlement actions are an embrace or an evasion by states of their protection obligation.

Resettlement Realities

The UNHCR identifies refugees for resettlement based on objective need rather than on the subjective desire of refugees themselves or other actors such as host states or resettlement states.[84] Integration considerations are explicitly irrelevant.[85] The criteria used by the UNHCR to assess resettlement need are legal and physical protection needs; medical needs; family reunification; whether the refugees are women and girls at risk, children and adolescents at risk, or survivors of violence and torture; and whether there is a lack of foreseeable alternative durable solutions.[86] Canada's resettlement program is open to both convention refugees and other individuals outside their countries of nationality and habitual residence who have been, and continue to be, seriously and personally affected by civil war, armed conflict, or massive violation of human rights.[87] While the Canadian *Immigration and Refugee Protection Regulations* include special provision for cases of vulnerability or urgent need of protection, they do not provide the same examination of need prioritization as does the UNHCR.[88] The UNHCR's referrals are the primary source for government and blended resettlement to Canada, while privately sponsored individuals are more broadly selected.[89]

Resettlement reached a twenty-year high in 2016 when the UNHCR submitted 163,200 refugees for resettlement. While resettlement offered a solution for 102,800 refugees worldwide in 2017, based on government statistics,[90] there was also a significant decline in the number of resettlement places available. In 2017, there was a 54 percent decrease in UNHCR resettlement submissions compared with 2016 and a 94 percent gap between the resettlement places available and the approximately 1.2 million refugees in need of resettlement.[91] Despite these declining numbers, an increasing number of states accepted resettlement submissions in 2016 and 2017, with thirty-five countries participating in the UNHCR's referred resettlement.[92] Much of the remainder of the global population waits in limbo in increasingly protracted situations. Protection simply does not automatically lead to a solution. Alexander Betts and Jean-François Durieux have suggested that the gap between the structure of asylum and that of burden sharing indicates the "half-complete" reality of the refugee regime.[93]

Protraction is defined by the UNHCR as 25,000 or more refugees of the same nationality in exile for five years or more in an asylum country. By this definition, an estimated 13.4 million refugees – two-thirds of the global total – were in protracted situations across forty host countries in 2017.[94] Even so, this definition is static and inadequate. It fails to encompass the chronic, irresolvable, and recurring character of protracted refugee situations or articulate the long-term political consequences of protraction.[95] A 2009 conclusion by the UNHCR's Executive Committee removed the numerical minimum of 25,000 and strongly called on states and other relevant actors to commit themselves to addressing the root causes of protraction.[96] Protracted situations represent the failure of local integration, voluntary repatriation, and resettlement. Protraction is the antithesis to solution.[97]

But the reality remains that resettlement will never be the "solution" to the refugee problem. In fact, it is the smallest piece of the puzzle, which is, arguably, as it should be. The relocation of people from their homes, their families, their regions, their languages, or their cultures is by no means ideal. Nor would it be fair to assume that individuals, even those who have suffered tremendously in their countries of origin, do not ultimately desire to return home. There are many who argue that resettlement is a costly solution that acts as a "pull factor," inducing migration and creating greater problems in host countries, that it permits countries of origin to rid themselves of unwanted ethnic minorities, and that it hampers peace and stabilization possibilities through the permanent departure of citizens.[98] The argument has been made that attention and resources should focus proactively on "preventative protection" to diminish the causes of displacement and concentrate reactively on peace building.[99] Yet, even taking these programs at their unproblematic best, they are not enough. One can never simply assume that refugee flows will occur and therefore abandon efforts to curtail these flows, but neither can one ignore the remaining reality of these flows, nor can they necessarily be resolved in the regions. The reality of protracted refugee situations with refugees lacking any solution betrays the idealism of the above arguments. The enormity of the refugee dilemma is visible in this challenge of both refugee movement and protraction.

Granting Status

Individuals who do reach a state party to the *Refugee Convention* trigger a domestic refugee status determination process. The state must determine whether these asylum seekers, or refugee claimants, as they are known in Canada, in fact meet the refugee definition. Provisional figures show that states and the UNHCR rendered 1.5 million decisions on individual asylum applications during 2017 alone.[100] When the definition is met and status is recognized, refugees cannot be sent back *(refoulé)*. Short of a right to asylum,[101] or a right of admission, the right to remain is essentially indirectly acquired through *non-refoulement* because no other state, other than the state of nationality, is required to take the refugee back.[102] The recognition and power of a refugee status is unique in international and human rights law.

Jane McAdam suggests that status is the "'primary' feature of the Convention."[103] Beginning with the establishment of refugee law as part of international human rights law, she examines the duties that states owe to people under other human rights law instruments that complement the duties under the *Refugee Convention*. The distinguishing factor in the *Refugee Convention*'s obligation of *non-refoulement*, she argues, is the attachment of a refugee status.[104] Given that the basis of the protection need – *non-refoulement* – is the same, McAdam suggests that the *Refugee Convention* should be read as a "specialist law" and that its provision of legal status be read to extend to all those in need of international protection. Hathaway has similarly proposed to reconceive refugee law as human rights protection both to benefit the refugee regime and to address the "inadequacy" of human rights law.[105] The difficulty is that the focus on "status" that the convention creates for refugees fails to recognize the constraints that prevent refugees from obtaining this status. Hathaway and Michelle Foster describe this as "protection *lacunae* which are the inevitable result of the limited reach of international law."[106] The reality is that status is consequently meaningless for many of those to whom it currently applies.

While universally based on the international definition, even refugee recognition can vary significantly between adjudicators and between states. Rebecca Hamlin's study of refugee status determinations in Canada, the United States, and Australia outlines how differences in process, institutional players, and administrative insulation or oversight affect the scope and level of protection provided.[107] Sean Rehaag's work in Canada has illustrated extensive variance even between decision-makers in the same system.[108] Refugee "law" – the international definition and its application in signatory states – may be the cornerstone of international protection, but states and the UNHCR rendered only 1.5 million substantive decisions on individual asylum applications in 2017, with about 3.1 million asylum seekers awaiting a decision at the end of the year.[109] Compared to the growing populations of displacement, these numbers are minimal.

Properly understanding protection requires the recognition of the moving pieces of refugees' realities – accessing asylum, getting stuck in protraction, and grasping at the options of local integration, repatriation, and resettlement. Resettlement and state-based status determinations are both triggered by a state's willingness to accept refugees through the obligation of *non-refoulement* or the decision to resettle from a third country. Status determinations and resettlement both result in the refugee's settlement in the host state. While similar in movement and consequence, they are separated by law, and the following discussion seeks to understand this separation.

The next chapter examines Canada's commitment to refugee protection and the relation between asylum and resettlement.

3

History, Humanitarianism, and Law

The day before Citizenship and Immigration Canada introduced the legislative package to reform Canadian refugee law in 2010, the ministry announced an expansion of Canada's resettlement program to bring over more needy refugees from camps and urban slums.[1] According to Citizenship and Immigration Canada, the expansion amounted to a potential increase of 2,500 resettlement places per year.[2] The fact that this announcement preceded the introduction of Bill C-11, *Balanced Refugee Reform Act*,[3] by one day demonstrates two important points. First, refugee resettlement is distinct from refugee law, and, second, resettlement sits in juxtaposition to in-country asylum.

The announced increase in resettlement numbers was not a legislative change. In fact, all that the announcement amounted to was a willingness by the government to increase the number of resettled refugees it voluntarily accepts each year. For refugee advocates, increased resettlement was a positive move. Refugees themselves cheered.[4] The Canadian Council for Refugees likewise welcomed the government's commitment to increased resettlement.[5] The legislated reform, in contrast, received significant criticism. While it professed to reduce delays and abuse, advocates argued it tightened borders and significantly reduced access to asylum.[6] The resettlement announcement, made in advance of the legislative change, served to counter allegations that government reform signalled a move away from refugee protection. The concluding line was forthright: "Providing increased support for resettled refugees clearly demonstrates Canada's ongoing humanitarian commitment and affirms our long-standing tradition as a leader in international refugee protection."[7] The narrative was clear even if the law was debatable.[8]

In the late 1990s, Canada was reconsidering its immigration and refugee laws and policies. The authors of the legislative review began with the recognition that "[m]any prevailing assumptions about immigration eventually reach the level of myth, which is an opinion, a belief, or an ideal that has no basis in truth or fact. Unfortunately, it requires much more effort (and recognition) to refute a myth than to create one."[9] The thread that links Canadian refugee policy from its inception to the present is the acknowledgment of Canada's "humanitarian tradition." The overseas processing manual that guides Canadian visa officers in resettlement admission determinations begins with this statement:

> The objective of Canada's Refugee and Humanitarian Resettlement Program is to uphold Canada's humanitarian tradition in the resettlement of refugees and persons in "refugee-like" situations. It is a discretionary program that complements Canada's in-Canada refugee determination system, which fulfils Canada's obligations under the *1951 Convention Relating to the Status of Refugees* (the Refugee Convention) to provide asylum and protection to Convention refugees who arrive on Canadian soil.[10]

The positioning of the resettlement scheme as "humanitarian" and "discretionary" sits in contrast to the obligatory basis of in-Canada asylum.[11] Canada's tradition of refugee protection is examined, clarifying the relationship between asylum and resettlement and outlining the interwoven rhetoric of legal obligation and voluntary action that dictates refugee policy in Canada.

Humanitarianism and Half-Open Doors

From the time of Confederation, Canadian officials sought to populate Canada. Canada's population was just over five million in 1901.[12] There was a demand for people to inhabit the country. As a consequence of this need for farmers and settlers, immigration was relatively open to incomers. Gerald Dirks reports that, "[f]or most of Canada's immigration history, neither politicians nor officials made any distinction between immigrants and refugees. The reasons for people's departures from their homelands seldom interested officials responsible for processing those who wanted to settle in Canada."[13] And, yet, many who settled in Canada during the first half of the twentieth century were indeed refugees fleeing persecution, according to the international refugee definition, including former American slaves, persecuted Hutterites, Mennonites, and Doukhobors, and Eastern European Jews.[14] Canada's first pieces of immigration legislation in 1869, 1906, and 1910 contained no recognition of refugees as an immigrant class.[15] There was no need for such a law. Even by mid-century, when the international recognition and protection of refugees was well under way, Canada's new 1952 *Immigration Act* made no reference to refugees.[16]

Despite the absence of legislative recognition, Canada was a proactive partner in the international resettlement of refugees. Active involvement in a refugee scheme, however, did not signify a true distinction between refugees and immigrants in the minds of the Canadian officials coordinating the resettlement program. Writing in 1957, David Corbett provided a telling critique of Canada's resettlement selections during this period:

> The degree of generosity which Canada has shown in her international relations is reflected in the admission of refugees. In 1949, the peak year of overseas resettlement by the International Refugee Organization, the United States accepted almost five times as many refugees as Canada; Australia more than three times as many; and Israel twice as many. In 1950, Canada took even fewer refugees than the previous year; however, in 1951 our total increased significantly to thirty thousand, one-third of the American total ... From 1952 to the middle of 1954, Canada's reception of refugees was second only to the United States and amounted to eleven thousand, nearly half the American total. All told, we have accepted about one hundred thousand refugees. *However, they have been carefully selected, and most of them would have satisfied our standards if they had been applying as immigrants.* The I.R.O. did not keep a record of the numbers of the so-called "difficult cases" which the receiving countries accepted. The "difficult cases" were people who for various reasons including ill-health and age would not normally be acceptable by immigration countries. On the other hand, *records were kept of the number of refugees requiring permanent care in institutions whom the receiving*

countries accepted. Of the nearly ten thousand such cases resettled, Canada accepted so few that she was not even listed among the countries which received two hundred cases or more, in a report issued by the Office of the United Nations High Commissioner for Refugees.[17]

Resettlement to Canada continued, absent legislated refugee recognition, throughout the 1950s, 1960s, and 1970s. Admissions were based on ad hoc decisions and Cabinet orders-in-council.[18] Elsewhere refugee policy was described as "unplanned and in a sense represented reactions to political emergencies or in response to humanitarian considerations."[19] Decisions tended to be ideological and strategic. As Soviet "escapees," approximately 37,000 refugees were admitted to Canada from Hungary in 1956 and 1957, and 11,000 from Czechoslovakia in 1968.[20] Sharryn Aiken contrasts the admission of "7,000 highly skilled and educated Asian refugees," following their expulsion from Uganda by Idi Amin in 1972, to the "closed door" that met the less desirous Tibetan agriculturalists when China annexed Tibet in 1959 and the "lethargic response to Chilean refugees, many of whom were suspected Marxists, fleeing Pinochet's coup in 1973."[21] Mike Molloy, working as a Canadian immigration officer at the embassy in Beirut in 1972 when Idi Amin issued his expulsion order, recalls that, while Ugandan Asians "were formally selected under the 'point system,' by the end of September every communication and visitor from Manpower and Immigration Headquarters carried the same message: humanitarian considerations were to be paramount in the selection process."[22] Through an informal resettlement program, the Canadian government maintained complete and selective control over those it chose to admit and protect.

In contrast to selective control, Article 33 of the *Convention Relating to the Status of Refugees (Refugee Convention)* obliges state parties to not send back refugees who have arrived within their territories.[23] A Canadian, Leslie Chance, chaired the ad hoc committee of the UN Economic and Social Council that drafted the convention in 1950.[24] Canada supported the UNHCR financially from its inception and has served as a member of its governing Executive Committee since 1957.[25] And, yet, Canada did not ratify the *Refugee Convention* or its *Protocol Relating to the Status of Refugees (1967 Protocol)* until 4 June 1969.[26] While the *Refugee Convention* permits states the possibility of limiting their obligations under the convention to persons who had become refugees as a result of events occurring in Europe, the *1967 Protocol* removes both the dateline and possible geographic limitations of the *Refugee Convention*, making it more relevant to Western states such as Canada. Ratification of the *Refugee Convention* and adoption of the obligation of *non-refoulement* in Article 33 required Canada to relinquish absolute control of its borders – the ability to turn away any foreigner for any reason and to make individual evaluations on admission. Reportedly, at the time of the *Refugee Convention*'s drafting, and the concluding conference of interested governments that took place in Geneva in July 1951, Chance, as head of the Canadian delegation, was directed not to sign the convention since the Canadian government "had certain reservations because some sections of the convention appeared to prohibit states from deporting 'bona fide' refugees, even on grounds of national security."[27] Christopher Anderson's review of government documents and debates from the time points to larger concerns that "non-citizens might gain rights in Canada that could be used to challenge government border control policy."[28] In terms of Canada's "humanitarian tradition," this eighteen-year period between the drafting of the *Refugee Convention* and Canada's ratification of the instrument can be considered a period of humanitarian hesitation.

While Canada hesitated, fifty-three countries became state parties to the *Refugee Convention*.[29] Table 2 sets out the states that signed before and after Canada. North America represented a major absence in the convention's coverage at the outset. The United States, while never signing the *Refugee Convention*, did ratify the *1967 Protocol* in November 1968, almost a year before Canada's ratification of both the convention and the protocol in June 1969.[30] Australia, the third of the major resettlement countries, was an early party to the *Refugee Convention* in 1954.[31]

With the eventual decision to ratify the *Refugee Convention*, Canada signalled to the world its commitment to refugee protection. Without any reference to the delay, the Canadian government announced in 1969: "Although Canada's treatment of refugees has been, as a matter of policy, in accordance with the letter and spirit of the international instruments for the protection of refugees, the act of acceding will denote official acceptance of the international standards for the protection of refugees and the approved international and universal definition of the term

TABLE 2
Refugee Convention state parties, 1951–2018

Year	State parties
1952	Denmark
1953	Belgium, Germany, Luxembourg, Norway
1954	Australia, Austria, France, Israel, Italy, Monaco, Sweden, United Kingdom
1955	Ecuador, Iceland, Switzerland
1956	Holy See, Ireland, Morocco, Netherlands
1957	Liechtenstein, Tunisia
1960	Brazil, Greece, New Zealand, Portugal
1961	Argentina, Cameroon, Colombia, Côte d'Ivoire, Niger
1962	Benin, Central African Republic, Congo, Togo, Turkey
1963	Algeria, Burundi, Cyprus, Ghana, Senegal
1964	Gabon, Jamaica, Liberia, Peru, Tanzania
1965	Democratic Republic of Congo, Guinea
1966	Gambia, Kenya
1967	Madagascar, Nigeria
1968	Finland
1969	Botswana, **Canada**, Ethiopia, Zambia
1970	Paraguay, Uruguay
1971	Malta
1972	Chile, Fiji
1973	Mali
1974	Sudan
1976	Guinea-Bissau, Iran, Uganda
1977	Djibouti
1978	Costa Rica, Dominican Republic, Panama, Sao Tome and Principe, Somalia, Spain, Suriname
1980	Burkina Faso, Nicaragua, Rwanda, Seychelles, Yemen
1981	Angola, Chad, Egypt, Japan, Lesotho, Philippines, Sierra Leone, Zimbabwe
1982	Bolivia, China
1983	El Salvador, Guatemala, Mozambique
1984	Haiti
1986	Equatorial Guinea, Papua New Guinea, Tuvalu
1987	Malawi, Mauritania
1988	Samoa
1989	Hungary
1990	Belize
1991	Poland, Romania
1992	Albania, Cambodia, Croatia, Honduras, Republic of Korea, Slovenia

(Continued)

TABLE 2 (Continued)

Year	State parties
1993	Armenia, Azerbaijan, Bahamas, Bosnia and Herzegovina, Bulgaria, Czech Republic, Russian Federation, Saint Vincent and the Grenadines, Slovakia, Tajikistan
1994	Dominica, Macedonia
1995	Antigua, Barbuda, Namibia, Solomon Islands
1996	Kyrgyzstan, South Africa
1997	Estonia, Latvia, Lithuania
1998	Turkmenistan
1999	Georgia, Kazakhstan
2000	Mexico, Swaziland, Trinidad and Tobago
2001	Belarus, Serbia
2002	Republic of Moldova, Saint Kitts and Nevis, Ukraine
2003	Timor-Leste
2005	Afghanistan
2006	Montenegro
2011	Nauru

Source: Based on "States Parties to the Convention and the Protocol," online: UNHCR <www.unhcr.org/pages/49da0e466.html>.

refugee."[32] The obligations of the *Refugee Convention* were not immediately enforceable. Canada operates under a dualist model, in which a treaty that has been ratified by the executive still requires implementation through domestic law to be enforceable at the national level. Legislation was required to reflect Canada's acceptance of the convention's obligations.

On 17 September 1973, Robert Andras, Canada's minister of manpower and immigration, announced actions to design a new immigration policy.[33] For the initial stage of legislative review, a task force was appointed to study policy options and organize the review process, which was followed by the publication of a green paper to guide further consultations. Interestingly, the minister's four-and-a-half-page statement in 1973 announcing the new immigration policy plans contains only a single line in reference to refugees and makes no mention of Canada's signing of the *Refugee Convention* whatsoever.[34] The eventual green paper recommended that the new *Immigration Act* contain specific provisions for the selection and processing of refugees.[35]

While not part of the international legal obligation, resettlement was an unquestioned aspect of Canada's refugee protection. Allan Gotlieb, deputy minister of manpower and immigration at the time of the legislative reform, stated: "Canadian Immigration law has even less to say about admission for first asylum than about resettlement."[36] The contrast here is telling. Law dictated the voluntary act of resettlement, but there was little need to consider the actual legal obligations of asylum. While Gotlieb spoke of the future potential for Canada to become a country of first asylum,[37] such a reality had not yet hit when he was writing in 1975. Resettlement was the norm because access to asylum at a port of entry was difficult in Canada. Canada is bookended by oceans on its east and west coasts, with the Arctic Ocean to the north – what Jennifer Hyndman, William Payne, and Shauna Jimenez term "cold ocean geography"[38] – and the United States to the south. Even in the present era of international travel and detailed laws surrounding asylum, Canada is far removed from refugee-producing countries.

Following extensive consultations, the *Immigration Act, 1976*[39] was the first piece of Canadian legislation to place government refugee policy in statutory form. Refugees were recognized as an immigrant class, with a process for admissions.[40] This marked Canada's evolution from refugee policy to refugee law. The non-legal aspect of Canada's refugee protection scheme continued nonetheless. Resettlement, as essentially a continuation of the status quo, was recognized but with less hype and commitment than in-Canada refugee status determinations. Reviewing the legislation in 1984, Dirks wrote:

> The advisory committee [tasked with assessing the validity of in-Canada refugee claims] had no role to play for individuals outside of Canada claiming to be bona fide refugees seeking to gain entry to this country. Verifying these claims to refugee status was a responsibility left to the immigration officers in the overseas posts. The exclusion of overseas claimants from the advisory committee process has not been a particularly contentious issue either at the time the 1976 legislation was being debated or since.[41]

Nonetheless, of the two approaches to refugee status in Canada, "bona fide refugees being selected by overseas Canadian visa officials from pools of individuals already in states of first asylum" was the approach "expected by the Act's drafters to be the *normal* entry route."[42] While an addition to its international obligation, the inclusion of resettlement can also be interpreted as a reflection of Canada's overall immigration policy, a policy premised on overseas selection.[43]

The *Immigration Act, 1976* incorporated the *Refugee Convention*'s refugee definition and the principle of *non-refoulement*.[44] From its first appearance, Canada's refugee legislation stated as an objective "to fulfil Canada's international legal obligations with respect to refugees and to uphold its humanitarian tradition with respect to the displaced and the persecuted."[45] The legislation later noted in terms of selection that

> [a]ny Convention refugee and any person who is a member of a class designated by the Governor in Council as a class, the admission of members of which would be in accordance with Canada's humanitarian tradition with respect to the displaced and the persecuted, may be granted admission subject to such regulations as may be established with respect thereto and notwithstanding any other regulations made under this Act.[46]

Even with this legislated recognition and humanitarian declaration, the 1984 review of the legislated refugee scheme concludes that "refugees seeking the right to permanent residence in Canada are informally, if not formally, evaluated in the light of criteria developed for gauging the adjustment potential of regular immigrants," and, ultimately, "neither formal legislation nor authoritative administrative structures guarantee humanitarian and compassionate refugee admission programmes."[47] As a country of immigration, Canada was welcoming, but decision-makers were selective even with refugee admissions. The program was generous but not necessarily humanitarian, with a focus on integration in Canada that trumped protection needs.[48]

Despite these critiques, from a global burden-sharing perspective, Canada was accepting a significant number of resettled refugees. With the fall of Saigon in 1975 and the eruption of an Indochinese "boat people" crisis, Canada admitted approximately 60,000 Vietnamese, Laotian, and Cambodian refugees between 1979 and 1980 alone.[49] In 1986, the UNHCR honoured the Canadian people with the Nansen Medal for their contribution to the refugee cause.[50] In total, Canada resettled more refugees from overseas camps than any other country on a per capita measurement, with over 150,000 refugees resettled between the eruption of the Indochinese crisis and Canada's receipt of the Nansen Medal in 1986.[51] This period marked the height of resettlement in Canada until the Syrian resurgence in resettlement in late 2015. It was mostly the result of the actions and energy of private citizens pushing and challenging the government. Both the Indochinese and the Syrian resettlements will be examined later in the discussion on private sponsorship, but it is important to note here as well. The government enabled the private sponsorship in a manner that has happened nowhere else in the world, and it was a monumental moment in Canadian refugee policy.

Enthusiasm was short-lived. The peak of recognition also marked a significant downturn in Canadian receptiveness to refugees. The Canadian Employment and Immigration Advisory Council reported in 1988 that most business and labour leaders felt the government had "lost control of the border."[52] In 1989, public opinion polls showed that 31 percent of Canadians felt that too many refugees were being admitted; by 1991, this number jumped to 49 percent.[53] While the Indochinese resettlement program highlighted the value of resettlement, it also raised concerns that the availability of resettlement was acting as a "pull factor" and encouraging people to flee.[54] At the same time, refugees were increasingly able to reach asylum countries on their own. Beginning in the late 1980s and mirroring the UNHCR's position at the time,[55] resettlement came to be viewed as a less preferred solution for refugees, while access to asylum in Canada became increasingly possible.[56]

A review of Canada's annual reports to Parliament on immigration highlights this movement from a resettlement-based program to an in-Canada asylum focus. Even after Canada signed the *Refugee Convention* and legislation was in place, overseas protection remained the only aspect of refugee protection considered in the reports. In both 1986 and 1987, the reports specifically state that "Canada's refugee program is directed primarily toward persons in legitimate need of third country resettlement; that is, people who cannot be repatriated voluntarily or settled in first-asylum countries."[57] Not until the 1990 report did Canada acknowledge that it "has become a country of first asylum for thousands of people."[58] The acknowledgment was tied to the implementation of a new in-Canada refugee determination system on 1 January 1989.[59] The new system was the result of the Supreme Court of Canada's 1985 decision in *Singh v Canada (Minister of Employment and Immigration)*, in which the Court considered the procedural rights of refugee claimants and held that inland claimants were entitled to oral hearings.[60] The follow-up annual report in 1991 was the first to include a new section on the "Refugee Determination System."[61] It acknowledged the shifting focus of the program from resettlement to asylum:

> The government remains committed to its program for resettlement of refugees from abroad. However, Canada's program is moving away from resettling mass movements of persons ... towards emphasis on protection cases. At the same time, the UNHCR is focusing its efforts on voluntary repatriation and local resettlement of refugees. Third country resettlement is considered only in exceptional cases.[62]

In Canada, asylum took centre stage, and resettlement became a subsidiary consideration. This is important. Resettlement in Canada developed in a vacuum during which asylum flows or any sense of an asylum crisis was far from the Canadian consciousness or Canada's borders.

Asylum's Ascendance

Following more than thirty amendments to the *Immigration Act, 1976*, Canada was again rethinking its immigration and refugee framework in anticipation of introducing new legislation as the 1990s drew to an end. The 1997 legislative review, *Not Just Numbers: A Canadian Framework for Future Immigration*, recommended that refugee and immigration concerns should be divided into two separate acts.[63] The proposal highlighted the differing goals of immigration and refugee protection – the former a means of serving national interests and the latter an international legal obligation – and argued that the two "sit uncomfortably" with each other.[64] By framing the contrast between national interests and international law, the authors positioned in-Canada claims for asylum based on the international legal obligation of *non-refoulement* as the cornerstone of refugee protection and gave little regard to the voluntary aspect of resettlement. The report did recommend that the processing of overseas and inland refugee claims be unified within a single system with shared decision-makers for both of them.[65] A single system reflects the desire for more consistent decision-making on refugee status but brushes over the additional necessity of the selection aspect in overseas resettlement.

Counter to the recommendation, immigration and refugee decisions remained contained within a single act with the introduction of the *Immigration and Refugee Protection Act (IRPA)* in 2001.[66] While the *IRPA* was awaiting proclamation, the editors of the final *Annotated Immigration Act of Canada* noted in their preface that the new act would "distinguish between objectives of the law that apply to immigration and those objectives that apply to the law pertaining to refugees."[67] "It may be," they continued, "that the confusion of immigration and refugee law principles has impeded the development of the law in both areas."[68] The editors were overly optimistic. The new act arguably only furthers the confusion that a shared system created. The *IRPA* contains twenty-five separate paragraphs addressing the objectives and application of the act, adding to the contradictions and confusions.[69] In arguing for a separate protection act, the authors of the legislative review noted that the "protection of persecuted persons is based on rights; it is inseparable from the notion of human rights. The caring and compassionate nature of Canadians should be at the root of these agreements."[70] In maintaining a single act, the legislators chose instead to preserve and perpetuate the tangled roots of immigrant selection and refugee protection. Nor did they merge inland and overseas decision-making processes. Resettlement, which reflects immigration decisions in its selection model for refugee protection, sits at the crux of the conflict.

The depth of the convolution reaches even deeper when one steps back to reconcile the linkage between human rights and compassion made by the authors of the legislative review. The statement merges actions based on legal obligation and those based on a voluntary act of compassion. The two are not the same. The former is based on equality and the latter on inequality.[71] *Non-refoulement* is a right; resettlement is not. Placed within the context of humanitarianism, resettlement results from compassion, not rights.[72] And, yet, the distinction between the compassionate basis of refugee protection and the strategic self-interest that underlies immigration selection remains valid. Notions of *non-refoulement* and resettlement are already intertwined. The legal obligations to refugees that states take on results from the same humanitarian compulsion that propels voluntary resettlement. States voluntarily opt to commit themselves to the international law by signing the *Refugee Convention*.[73] Resettlement is an extreme act of compassion because it is not compelled, and yet it is also the closest that refugee protection comes to mirroring immigration and strategic state self-interest specifically because of that lack of compulsion. Indeed, like resettlement, the immigration program is a voluntary program pursued by the government at its own discretion. Resettlement thus tugs at, and is tied to, both the law of asylum and immigration law.

Boatloads, Back Doors, Rhetoric, and Reform

The *IRPA* continued the custom of framing Canadian refugee law within a "humanitarian tradition" but tied this to proposals to be "tough on those who pose a threat to Canadian security."[74] The perceived threats were those individuals entering Canada on their own to claim asylum. The first bill was introduced in 2000,[75] following the arrival of four boats carrying 599 Chinese migrants off the coast of British Columbia in 1999.[76] At the time, local news reported:

> With each Chinese migrant rustbucket that shows up off British Columbia's coast, a bizarre form of behaviour becomes more commonplace on the streets of Vancouver. Total strangers will accost you and shout these things into your face: (a) The House of Commons should be recalled for an emergency debate; (b) Parliament should invoke its special powers to override the Constitution to deal with the "crisis"; (c) the Constitution should be amended, if needs be, to deal with these people.[77]

Reviewing the first incarnation of the *IRPA* legislation, Michael Casasola, a UNHCR resettlement officer in Canada, noted:

> Unfortunately, the most negative aspect of the legislative package was that the many positive resettlement initiatives were presented as a counter to some of the more punitive actions the government planned in order to limit access to the refugee determination system in Canada. In fact, the resettlement initiatives became an important part of the selling of the

bill to the Canadian public ... Resettled refugees were presented as part of the refugees using the "front door." And by providing refugees greater access, Canada suggested it had the moral authority to limit access to those refugees described as using the "back door."[78]

By the time amended legislation was passed by Parliament in November 2001, a new awareness of terrorism following the 11 September 2001 terrorist attacks in the United States heightened the desire to curtail the arrival of unwanted migrants and the suspicion and fear attached to their motives.

In the introduction to the publication on the UNHCR's global consultations in 2003, the editors note that "it has been noticeable that the post-September 11 context has been used to broaden the scope of provisions of the *Refugee Convention* allowing refugees to be excluded from refugee status and/or to be expelled. The degree of collaboration between immigration and asylum authorities and the intelligence and criminal law enforcement branches has also been stepped up."[79] At the same time, many pointed to this securitized turn as an opening for resettlement. Both the academic and the advocacy sides identified an opportunity for renewed conversation on resettlement.[80] John Fredriksson argued that "[i]n the aftermath of the tragic events of 11 September, [resettlement] may prove to be one of the most useful tools in the protection kit."[81] Joanne van Selm similarly suggested that the post-9/11 security measures "could in fact benefit some of those people seeking asylum and refuge by ensuring other, safer, means of arrival, including the expansion of resettlement."[82] James Hathaway noted a "recent renaissance of interest by some governments" in resettlement schemes.[83] And, indeed, resettlement proved quite attractive to states, albeit in an altered form. In 2003, the international community defined the "strategic use of resettlement" as "the planned use of resettlement in a manner that maximizes ... directly or indirectly ... benefits other than those received by the refugee being resettled."[84] The focus is therefore on using resettlement as a tool to achieve durable solutions other than resettlement.

In Canada, while professing the continuance of an imagined tradition, the *IRPA* shed many of the pretenses of humanitarianism in Canadian refugee law as the threat but, more so, the fear of terrorism granted the government justification and support for restrictive policies. Resettlement initiatives were at the forefront of this readjustment since they offered predictable, controlled screening.[85] Ironically, in so doing, the *IRPA* moved Canadian refugee law back closer to its resettlement-focused origins. The difference here is that, at the outset, resettlement arose due to the absence of asylum claims in Canada, and its return stemmed from a desire to reduce the number of claims.[86]

In the United States, one response to the terrorist attacks of 11 September 2001 was a complete freeze of the US resettlement program for three months, after which acceptance rates slowed. With the largest resettlement program in the world, tens of thousands of refugees lost the opportunity to be resettled as a consequence.[87] The year 2002 marked the lowest year in US resettlement since the country's current program began in 1980.[88] This halt is a significant reminder of the fragility and vulnerability of state resettlement programs in contrast to asylum. They can disappear. There is irony in the re-embrace of resettlement that the same terrorism triggered. Fear of outsiders drew governments towards the selective control that resettlement offers over the unpredictability and lack of control that is inevitable with asylum entrants, but this same fear also allowed the US government to stop resettlement entirely. The precarity of refugee protection has heightened in the United States since the 2016 presidential election. Overall, refugee admissions have been halved, while executive orders seek to pause resettlement entirely.[89]

With more recent Canadian refugee reform, the government has strengthened the distinction between asylum and resettlement. A boatload of Sri Lankans arrived on the coast of British Columbia in October 2009, travelling in the bottom of a decrepit cargo ship, the *Ocean Lady,* with limited supplies and facilities. In the ten years between this arrival and the previous four boats in 1999, not a single boatload of migrants had arrived on Canada's coasts.[90] Minister of Citizenship and Immigration Canada Jason Kenney nonetheless suggested that the arrival of the Sri Lankan men put Canada at risk of developing "a two-tier immigration system – one tier for legal, law-abiding immigrants who patiently wait to come to the country, and a second tier who seek to come through the back door, typically through the asylum system."[91] The statement belies the fact that Canada has an *"Immigration" and "Refugee" Protection Act* that legislates the entrance of both immigrants and refugees. There is no back door. There is an immigration door, and there is an asylum door. While there is a clear legal process for entering Canada as an immigrant, the *Refugee Convention* specifically acknowledges that asylum seekers cannot be penalized for illegal entry.[92] Nor does Canadian law in fact penalize entrants.

Often, refugee claimants who enter irregularly are presumed to be violating Canadian law. More than a decade ago, Audrey Macklin labelled this process a "discursive disappearance" of the refugee as border-crossing refugees share the discursive space with other border crossers.[93] Macklin's work was premised on the negotiation of the *Safe Third Country Agreement* between Canada and the United States.[94] The agreement allows each state to return refugee claimants back to the other state from which they directly came. The return is only triggered where a refugee claim is made at a land port of entry and not when a refugee claim is made inland. From the outset, there were warnings that this distinction would increase reliance on smugglers and surreptitious border crossings.[95] A consequent report by the Harvard Immigration and Refugee Law Clinical Program in 2013 confirmed that the *Safe Third Country Agreement* triggered a rise in unauthorized border crossings and human smuggling between Canada and the United States.[96] It is common in public discourse, media reporting, and political debate to refer to these crossings as illegal. Even the spokesperson for the Royal Canadian Mounted Police has stated: "We can assure you that the only law they've broken is entering the country illegally."[97] Resistance to this articulation of crossings has come from both advocates and scholars.

Looking at the specific legal provisions in the *IRPA*, those seeking to enter Canada must appear for examination to determine their right to enter (section 18(1)); foreign nationals seeking entrance must first apply for a visa or other document required by the regulations (section 11); and it is a broad general offence to contravene a provision of the act (section 124(1)(a)).[98] The act must be read alongside the *Immigration and Refugee Protection Regulations*, which specify that "a person who seeks to enter Canada at a place other than a port of entry must appear without delay for examination at the port of entry that is nearest to that place."[99] The idea of appearance "without delay" connects to Article 31 of the *Refugee Convention*, which states that refugees should not be penalized for illegal entry "provided they present themselves without delay to the authorities and show good cause for their illegal entry or presence."[100] The *IRPA* further notes that decision-makers must take into account a refugee claimant's "reasonable explanation for the lack of documentation" (section 106). Both international and domestic law recognize that refugees may need to enter a country irregularly and without proper identification in order to access protection. Irregular border crossers are avoiding the port of entry to avoid triggering the *Safe Third Country Agreement*, but they are presenting themselves on arrival to make their claims. A *Toronto Star* article from 2017 contains the heading "New Data Show 69% of Illegal Border-Crossers Are Being Granted Asylum."[101] The article maintains the notion of illegality even while acknowledging an almost 70 percent acceptance rate, which puts these refugees on the same legal route to permanent residence as resettled refugees.

Arguably much of the fear, skepticism, and law-focused arguments against asylum and refugee claimants connects back to the 2009 arrival of the *Ocean Lady* and the legal mechanisms that taint refugee claimants with illegality. Both the boat's arrival and the minister's responding statement occurred during the build up to reform. In March 2010, a minority Conservative government introduced Bill C-11, the *Balanced Refugee Reform Act (BRRA)*.[102] The act sought to streamline the refugee status determination system for asylum seekers. When it was first proposed, the Canadian Bar Association noted: "Expeditiousness without fairness leads to capriciousness and possible injustice. Fairness without expeditiousness leads to legitimate claims languishing in the system and encourages the proliferation of unmeritorious claims."[103] But what is the right balance between fairness and expediency? Following extensive debate that resulted in "less than any party wanted but enough for all to support," an amended version of the act was approved by both houses and received royal assent in June 2010.[104] The act was set to come into force on 29 June 2012.

Another ship, the *MV Sun Sea*, arrived in August 2010 and provided further opportunity to promote the dichotomized rhetoric. As the vessel neared Canadian waters, the spokeswoman for Citizenship and Immigration Canada used its approach to reiterate: "Our government is committed to cracking down on bogus refugees while providing protection to those that truly need our help."[105] The implication, once again, was that those who approach Canada on their own to access the asylum system are not genuine refugees. Upon the ship's arrival on 13 August 2010, the minister of public safety, Vic Toews, pledged future legislation to distinguish between refugee claimants arriving by boat and those by other means.[106] An editorial in the *Globe and Mail,* one of Canada's national newspapers, suggested that the solution was for the Canadian government to resettle "legitimate" Tamil refugees.[107] The inference was that the legitimate refugees would not be found on the boat nor be dependent on smugglers but would still be in Sri Lanka or neighbouring countries.[108]

Following Minister Toews's pledge, reform continued with the introduction of Bill C-49, *Preventing Human Smugglers from Abusing Canada's Immigration System Act*, in October 2010.[109] This initial bill died when an election was called but was reintroduced with no changes by the then majority Conservative government in June 2011. In February 2012, the government introduced omnibus Bill C-31, entitled *Protecting Canada's Immigration System Act (PCISA)*, which incorporated the anti-smuggling bill with minor changes.[110] The *PCISA* further amended the *BRRA*, before it came into force, to reinsert many of the most contested sections that had been negotiated out in June 2010. As the short titles of the three acts make clear, the purpose of the legislative reform was to balance and protect Canada's immigration and refugee system from abuse – abuse from human smugglers and the backlog created by unfounded refugee claims. The reforms created disincentives for asylum seekers to come, fast-tracked the processing of many who were still arriving, detained some, and limited access to appeals. As Stephanie Silverman cautions, the implementation of "risk-based categories" of asylum seekers inevitably shifts how refugees are perceived and treated.[111]

The reforms established the authority for the government to differentiate between asylum seekers in two critical ways. First, the minister of immigration could now develop a list of "designated countries of origin" (DCO) that was less likely to produce "real" refugees. The designation was based on a quantitative measure of rejection, abandonment, and withdrawal rates or, for countries with a low number of claims, a qualitative checklist concerning respect for human rights and the availability of state protection.[112] Second, the minister of public safety could classify a group of two or more asylum seekers who arrive together as an "irregular arrival," making those individuals "designated foreign nationals" (DFN).[113] As a result of the *BRRA* and the *PCISA*, a system of differential treatment could apply to refugees depending on their country of origin and method of arrival in Canada. Countries identified under the DCO list are presumed "safe," with the implication that DCO refugee claims are likely "bogus."[114] The reforms inserted protectionist and negative attitudes into the legal framework.[115] Concern and criticism grew among refugee scholars and advocates over the lack of transparency and significant discretionary power given to the minister that was inherent in the provisions.[116] The minister's decision to put Hungary on the DCO list in 2012 illustrates such concerns. Refugee advocates and government often present conflicting narratives about claimants coming from Hungary, despite the common acknowledgment that minority groups – in particular, Roma populations – lack state protection.[117]

DCO claimants have their claims processed faster than regular refugee claimants (thirty to forty-five days as opposed to sixty days) and have no access to a pre-removal risk assessment (PRRA) for thirty-six months.[118] In contrast, those who have had their refugee claim rejected by the Immigration and Refugee Board can apply for a PRRA within fifteen days of being notified by the Canadian Border Services Agency (CBSA). Claimants re-applying for a PRRA may do so after only one year has passed, which is assessed based on the risks arising since the previous PRRA.[119] The expedited timelines under the current provisions place significant pressure on claimants attempting to submit an asylum application and expose them to increased risks of rejection and deportation.[120] Jennifer Bond and David Wiseman have argued that the restriction on PRRAs "raises serious concerns" as it is the only procedural mechanism that safeguards against returning refugees to their country of origin where they may face serious danger.[121] The authors argue that the impact of the reforms on access to justice for refugee claimants is "particularly troubling," noting that Legal Aid Toronto has reported that the new legislation compounds the already existing legal aid crisis.[122]

The provisions also impose harsh restrictions on DFN claimants. This includes a five-year suspension before being eligible to apply for permanent residency, temporary residency, or permanent residency on humanitarian and compassionate grounds.[123] There are "practical consequences" to such delays.[124] Even if recognized as refugees or someone in need of protection,

DFNs still find themselves in a state of limbo without the rights and protections of being a permanent resident, a legal status that other successful refugee claimants can apply for without restrictions. The *PCISA* reforms further established a mandatory detention regime for DFNs. Under these reforms, a DFN claimant sixteen years of age or older will be detained upon arrival in Canada or will be arrested and detained after entry into Canada. DFNs are the only refugee claimants subject to mandatory detention.[125] Furthermore, DFN claimants are detained until a final refugee status determination decision is rendered or until the Immigration Division of the Immigration and Refugee Board or minister orders their release.[126] Detention raises exceptional challenges for claimants and legal counsel, including access to holding centres and jails where claimants are detained and navigating the legal issues of both detention and the refugee claim.[127] DFNs are also subject to a specific and less frequent detention review process.[128]

If unsuccessful in their refugee claims, DFNs are not eligible to appeal a negative decision to the Refugee Appeal Division (RAD) and do not receive an automatic stay of removal if they seek judicial review at the Federal Court.[129] The denial of appeal to DFNs has been criticized for being unfair and not in line with international law.[130] Even if recognized as refugees, DFNs are treated with skepticism. DFNs granted refugee protection are required to report to an immigration officer within thirty days of a positive protection decision and once per year for a period determined by an officer or upon request.[131] Their mobility is monitored, as DFNs are required to report a change of address as well as any departure from Canada and return to Canada.[132] Nor are DFNs issued travel documents until they become permanent residents, a process that is delayed for them by five years. This restriction creates an ambiguous legal status and distinguishes between types of refugee claimants and the extent to which international law applies to them.[133] In reviewing this scheme, the UNHCR "advise[d] against setting up a two-tiered system of recognized refugees."[134] Two tiers may be an understatement as claimants, lawyers, and advocates must navigate the complicated web of differential timelines, detention, appeal access, and other consequences attached to each designation.

On 5 December 2012, the minister of public safety declared five groups of Romani refugee claimants, arriving in Canada from the United States over the course of several months, as DFNs. The groups were designated on the basis that the arrivals were linked to a human smuggling operation.[135] Eighty-five people were designated, including thirty-five children, and those located were detained.[136] Ultimately, the groups agreed to go back to their country of origin instead of being detained for one year. Many were concerned that genuine refugees were amongst the group of DFNs.[137] It does not appear that the designation has been applied since this time.

These new refugee tiers have not proceeded without challenge. In 2014, the Federal Court ruled in favour of DCO claimants, finding that the Interim Federal Health Program (IFHP) reforms, which denied claimants in that group basic health-care coverage, were unconstitutional.[138] Under the original reforms, DCO claimants would only receive "public health or public safety health-care coverage" in situations that posed concerns to public health. This excluded "essential care" services, even while a refugee's claim was pending.[139] Under the 2012 cuts, benefits were limited to "urgent and essential health-care services." All rejected refugee claimants would no longer be eligible for IFHP benefits except for public health or safety reasons, and all PRRA applicants who had not applied for refugee protection were to receive no IFHP benefits.[140] In her judgment regarding the IFHP cuts, Justice Anne Mactavish powerfully noted that any suggestion that a small number of successful claims from DCOs implied that "claims were all 'bogus,' brought by queue jumpers and cheats seeking to abuse the generosity of Canadians," was "a grossly simplistic understanding of the refugee process."[141] And, yet, this suspicion pervades the DCO design.[142]

A further provision denied refugee claimants from DCOs access to the RAD.[143] The Federal Court ruled in July 2015 that the differential access to the RAD violated section 15 of the *Canadian Charter of Rights and Freedoms*.[144] In this case, Justice Keith Boswell noted the challenged law "draws a clear and discriminatory distinction between refugee claimants from DCO-countries and those from non-DCO countries."[145] Despite this remedial measure, the designation still risks being a sweeping overgeneralization and, ultimately, goes against the "fundamental principles of refugee determination."[146] As of October 2014, the number of DCOs had risen to forty-two.[147] In 2015, when the Liberal government came to power, the prime minister outlined top immigration priorities, including setting up a human rights tribunal to determine DCOs, reinstating DCO claimants' access to appeals, and fully restoring IFHP benefits to refugee claimants.[148] Despite being within his mandate, this task was not completed by John McCallum during his tenure as the minister for citizenship and immigration and was not included in the mandate letter when Ahmed Hussen became minister in January 2017.[149] The government has been silent on DFNs and their mandatory detention. While the government does not seem inclined to employ the DFN designation to current border crossings, the fact remains that the provisions have not been repealed.

Both the DCO and the DFN frameworks demonstrate the growing and concerning trends of immigrant detention and the criminalization of asylum seekers.[150] The framing of DCO and DFN refugee claimants as "different," if not "dangerous," serves as a justification for the government to enact more punitive measures. The *Ocean Lady* and *Sun Sea* boat arrivals represent a form of migration that governments want to deter because they lack control over who, when, and where asylum seekers arrive.[151] While the DFN provisions specifically allowed for retroactive designation of arrivals that had occurred as early as March 2009,[152] the passengers from the *Ocean Lady* and *Sun Sea* were never designated. The CBSA, however, did issue an internal memo indicating that detention is "an effective tool against those who circumvent the immigration process," and, as such, agents would "take maximum advantage of this tool" and initially detain the arrivals for further investigation.[153] Passengers were arguably treated similarly to how DFNs can be treated under the reforms. The rhetorical use of these provisions to suggest more suspicion be placed on some refugee claimants over others, and the looming potential to designate, frame Canada's refugee system as one that is weary and mistrusting of refugee claimants. This messaging reaches into political discourse, media reporting, and pubic understanding of refugee flows.

Beyond DCOs and DFNs, Canada has adopted an interdiction strategy with the explicit goal of "pushing the border out" in the CBSA's own language.[154] This strategy is officially motivated by the desire to control and monitor the arrival of people and goods in Canada; however, the strategy also obstructs asylum seekers and refugees.[155] The interdiction is accomplished by using visa requirements, intelligence services, multinational agreements, and international liaison officers to bring prospective migrants into contact with the Canadian "border" before they reach a genuine, physical point of entry to the country.[156] Thus, the border is effectively "reconceived as any point at which the identity of the traveler can be verified."[157] Prospective migrants are screened before they trigger the protections of Canadian law and are thereby pushed into "ambiguous thresholds where their legal status and entitlements can more easily be denied."[158] Canada is not alone in employing such strategies. Australia has attracted considerable international attention and condemnation for employing interdiction strategies to obstruct and detain thousands of prospective migrants from southeast Asia,[159] and European nations have employed similar strategies.[160] The combined messaging of these efforts is *stop them before they get here, penalize them if they get here*, and, with the DFN regime, *continue these penalizing disincentives to arrival even if they turn out to be legitimate refugees.*

In the fall of 2015, the newly elected Liberal government of Justin Trudeau came to power with a message of welcome for refugees. The hashtag #WelcomeRefugees set out the government's Syrian resettlement numbers.[161] The new government discontinued appeals on both the IFHP[162] and the exclusion of DCO claimants from access to an appeal[163] and returned the age of dependency for all immigration applications back to twenty-one.[164] The federal government also committed to clear the remaining 5,500 backlogged legacy refugee claimants through the creation of a Legacy Task Force in April 2017.[165] However, staffing shortages remain at the Immigration and Refugee Board,[166] there have been no changes to the DFN regime, which was brought in by the previous government, the private sponsorship backlog is growing,[167] and concerns with detention, particularly of children with their parents, are receiving increasing criticism.[168] The change in government in the United States at the start of 2017 commenced with anti-refugee messaging and swiftly led to a changed atmosphere for refugees and asylum seekers in that country.[169] An increase in border crossings between the United States and Canada has triggered calls and legal action to suspend or end the *Safe Third Country Agreement* between the two states, and a challenge to the agreement is now under way in the Canadian Federal Court.[170] While the Canadian government continues to promote resettlement globally and has announced new goals for the resettlement of Yazidi refugees,[171] it has been resolute in its unwillingness to suspend the agreement even in the face of death and amputation along the border.[172] As this book goes to press and a fall federal election looms once again, the government has initiated significant changes to refugee law. On the one hand, the government has removed all countries from the DCO list with the intent to repeal the policy through "future legislative changes."[173] On the other hand, included in an almost 400-page omnibus budget bill is a new ground of ineligibility which will limit access to make a refugee claim.[174] Despite a rhetorical tendency to conflate the protection categories of asylum and resettlement and present them as being interchangeable, access to asylum is increasingly challenging. The realities of the numbers, access, and rights are explored in the next chapter.

4

Numbers, Access, and Rights

The Canadian resettlement program consists of both government-assisted refugees who receive government support and sponsored refugees who are supported by private groups. The government-assisted refugee (GAR) program traditionally made up the majority of resettled refugees with the private sponsorship of refugees (PSR) program amounting to 40 percent of yearly resettlement in 2009 and an average of just over 30 percent in the preceding four years. The resettlement increase announced in advance of the 2010 reform was a commitment to resettle 2,500 more refugees. However, only 500 of these refugees were from the GAR program, with the remaining 2,000 coming from the PSR program. By 2011, 42 percent of resettled refugees were privately sponsored. With the 2012 budget, the government shifted 1,000 refugee spaces from the GAR program to private sponsorship and created a new category of blended visa office–referred (BVOR) refugees.[1] As of 2015, the two categories – GAR and PSR – were almost equal. The 2016 numbers significantly increased overall quotas and firmly put government resettlement back in the lead, but these results were reversed in 2017, and projected plans show privatized protection doubling the government commitment by 2020 (see Table 3).

Every year, the government announces a numeric range for resettlement and aims to resettle within that range. The immigration minister establishes annual targets following consultations with the immigration department, provincial governments, Canadian non-governmental organizations, and the United Nations High Commissioner for Refugees (UNHCR). The annual resettlement target is then allocated among visa offices on the basis

TABLE 3
Government-assisted/private sponsorship ranges and landings, 2001–21

Year	Government-assisted range	Government-assisted numbers	Private sponsorship range	Private sponsorship numbers
2001	7,300	8,697	2,800–4,000	3,576
2002	7,500	7,505	2,900–4,200	3,041
2003	7,700	7,508	2,900–4,200	3,252
2004	7,400	7,411	3,400–4,000	3,116
2005	7,300–7,500	7,424	3,000–4,000	2,976
2006	7,300–7,500	7,326	3,000–4,000	3,338
2007	7,300–7,500	7,572	3,000–4,500	3,588
2008	7,300–7,500	7,295	3,300–4,500	3,512
2009	7,300–7,500	7,425	3,300–4,500	5,036
2010	7,300–8,000	7,264	3,300–6,000	4,833
2011	7,400–8,000	7,364	3,800–6,000	5,582
2012	7,500–8,000	5,430	4,000–6,000	4,224
2013	6,800–7,100	5,781	4,500–6,500	6,392
2014	6,900–7,200	7,573	4,500–6,500	4,560
2015	5,800–6,500	9,411	4,500–6,500	9,350
2016	24,000–25,000	23,523	15,000–18,000	18,362
2017	5,000–8,000	8,823	14,000–19,000	16,873
2018	6,000–8,000		16,000–20,000	
2019	7,000–9,000		17,000–21,000	
2020	8,500–10,500		18,000–23,000	
2021	9,000–11,000		18,000–23,000	

Source: Citizenship and Immigration Canada, *Pursuing Canada's Commitment to Immigration: The Immigration Plan for 2002*, online: <http://publications.gc.ca/pub?id=9.663259&sl=0>; Citizenship and Immigration Canada/Immigration, Refugees and Citizenship Canada, *Annual Reports to Parliament on Immigration* (2002–18); Immigration, Refugees and Citizenship Canada, *Notice: Supplementary Information 2019–2021 Immigration Levels Plan* (31 October 2018), online: <www.canada.ca/en/immigration-refugees-citizenship/news/notices/supplementary-immigration-levels-2019.html>.

of estimated resettlement need, although additional places can be requested.[2] The range given in the 2009 annual report to Parliament for government-assisted refugees in 2010 was from 7,300 to 8,000, which reflects the announced increase of 500 GARs.[3] The lower number of 7,300 had been maintained since 2005. The 2010 range marked an increase to the upper number, although, as Table 3 sets out, the increase was short-lived. By 2013, the quota was decreased, and targets were maintained at the lesser range in 2014 and further decreased in 2015. Actual numbers, however, increased in 2014 and significantly beyond the quotas in 2015 with the year-end change of government.

Despite recent rising numbers, there is no guarantee of actual increased resettlement, particularly without an increase to the lower end. Even with such a lower-end increase, the government failed to meet the lower threshold of 7,300 in 2010, resettling only 7,264 refugees. Despite not meeting this target in 2010, the lower threshold was raised to 7,400 in 2011, with only 7,364 refugees resettled, and again raised to 7,500 in 2012, although only 5,412 refugees were resettled. The 2010 range for private sponsorship was from 3,300 to 6,000. While there was no change from the two previous years in the lower end of this range, the upper end marked an increase from the limit of 4,500 of the previous three years. This upper limit remained constant for 2011 and 2012 but increased to 6,500 in 2013. In 2007, the Standing Committee on Citizenship and Immigration released a report in which the committee addressed the government's tendency to change upper, but not lower, thresholds. The standing committee recommended that the government increase the lower threshold for private sponsorship from 3,000 to 4,000.[4] The government responded with a reduced increase of only 300 in 2008, raising the threshold to 3,300 and then to 4,500. The upper limit remained at 6,500 in 2014 and 2015, although actual numbers more than doubled to 9,743 in 2015 with the change in government. The actual resettlement numbers in 2015 and the significantly increased targets in 2016 and 2017 onward to 2021 capture the political malleability of intentions and results.

Just Numbers

Former UNHCR High Commissioner Ruud Lubbers noted that while the "1951 Refugee Convention remains the cornerstone of the international refugee protection regime ... it alone does not suffice."[5] And, to an extent, under his leadership, an addition to the *Refugee Convention* was envisioned in the concept of "Convention Plus."[6] The *Agenda for Protection,* arising out of the global consultations on the *Refugee Convention*'s fiftieth anniversary in 2001 and addressing the increasing challenges to the convention's relevance, introduced the notion of Convention Plus in 2002.[7] Two key interrelated components of the "plus" were improved burden sharing and increased resettlement.

The first paragraph of the preamble to the 2004 *Multilateral Framework of Understandings on Resettlement (MFU)*, which resulted from the UNHCR's Convention Plus initiative, recognizes the "need to expand resettlement opportunities."[8] The *MFU* later states: "Expanding resettlement opportunities is an ambition of this framework."[9] As co-chair of the resettlement strand of Convention Plus, Canada led the authorship of the *MFU*. Canada's annual resettlement numbers, however, remained essentially static and minuscule in comparison to the overall issuance of yearly permanent resident visas for the following decade. Government-assisted resettlement averaged 7,000 refugees per year between 2006 and 2014 – an average of 2.7 percent of the number of permanent resident visas issued annually.[10] The Canadian Council for Refugees has noted that, while the 2009 private sponsorship numbers marked a significant increase, the total number of refugees granted permanent residence in 2009 was significantly lower – at 22,844 – than the decade average of 28,000.[11] The counterargument is that, with the *Immigration and Refugee Protection Act (IRPA)*, Canada moved to more protection-focused, needs-based resettlement of vulnerable refugees and has put a focus on protracted refugees, populations with higher settlement costs, and medical needs.[12]

Legislative and Policy Framework

Whether the numbers are understood as moderate or minute, the active resettlement of thousands of refugees per year within a voluntary burden-sharing scheme nonetheless places Canada near the top of a small group of approximately only thirty countries worldwide willing to offer refugee protection through resettlement in addition to the promise of *non-refoulement* in the *Refugee Convention*.[13] The *IRPA*, like its predecessor act, also takes Canada beyond the obligations of international law by enabling claims for refugee protection to be made outside of Canada.[14] The legislation further expands beyond the "convention refugee" definition, which imports the international refugee definition from the *Refugee Convention* directly into Canadian legislation,[15] to include those who do not meet this narrow definition but are a "person in need of protection" due to torture or cruel and unusual treatment.[16]

Until 2011, there were three classes of persons that could be considered for resettlement to Canada: the convention refugee abroad class;

the country of asylum class; and the source country class.[17] The country of asylum class and the source country class were subclasses of the humanitarian protected persons abroad class.[18] Members of each class must be in need of resettlement, meaning that there is no other reasonable prospect of another solution at the time of assessment or in the near future. Members of the convention refugee abroad class must meet the convention's refugee definition. Members of the country of asylum class must be outside their own country and must have been, and continue to be, seriously and personally affected by civil war, armed conflict, or a massive violation of human rights. While the country of asylum class moves beyond the refugee definition, the criteria of the class are distinct from the inland "person-in-need-of-protection" expansion noted earlier. When speaking of resettlement "refugees," I am encompassing both those within the convention refugee abroad class and the country of asylum class. Members of the source country class were required to be living in one of the specifically listed countries and to be seriously and personally affected by civil war or armed conflict in that country; to have been detained or imprisoned as a result of legitimately expressing themselves or exercising their civil rights; or to meet the convention's refugee definition aside from not being outside of their home country. In 2011, however, the source country class was removed as an option.[19]

It is no longer possible for foreign nationals to independently apply directly for a permanent resident visa under these classes.[20] An "undertaking" or "referral" is required.[21] Referral organizations must have a working knowledge of the *IRPA*'s protection criteria and the ability to locate and identify convention refugees abroad.[22] The UNHCR referrals come by way of a resettlement registration form outlining the protection and resettlement needs on which the referral is based.[23] Canadian visa officers decide on the success of resettlement applications. Canada's overseas processing manual instructs visa officers to "be proactive in requesting referrals of appropriate cases."[24] The referral system, in its current design, is a duplicative process whereby refugees are often doubly screened for credibility and resettlement eligibility by both the resettlement organization and the Canadian government. The trust Canada places in referral agencies and the UNHCR is essentially revoked by the independent review then conducted by the visa officer.

Following a referral, eligibility for the permanent resident visa requires specific conditions set out in the *Immigration and Refugee Protection Regulations (IRPR)* to be met.[25] It is worthwhile to set out these conditions in detail:

139(1) A permanent resident visa shall be issued to a foreign national in need of refugee protection, and their accompanying family members, if following an examination it is established that
(a) the foreign national is outside Canada;
(b) the foreign national has submitted an application for a permanent resident visa under this Division in accordance with paragraphs 10(1)*(a)* to *(c)* and (2)*(c.1)* to *(d)* and sections 140.1 to 140.3;
(c) the foreign national is seeking to come to Canada to establish permanent residence;
(d) the foreign national is a person in respect of whom there is no reasonable prospect, within a reasonable period, of a durable solution in a country other than Canada, namely
 (i) voluntary repatriation or resettlement in their country of nationality or habitual residence, or
 (ii) resettlement or an offer of resettlement in another country;
(e) the foreign national is a member of one of the classes prescribed by this Division;
(f) one of the following is the case, namely
...

 (ii) in the case of a member of the Convention refugee abroad class, financial assistance in the form of funds from a governmental resettlement assistance program is available in Canada for the foreign national and their family members included in the application for protection, or
 (iii) the foreign national has sufficient financial resources to provide for the lodging, care and maintenance, and for the resettlement in Canada, of themself and their family members included in the application for protection;

(g) if the foreign national intends to reside in a province other than the Province of Quebec,[26] the foreign national and their family members included in the application for protection will be able to become successfully established in Canada, taking into account the following factors:
  (i) their resourcefulness and other similar qualities that assist in integration in a new society,
  (ii) the presence of their relatives, including the relatives of a spouse or a common-law partner, or their sponsor in the expected community of resettlement,
  (iii) their potential for employment in Canada, given their education, work experience and skills, and
  (iv) their ability to learn to communicate in one of the official languages of Canada.

Over the years, the Canadian government has received pointed criticisms of its overseas requirements. Critiques have amounted to accusations of cherry-picking and selecting refugees for resettlement who most resembled independent immigrants.[27] Little seems to have changed since the program's origins in the 1950s. Indeed, in their earlier incarnation, the regulations did reflect more closely the immigration scheme. Section 7 of the former *Immigration Regulations*, which were in force until they were replaced by the current regulations, contained the following criteria for successful establishment in resettlement applications:

7(1)(c) where the person and the accompanying dependants intend to reside in a place in Canada other than the Province of Quebec, a visa officer determines that the person and the accompanying dependants will be able to become successfully established in Canada, taking into consideration:
  (i) the ability of the person and the accompanying dependants to communicate in one of the official languages of Canada,
  (ii) the age of the person,
  (iii) the level of education, the work experience and the skills of the person and the accompanying dependants,
  (iv) the number and ages of the accompanying dependants, and

(v) the personal suitability of the person and their accompanying dependants, including their adaptability, motivation, initiative, resourcefulness and other similar qualities.[28]

Evaluation under section 7 followed the "points system" assessment for independent immigrants.[29] In terms clearly asserted in the 1990 annual report to Parliament on future immigration levels, refugees selected abroad were assessed on "their need for protection and their potential for eventual self-sufficiency in Canada."[30] The legislative review of the 1990s suggested "our requirements sometimes deny us the very tools we require to select those in greatest need, by screening them out."[31]

With the enactment of the *IRPA* in 2001, the government of Canada claimed a shift in Canadian resettlement policy towards protection rather than the ability to establish.[32] With the new regulations, the "successful establishment" assessment is made only of the foreign national applicant and not of accompanying dependants. Both versions reference "education, work experience and skills," although the current phrasing also directly links these criteria to "employment potential," which is arguably a higher standard. Age has been removed as a criterion, and "ability to communicate" in one of the official languages has been replaced with the less demanding "ability to learn to communicate" in one of the official languages. The *IRPR* no longer reference "personal suitability," and the list of "adaptability, motivation, initiative, resourcefulness and other similar qualities" was replaced with "resourcefulness and other similar qualities that assist in integration." Yet, in the context of discretionary decision-making, this change is practically meaningless. The government has taken the position that these requirements are "rarely" used as the basis of refusals.[33] The fact that they remain in the regulations, however, means that they can be used as a basis of refusal in as many cases as desired. Thus, despite some reworking of the criteria, the successful establishment criteria in the regulations continue to reflect the desired qualities of economic immigrants.

A significant exception was added to the long list of requirements in section 139. The "successful establishment" requirement of paragraph 139(1)(g) is tempered by subsection 139(2) where it is noted: "139(2) Paragraph (1)(g) does not apply to a foreign national, or their family members included in the application for protection, who has been determined by an officer to be vulnerable or in urgent need of protection." Definitions of "vulnerable" and "urgent need" are found in section 138:

> 138 The definitions in this section apply in this Division and in Division 2. "[U]rgent need of protection" means, in respect of a member of the Convention refugee abroad or the country of asylum class, that their life, liberty or physical safety is under immediate threat and, if not protected, the person is likely to be
> (a) killed;
> (b) subjected to violence, torture, sexual assault or arbitrary imprisonment; or
> (c) returned to their country of nationality or of their former habitual residence *(besoin urgent de protection)* ...
> "[V]ulnerable" means, in respect of a Convention refugee or a person in similar circumstances, that the person has a greater need of protection than other applicants for protection abroad because of the person's particular circumstances that give rise to a heightened risk to their physical safety *(vulnérable)*.

The government developed an urgent protection program (UPP) to offer rapid resettlement where requested by the UNHCR in emergency situations. In these cases, a decision is made within twenty-four hours following a referral, and Citizenship and Immigration Canada tries to ensure accepted individuals are en route to Canada within one week.[34] Cases of vulnerability do not lead to emergency processing but will be prioritized over regular cases for expedited processing between one and four months.[35] Refugees admitted through the UPP or deemed to be vulnerable do not need to meet the successful establishment requirement. While a clear shift towards need-based protection in theory, Michael Casasola notes that, in the years preceding the *IRPA*'s enactment, "the number of refugees facing urgent or emergency protection concerns [was] actually quite small."[36] He reports that in 1999 the UNHCR referred only 114 urgent and emergency submissions across all resettlement countries.[37]

The legislative changes shifted the nature of Canada's resettlement, enabling more refugees with medical needs and needs associated with psychological trauma to be resettled.[38] Refugee settlement services have reported a significant change and increased need in the refugees arriving under the *IRPA*.[39] Low literacy levels in original languages, increased physical and mental health issues, larger households, more single parent-led (mostly female) households, and youth with limited formal education create new or heightened barriers to settlement.[40] From a settlement perspective, the *IRPA* has shifted Canadian resettlement from a settlement framework to a protection framework.[41]

In addition to vulnerable persons and those in need of urgent protection, Canada has operated a women at risk (AWR) program since 1988.[42] Women at risk are "without the normal protection of a family unit who find themselves in precarious situations where the local authorities cannot ensure their safety."[43] The overseas processing manual notes that women at risk "usually receive priority processing" and "may not *fully* meet the requirement to demonstrate an ability to establish themselves in Canada in the short or medium term."[44] Women at risk may fall within the urgent or vulnerable categories and benefit from priority processing and having the successful establishment requirement waived. However, a woman may fall within the AWR program without being considered to be vulnerable or in need of urgent protection. In these cases, the successful establishment criteria are to be applied by visa officers on a "sliding scale."[45] Canada touted the AWR program as a means "to provide women applicants with more equitable access to resettlement opportunities."[46]

Unlike economic migrants, whose admission to Canada is overtly strategic and self-serving from a national need perspective, and family reunification, where the personal interests of Canadian citizens are being met, refugee admissions are premised on international burden sharing and a vague humanitarian notion. And, yet, in requiring resourcefulness, relatives, employment potential, and language skills, the successful establishment criteria can still apply and closely mimic non-humanitarian migration selection in Canada.[47] Recognizing this reality behind Canadian resettlement brings government positioning into harsher contrast. As the former government pushed to limit asylum based on justifications of abuse and present resettlement as an interchangeable alternative means of protection, it is necessary to remember that little numeric increase is in fact guaranteed and that the selection process for resettlement is precisely that

– a selection process. Moreover, even when done fairly, resettlement is not an all-encompassing answer. With 10.4 million global refugees at the close of 2011,[48] the combined government (7,364) and private sponsorship (5,582) resettlement to Canada in 2011 amounted to offering a solution to 0.1 percent of the global refugee population. A projected 19.9 million refugees were under the UNHCR's mandate at the close of 2017.[49] Canada's resettlement targets in 2018 for government (6,000–8,000) and private sponsorship (16,000–20,000) pale in comparison to the refugee population under the UNHCR's mandate.[50] This minor movement of people cannot adequately alleviate refugee flows so as to abandon the need for in-country asylum claims.

Opportunities for Review

While no international legal obligation exists for countries to resettle refugees, in creating a legislative scheme for resettlement, Canada has triggered certain legal rights, although not a right to resettlement, and obligations that are subject to judicial review before a Canadian court. Judicial review enables a court to review the decision-making of a public body or administrative decision-maker. Judicial review in the Canadian Federal Court is permitted under the *IRPA*, but it is not automatic. This means that any person subject to a decision under the *IRPA* may apply to the Federal Court for permission ("leave") to commence proceedings.[51] A decision not to grant leave cannot be appealed. If leave is granted, the Federal Court does not rehear the case but reviews the decision-making for errors or failure to observe a principle of natural justice or procedural fairness.[52] The merits of the case are not reviewed. As it is a review and not a rehearing, the Federal Court will not re-decide the case but may set aside or quash the decision and refer it back to the decision-maker in accordance with certain directions for redetermination.[53] In resettlement decisions, the decision-maker is a visa officer, and a redetermination is made by a different visa officer. An appeal of a judicial review from the Federal Court to the Federal Court of Appeal on immigration matters may only proceed if the Federal Court certifies that there is a "serious question of general importance" to be resolved and states the question.[54] If the Federal Court of Appeal hears a case, a further application for leave to be heard by the Supreme Court of Canada may be made.

The starting point for all considerations of immigration law in Canadian jurisprudence is found in the Supreme Court of Canada's statement in *Chiarelli v Canada (Minister of Employment and Immigration)*: "The most fundamental principle of immigration law is that non-citizens do not have an unqualified right to enter or remain in the country."[55] Nonetheless, the decision as to whether a non-citizen enters, as opposed to remains, in Canada is approached very differently. While applicable to all non-citizens, this statement is particularly true, and visible, in the treatment of refugees within Canada in contrast to those outside Canada and desiring to enter. In a discussion paper prepared in the context of the international forum on the strategic use of resettlement, the government of Canada noted:

> It has been Canada's experience that resettlement can be effectively managed as an *administrative process*. As a result resettlement decisions are not subject to the same level of formality as asylum determinations. In addition to being *less costly* to administer, this allows for *quicker decision-making* than is the case for asylum adjudication.[56]

Canadian courts have confirmed that a legitimate legal distinction exists between asylum determinations and resettlement decisions premised on the individual's presence within or outside of Canada. In the landmark decision in *Singh v Canada (Minister of Employment and Immigration)*, where the Supreme Court of Canada determined whether claimants were entitled to oral hearings,[57] the court split three to three on whether entitlement derived from protection under the *Canadian Charter of Rights and Freedoms*[58] or the *Bill of Rights*.[59] All agreed that there must be an adequate opportunity for refugee claimants to state their case and know the case to be met. The resulting decision triggered the government of Canada's first redesign of its in-Canada status determination system.[60] However, when the argument was subsequently made in *Jallow v Canada (Minister of Citizenship and Immigration)*[61] that *Singh* should extend to resettlement determinations by visa officers, it was flatly rejected at the Federal Court:

> In reviewing *Singh*, ... it is clear to me that the process which was eventually put in place in Canada is not applicable to claimants outside the country. Wilson J. makes numerous references in her reasons wherein

she emphasizes the duty of fairness on decision makers but it is very clear to me that other consequences which flowed from the decision are only applicable to Refugee claimants within Canada.[62]

And, as Justice Paul Rouleau reviewed in *Jallow*, Justice Bertha Wilson clearly stated in *Singh*:

> The Act envisages the assertion of a refugee claim under s. 45 in the context of an inquiry, which presupposes that the refugee claimant is physically present in Canada and within the jurisdiction of the Canadian authorities. The Act and the Immigration Regulations, 1978, SOR/78-172, do envisage the resettlement in Canada of refugees who are outside the country but the following observations are not made with reference to these individuals ... I am prepared to accept that the term includes every human being who is physically present in Canada and by virtue of such presence amenable to Canadian law.[63]

While *Jallow* clarified that the decision in *Singh* was not applicable to claimants outside Canada, the application of *Singh* to resettlement decisions was again argued in *Oraha v Canada (Minister of Citizenship and Immigration)*.[64] Manhal Abed Oraha's counsel asserted that, by attending an interview at a Canadian embassy abroad, a convention refugee claimant effectively becomes a person claiming refugee status in Canada. Justice Frederick Gibson of the Federal Court rejected the argument, stating: "Persons such as the principal applicant file their applications outside Canada or, at the time of filing, are outside Canada. The fact that they may briefly attend at a Canadian embassy for an interview or other related purpose can in no sense be said to make them persons claiming refugee status from within Canada."[65] Unlike refugee claimants within Canada who are accorded a hearing before a quasi-judicial tribunal, resettlement applicants abroad, as the statutory framework above outlines, are within an administrative process.

Individuals seeking resettlement to Canada are subject to the considerable discretion of the visa officer reviewing the referral. In the resettlement case of *Qarizada v Canada (Minister of Citizenship and Immigration)*, the court noted: "[M]uch of the case law cited in support of their arguments by the applicants is of little assistance to the Court as it stems from proceedings of the Refugee Protection Division in a quasi-judicial context. Here, the officer was making an administrative decision."[66] The distinction between quasi-judicial and administrative decision-making illustrates why the suggestion by the legislative review to unify overseas and inland protection decisions as one decision-making scheme was not accepted. The government retains more freedom and less responsibility in the administrative scheme.

Despite the current distinction between administrative and quasi-judicial decision-making, the Federal Court of Appeal has noted in *Chiau v Canada (Minister of Citizenship and Immigration)* that "the statutory scheme under which immigration control is administered does not leave admission decisions to the untrammelled discretion of the Minister or her officials."[67] Where a visa officer has refused a resettlement referral, the UNHCR can initially request that the decision be reconsidered. In such cases, the immigration and program manager at the responsible visa office is contacted.[68] There is no formal appeal process through either the visa office or within Canada. This means that the resettlement application will not be reconsidered and reheard in its entirety by a new decision-maker. Judicial review, however, is provided for in the *IRPA*.

An application for judicial review of the visa officer's decision to refuse resettlement can be brought before the Federal Court, which permits limited review for procedural errors or bias. If errors are found, the court will not reverse a decision, but it will send the case back for a redetermination by a different visa officer. Procedural protections therefore apply even to administrative decisions on resettlement. The degree of protection is dependent on the facts of the case. In *Baker v Canada (Minister of Citizenship and Immigration)*, the Supreme Court of Canada indicated that a key factor in determining the content of the duty of fairness in administrative law is the importance of the decision to the individuals affected: "The more important the decision is to the lives of those affected and the greater its impact on that person or persons, the more stringent the procedural protections that will be mandated."[69] The Federal Court has repeatedly recognized that a visa officer deciding an application for permanent residence in Canada of a resettlement refugee has a duty to act fairly.[70] The decision of the visa officer is reviewable on a reasonableness standard, but questions of procedural fairness raised by such decisions are decided on a standard of correctness.[71] The decisions examine the level of procedural fairness accorded in making a determination as to whether an applicant meets the definition of a convention refugee and fulfills the admission requirements – they do not review the decision-making as to which convention refugees are to be selected for resettlement.

In *Oraha*, Justice Gibson, while confirming that the duty to act fairly applies in resettlement decisions, clarified that an applicant for refugee resettlement is not entitled to the same level of procedural fairness accorded to a refugee claimant in Canada:

> I am in agreement that a visa officer, in matters such as this, has a duty to follow the Immigration Act and to act fairly. That duty of fairness is, I think, somewhat limited by comparison with that owed Convention refugee claimants applying from within Canada by reason of the fact that persons such as the principal applicant are not in Canada and do not face the possibility of deportation by Canadian authorities to the country where they claim to fear persecution if their claims are disallowed.[72]

While involving a decidedly lesser threshold than is encountered by in-Canada claimants, the more recent decision in *Ha v Canada (Minister of Citizenship and Immigration)*, which was decided by the Federal Court of Appeal, followed the decision in *Baker* with the acknowledgment that "[t]he fact that the appellants are applying for permanent residence status as Convention refugees suggests that this decision is potentially of great importance in their lives."[73] The Court of Appeal further noted:

> According to *Baker, supra*, at para. 24, the fact that there is no right of appeal from the visa officer's decision suggests that greater procedural protections should be afforded to the appellants in this case. While people applying for permanent residence status as CRSRs [convention refugees seeking resettlement] may bring judicial review applications, importantly, the scope of the reviewing judge's authority may be limited with respect to the substantive issues of the case, and therefore cannot be equated to an appeal right.[74]

Muhazi v Canada (Minister of Citizenship and Immigration) appears to be the first case that considered the review of resettlement visa decisions under the *IRPA* as opposed to its predecessor, the *Immigration Act*.[75] Justice François Lemieux in *Muhazi* considered *Baker* and *Oraha* in his reasoning and made no distinction between the old and new legislation. Relying on *Oraha*, he equated an interview with a visa officer to a hearing and asked whether the hearing was "full and fair."[76] However, as Justice Karen Sharlow clearly outlines in *Mohamed v Canada (Minister of Citizenship and Immigration)*, "[u]nder the regulations that set out the requirements for admission to Canada for a Convention refugee seeking resettlement, the visa officer's negative assessment of Mr. Mohamed's prospects in Canada is enough, standing alone, to justify the visa officer's denial of Mr. Mohamed's application for admission to Canada."[77] The scope of intervention available through judicial review is limited.

Judicial review remains, however, the sole route of legal challenge to a negative resettlement decision by a visa officer. A search of "refugee," "resettlement," and "visa officer" in the Quicklaw database "All Canadian Court Cases" on 10 June 2016 resulted in 253 cases. Only sixty-five cases, however, involved challenges to resettlement decisions – the remainder of the cases simply contained the search words in quoted legislation that was relevant to another type of overseas visa application, and many cases were translated duplicates where the legislation was quoted in both English and French. A further twenty-two relevant cases were discovered by reviewing the subsequent judicial treatments of the sixty-five cases. For the most part, these were cases where the decision-makers were referred to as embassy officials or immigration officials rather than as visa officers, which caused them to be missed in the keyword search. In total, therefore, eighty-seven challenges to resettlement decisions were found. Recalling that the Federal Court must grant leave under subsection 72(1) of the *IRPA* in order for a judicial review application to be heard, eighty-seven resettlement challenges is a significant number.

The Federal Court provides statistics on the number of leave applications granted for all refugee applications for leave, but it does not break this number down further between refugee claimants in Canada and those overseas. Nor does it indicate the total number of leave applications made.[78] In 2005, the Canadian Council for Refugees received data from the

Immigration and Refugee Board of Canada that, between 1998 and 2004, 89 percent of applications to the Federal Court for judicial review of in-Canada refugee claim determinations were denied leave.[79] An analysis of applications for leave from in-Canada refugee determinations between 2005 and 2010 found a leave grant rate of 14.44 percent but a 43.98 percent success rate where leave was granted.[80] It is likely that the rates for overseas applications are similar.

Certain observations can be made about these cases that offer insight into Canadian resettlement. The eighty-seven cases span the years 1994 to 2016, with between zero and nine cases being decided each year.[81] Forty-two of the eighty-seven applications for judicial review – 48 percent of the cases – were allowed at the Federal Court, with the cases being returned for redetermination by a new visa officer. One of the forty-five applications that were dismissed at the Federal Court was reversed at the Federal Court of Appeal and returned for redetermination by a new visa officer.[82] These cases arose out of negative visa decisions by officers from twenty-nine countries where Canada has diplomatic missions abroad. Twenty-three cases (26 percent) challenged decisions from Pakistan, nine cases (10 percent) challenged the decisions of visa officers in Germany, seven cases (8 percent) challenged the decisions of visa officers in Kenya, and six cases (7 percent) challenged the decisions of visa officers in Egypt. Visa officers in England and India were each challenged in four cases (4.5 percent). The remaining twenty-three countries each had between one and three resettlement decisions challenged. While the type of resettlement decision was not always noted in the judgments, forty-four of the cases (51 percent) were identified as sponsored resettlement applications.

It is impossible to make any conclusive statements from these data as the search criteria were non-exhaustive and the number of cases where the application for leave was denied is unknown. It does appear that refugees in certain countries (Pakistan and Germany) are more aware of the judicial review options and that applications for judicial review are much more likely to be made when there is a Canadian sponsor with knowledge of, and access to, the Canadian legal system. The fact that almost 50 percent of these applications were successful does speak to the Canadian legal system's concern for fairness. However, without knowing the results of the redeterminations, the fact that the Federal Court found that more than half of the reviewed visa officer decisions breached procedural fairness should raise alarm with respect to the thousands of negative decisions made by visa officers each year that are not reviewed.[83]

In November 2009, ten applications for judicial review were filed at the Federal Court following a series of rejections of Eritrean refugee applicants claiming to be members of the Pentecostal Church at the Canadian visa office in Cairo.[84] One visa officer decided all of the cases. Frustrated Canadian sponsors and the Canadian Council for Refugees coordinated the reviews, which is a further signal that connection to Canadian organizations greatly increases the likelihood of a failed refugee applicant pursuing judicial review. Many more cases with the same profile were added. The cases were case managed, with three lead cases granted leave in January 2011 and heard on 6 April 2011.[85] In its report *Concerns with Refugee Decision-Making at Cairo*, the Canadian Council for Refugees stated:

> The CCR [Canadian Council for Refugees] has long been concerned about inconsistencies in the quality of decision-making at visa offices abroad for refugees seeking resettlement to Canada. Not all visa officers have been adequately trained on refugee determination: this lack of preparation shows in some of the errors made. When mistakes are made, there is little opportunity for them to be corrected or for visa officers to learn from them, as there is no appeal and few cases are reviewed by the Federal Court. It is much more difficult for people in Canada to gather information on refugee decisions made at visa offices, compared to those made in Canada, and little attention is paid to the area by politicians, academics or the media.[86]

The Federal Court released judgments in four lead cases on 5 May 2011, each overturning the visa officer's decision.[87] The remaining cases, numbering close to forty, had been held in abeyance pending the outcome of the initial cases. The minister ultimately consented to judgment, with all of the cases being sent back for reconsideration.[88] Justice Judith Snider presided over each of the four lead cases. Her judgment in *Ghirmatsion v Canada (Minister of Citizenship and Immigration)* provides the most detailed reasons.[89]

The bulk of the decision in *Ghirmatsion* falls within general judicial review considerations on the unreasonableness of the officer's decision and is not specifically relevant here. Justice Snider does recognize the precarious situation of refugee claimants abroad: "[T]he situation faced by the Applicant cannot be ignored; he is a refugee claimant abroad, without counsel and without the various systems to protect his rights that would be found in Canada."[90] Again, however, the distinction between refugee claimants abroad and those in Canada is clearly drawn. One interesting aspect of this challenge was the submission that the visa officer erred in failing to give any consideration to the UNHCR's recognition of refugee status in her determination.[91] Showing the disjuncture between the Canadian and international systems of protection, Henok Aynalem Ghirmatsion, as well as the three other applicants, were recognized as convention refugees by the UNHCR.[92] However, UNHCR status is not determinative of Canadian eligibility, and Canadian law guides the officer's decision.

The operational manual for overseas processing does set out the eligibility criteria an officer should consider in assessing whether the convention refugee abroad class is met. The criteria include "a decision by the UNHCR or a signatory country with regard to an applicant's refugee status."[93] In *Ghirmatsion*, Justice Snider stated: "In my view, the Applicant's status as a UNHCR refugee was a personal and relevant consideration."[94] She held: "The Officer, faced with a UNHCR refugee, should have explained in her assessment why she did not concur with the decision of UNHCR."[95] This reassertion by the Federal Court of the operational manual's recognition of the relevance of the UNHCR's status determination is important for aligning the work of the UNHCR with the Canadian process. However, UNHCR status is not determinative in Canadian law, as *Ghirmatsion* confirms, and these cases illustrate the failure of visa officers to even reference it in their decision-making. The idea of refugee resettlement as a complementary mechanism to the internationally agreed upon refugee protection through asylum cannot be fully supported when these connections appear so tenuous.

Even more telling is Justice Snider's subsequent decision that an award of costs was warranted in these cases. The awarding of costs for judicial review in a refugee case requires special circumstances.[96] In *Ghirmatsion*, Justice Snider found there had been unnecessary prolongation of proceedings and blatant errors in the decision-making.[97] In this brief decision on costs, which in many ways is less legally significant than the substantive decision, Justice Snider spoke emphatically on both the failure and the power of the law. The law failed with the visa officer's decision-making, and the "magnitude" of errors and "her lack of adequate training and support" were evident on cross-examination.[98] Justice Snider also acknowledged the rarity of the application of the law in resettlement cases where the refugee remains outside of Canada: "The four representative Applicants and all of the remaining applicants are refugees in a dangerous foreign country without the resources to finance the judicial review of their claims in Canada."[99] Financial resources as well as access to, and awareness of, the law make cases such as *Ghirmatsion* unlikely. However, Justice Snider concluded with a powerful statement on the potential of law: "In such a situation, costs may be appropriate to encourage CIC [Citizenship and Immigration Canada] to review, and perhaps modify, the training and practices of visa officers in overseas posts."[100] Here, it is not the refugee's rights nor the state's obligations that may lead to better resettlement practices but, rather, the court's ability to make a financial order against the government.

In 2012, the *IRPR* were amended to formalize resettlement application procedures in response to low approval rates, large inventories, and long processing times.[101] The amendments limited eligibility for group-of-five and community sponsorship to refugees recognized by the UNHCR or a state. Under the sponsoring requirements set up in section 153(1), subsection (b) now requires that a sponsor

> must make a sponsorship application that includes a settlement plan, an undertaking and, if the sponsor has not entered into a sponsorship agreement with the Minister, a document issued by the United Nations High Commissioner for Refugees or a foreign state certifying the status of the foreign national as a refugee under the rules applicable to the United Nations High Commissioner for Refugees or the applicable laws of the foreign state, as the case may be.

Since the requirement only applies to group-of-five and community sponsors, but not to sponsorship agreement holders (SAH), it affects less than

50 percent of private sponsorship applications.[102] The intended goal was to increase sponsorship acceptance rates by ensuring applications meet Canadian requirements for resettlement. The changes have been criticized as going too far by requiring a recognition that is more rigid than Canadian protection and eligibility for resettlement, therefore risking the exclusion of certain individuals and groups in need of protection.[103] In numeric terms, the consequence was a reduction in group-of-five and community sponsorships and increased SAH sponsorships.[104]

Law's challenge here is in finding the appropriate line between overly broad discretion and overly stringent requirements. Given the huge levels of refugee protraction and the need for the efficient processing of applications, the government is right to seek a means of ensuring applications are likely to be successful.[105] In not making this a blanket requirement on all sponsorship applications, there remains a capacity to resettle those who might otherwise be excluded. This is a positive step towards better aligning resettlement with refugee protection. It should be supported by the grant of greater deference to these refugee status decisions by the UNHCR or a foreign state. The overseas processing manual lists "a decision by the UNHCR or a signatory country with regard to an applicant's refugee status" as merely one of the "other factors" for a visa officer to consider in determining eligibility.[106] If proof of refugee status is being made a requirement on sponsorship applications, it should be presumptive of eligibility in the visa officer's decision-making, subject to evidence to the contrary.

Other changes in 2012 included the creation of a Centralized Processing Office in Winnipeg (CPO-W) in April 2012 and the introduction of annual global caps and regional sub-caps since January 2012 to limit the number of applications that SAHs can submit to visa offices in Islamabad, Nairobi, Cairo, and Pretoria.[107] The rationale for these changes is addressed in the 2016 program evaluation, where, alongside the limitations to group-of-five and community sponsorships, it is suggested that there should be "efforts to create efficiencies in PSR processing and address inventories," which were previously noted in the 2007 evaluation.[108] Critiques point to "geographical discrimination, prejudice, or racism in the processing of PSRs."[109]

Discretion and Legal Layering

Whereas a state's asylum system originates in the international law of *non-refoulement* and is replicated and implemented within the state's own legal system, resettlement originates only from an international sense of responsibility for burden sharing, tied as it may be to foreign policy and international relations.[110] There is no international legal framework to set state standards. As a result, the state has absolute discretion to resettle refugees or not. If refugees are resettled, it is the state's discretion to decide whom to resettle, from where, and how. Discretion not only on the use of resettlement but also on whom to select for resettlement places the program's structure between in-Canada asylum claims and Canada's immigration program. While resettlement is defined by a humanitarian impulse towards refugee protection and is undoubtedly influenced by a sense of international burden sharing, Canadian resettlement operates as an administrative process in overseas embassies and high commissions much the same way that immigration decisions are made, with visa officers often reviewing both sets of applications.

The discretionary basis of resettlement means that it is approached by a state differently than it approaches its legal obligations to refugees. In Canada, this can be seen through Canada's active use of resettlement long before it ultimately agreed to sign the *Refugee Convention* in 1969 and absent any refugee legislation; the exclusion of overseas resettlement from the advisory committee process even when the decision was made to implement legislation dealing with refugees; the more recent announcement of resettlement increases alongside of, but not part of, legislated reform of refugee law; the subsequent numeric shift to private sponsorship that has significantly reduced government-assisted resettlement; and the confirmation by Canadian courts that a legitimate legal distinction exists between in-country refugee determinations and resettlement decisions premised on the individual's presence within or outside of Canada.

In Canada, geographic realities mean that resettlement preceded a comprehensive in-Canada asylum system. As a consequence, the two refugee protection programs developed to play theoretically complementary roles. The absence of a legal foundation for resettlement, however, has increasingly placed the program in juxtaposition to and competition with in-Canada asylum through a selective assertion of law while failing to acknowledge other legal rights. This selectivity corrupts the complementarity of the programs. Resettlement puts into focus the fundamental tension in the concept of refugee protection. The 1997 legislative review clumped together human rights and compassion as the basis of Canada's protection program.[111] Yet protection subdivides into in-Canada asylum and overseas resettlement, with rights tied to the former and compassion tied to the latter. While compassion links back to the underlying basis for Canada's self-imposition of the legal obligation of *non-refoulement*, resettlement has never been legally imposed, merely legally framed. The same is true of Canada's immigration program, which is fundamentally based on self-interest.[112] While self-interest undoubtedly also influences compassionately defined decisions, there is likewise compassion inherent in immigration programming as well. The interesting thing is that, while compassion and self-interest intermingle, and both resettlement and the immigration program are structured through a discretionary legal framework, it is only *non-refoulement* that has acquired the status of legal obligation.

It is the strength of the law and the absence of discretion with *non-refoulement* that now necessitates the discretionary counterpoint of resettlement. For over a decade, the Canadian government positioned resettlement as the more valid form of protection. It did so by focusing on law. A 2011 Citizenship and Immigration Canada news release makes the positioning clear: "All of these individuals who immigrated to Canada through our resettlement programs waited patiently in the queue for the chance to come to Canada legally. They followed the rules."[113] This is not the law of asylum but, rather, the immigration laws that control who may legally enter Canada. Part 1 of the *IRPA* begins with the requirement that a foreign national must "apply to an officer for a visa or for any other document required by the regulations" before entering Canada.[114] Immigration law is premised on the principle that non-citizens cannot simply enter and remain in Canada. Refugees, by necessity, however, may have to enter irregularly. This has been used to discount their right to asylum; they are "bogus refugees"[115] whose entrance is unfair to "legal, law-abiding immigrants who patiently wait to come to the country."[116]

Within this rhetoric, resettlement, while the voluntary aspect of the program, is privileged for its legal framework and clear legal entry into Canada. In a statement by the government in a 2010 backgrounder to its proposed anti-human smuggling legislation, potential resettlement applicants are described as "waiting patiently and *legally* in the refugee queue to come to Canada. These refugees choose to wait for the chance to come to Canada *legally*, rather than pay human smugglers to help them jump the queue. The Government of Canada appreciates their *respect for our laws.*"[117] The rhetorical attempt is to replace refugees who claim asylum in Canada with those waiting for resettlement through the suggestion that resettlement refugees are obeying Canadian law, whereas asylum-claiming refugees break Canadian law by entering Canada. This positioning of the law completely obscures the reality that, on another legal plane, resettlement refugees have no legal right to resettlement, whereas asylum refugees do possess the right not to be sent back through the legal obligation of *non-refoulement,* set out in Article 33 of the *Refugee Convention* and confirmed in the *IRPA.*

Moreover, international law recognizes that refugees may need to enter a state illegally. The *Refugee Convention* is clear that

> [t]he Contracting States shall not impose penalties, on account of their illegal entry or presence, on refugees who, coming directly from a territory where their life or freedom was threatened in the sense of article 1, enter or are present in their territory without authorization, provided they present themselves without delay to the authorities and show good cause for their illegal entry or presence.[118]

Canada is a state party to the *Refugee Convention,* and the *IRPA* acknowledges both that an objective of the act is "to fulfil Canada's international legal obligations with respect to refugees"[119] and that an in-Canada refugee claimant may present with no documentation-establishing identity whatsoever.[120] Essentially, one layer of legality is being asserted to evade another layer of legal obligation. Recalling the review of Canadian judicial decisions, those potential resettlement refugees whom the government applauds for their respect for Canadian law are less entitled to legal review of their cases than in-Canada asylum claimants and are more squarely in an administrative, rather than quasi-judicial, framework. Even with those refugees who fall within the convention refugee abroad class, recognition by the UNHCR of their convention refugee status is only a tenuously connected criterion that, from a review of the cases reaching the Federal Court, is not even noted by certain visa officers.

There are those who argue that Canada's recent re-emphasis on resettlement is a return to the country's original position on refugee protection premised on overseas selection. While not incorrect, this position reflects a time when Canada was simply not a country of first asylum. Nor did resettlement selection at the time reflect a foremost concern with protection. The humanitarianism that is threaded through governmental policies, positioning, and legislation has never truly dictated behaviour. Resettlement is a small piece of the protection regime. Refugees cannot simply opt to wait for resettlement rather than boarding a boat or a plane or crossing a border to claim asylum. While the government's refugee program is influenced by international relations, burden sharing, and its in-country image, the next chapter looks at Canada's private sponsorship program, which is propelled by the interests of individual Canadians. A very different set of challenges pulls at this program and influences the perception and protection of refugees.

5

Privatized Protection

In addition to the government-directed resettlement of refugees is the potential to involve private citizens in a resettlement partnership. In Canada, this is enabled through private sponsorship, where sponsors provide the financial support to bring over additional resettlement refugees. Private sponsorship both adds to Canada's resettlement capacity and creates a division in resettlement between refugees entering through the government program and those brought to Canada by citizens and permanent residents. The interests and motivations of Canadians to involve themselves in refugee resettlement fundamentally influence the concept and breadth of resettlement. Private sponsorship brings to the forefront the relationship between citizens and the state and the ways in which law is used and confused by contrasting the various forms of resettlement. In September 2016, Canada announced a joint project with the United Nations High Commissioner for Refugees (UNHCR) and the Open Society Foundations to export the Canadian sponsorship model to interested states.[1] Already, interest and programs are commencing in the United States, the United Kingdom, Spain, and elsewhere.

Private Sponsorship in Canada

While global interest expands, Canada's long-standing private sponsorship program remains unique in the world. It enables groups of individuals (five or more) and private organizations (religious, ethnic, or community) to sponsor refugees for resettlement. Sponsorship entails that the group takes on the responsibility of providing the refugee with assistance, accommodation, and support for up to one year. In exceptional circumstances of trauma, torture, or women and children at risk, the assistance can be extended for up to three years.

Over 300,000 refugees have been privately sponsored in Canada.[2] Canadian private citizens have resettled more refugees than most governments, ranking fourth behind the United States, Canada, and Australia.[3] While the Canadian government covers the administrative costs of the program, it is individual Canadians who provide the financial support attached to settling the refugee in Canada. As a general guidance, the government suggests the level of support should equate to the prevailing rates for social assistance in the settlement community.[4] The sponsor essentially takes on the state's responsibility for social welfare. In 2006, the Canadian Council for Refugees assessed the annual financial costs of private sponsorship at $79 million, with an additional volunteer contribution of over 1,600 hours per refugee family.[5] A "Sponsorship Cost Table" prepared by Immigration, Refugees and Citizenship Canada in 2018 estimates the cost of sponsoring a single individual at $16,500.[6]

Critiquing private sponsorship is an uncomfortable task. The program gives individual Canadians a voice and policy power, demonstrates their generosity, and significantly increases Canada's annual resettlement numbers. The purpose of this discussion is not to argue against the program, particularly at a time when it is being both exported and embraced more broadly. Rather, my interest is to impose a check that the program in fact meets its objective to complement the government program and resettle additional refugees.[7] While most evaluations of private sponsorship focus on sponsor motivation, program functioning, and refugee integration, these discussions fail to situate sponsorship within the greater whole of the Canadian refugee program. My intent here is different. While cognizant that the structure of the program will have an effect on sponsorship appeal,[8] the focus here is on the effect of sponsorship on refugee protection. Sponsorship's influence on government-assisted resettlement, the inland asylum program, and international obligations and burden sharing are considered.

Private sponsorship has been a part of Canadian refugee policy since Canada first formally recognized refugees as a separate immigration class in the *Immigration Act, 1976*.[9] Included with this legislated recognition were innovative and rather incidental provisions for the private sponsorship of refugees (PSR).[10] Lobbying for the private sponsorship scheme within this legislation came predominantly from ethnic groups wanting to resettle refugees from the Soviet Union and Eastern Europe. As one example, the Jewish Immigrant Aid Services of Canada (JIAS) pushed to introduce private sponsorship into the act.[11] Commenting on the government's 1967 white paper on immigration, Joseph Kage, the JIAS's national executive vice-president, wrote: "We also suggest that consideration be given to provisions which would enable individuals or responsible voluntary social agencies to offer sponsorship or co-sponsorship to deserving cases of refugees."[12] In 1973, he suggested that in looking to revise the *Immigration Act* "that consideration be given to provisions which would enable individuals or responsible voluntary social agencies to offer sponsorship or co-sponsorship in deserving cases of refugees or other immigrants, which would come under the category of 'humanitarian immigration.'"[13] In fact, the JIAS advocated not only for private sponsorship but also for other resettlement models embraced under the categories of source country and group resettlement.[14]

Informal private assistance from religious organizations was already happening. Both the Mennonite Central Committee and the JIAS were founded following the First World War to assist in immigration to Canada.[15] An order-in-council on 2 June 1922 permitted Mennonites from the Soviet Union to come to Canada but required that the Canadian Mennonite community take responsibility for the care of the newcomers so that they would not become a burden on the state.[16] Following the end of the Second World War, the Canadian Christian Council for the Resettlement of Refugees (CCCRR) was created in 1946 to assist the government in the assembly and selection of refugees in Germany.[17] Through a government grant of up to $10,000 a month, the CCCRR's purpose was "to organize the assembly abroad, selection, presentation to Canadian Immigration offices, and onward movement to Canada of refugees and displaced persons who did not come within the mandate of the I.R.O. [International Refugee Organization]."[18] This action was at a time when Canada's overseas immigration program consisted of "a single immigration officer, whose office was in his suitcase and whose method of transportation was by thumbing rides from military or other vehicles on the German roads."[19] The CCCRR operated until the end of 1951 and was followed by the approved church program of 1953 and the National Inter-Faith Immigration Committee established in 1968.[20] The approved church program permitted the Canadian Council of Churches, the CCCRR, the Rural Settlement Society of Canada, the Canadian Jewish Congress, and Jewish Immigrant Aid Services to assist with the selection of unsponsored immigrants as well as the approval and processing of sponsor applications.[21]

The assistance capacity of religious groups to bring refugees to Canada was thus well established before the scheme was brought into law. In 1969, Kage wrote to R.B. Curry, the assistant deputy minister of immigration, to advocate on behalf of the JIAS to sponsor "de facto" refugees from the Middle East, North Africa, and Eastern Europe. In the letter, Kage states: "We assure your Department [of Manpower and Immigration] that we shall provide for the necessary reception, housing, financial assistance, referral to employment and other adjustment and integration services."[22] The "Immigration Service" of the JIAS was described at the time as "provid[ing] sponsorship and guarantees for certain applicants who would otherwise not be able to enter Canada."[23] In a further letter to Robert Adams, the assistant deputy minister of immigration in 1972, Kage noted: "In all cases where the sponsor or nominator cannot fulfil the requirements for satisfactory settlement arrangements, JIAS will offer a letter of co-sponsorship and thereby assume on behalf of the Jewish community, the responsibility for the post-arrival adjustment of the immigrant, with reference to the provisions of essential housing, referral to employment and such other social assistance that may be required to effect satisfactory settlement."[24] The idea of private sponsorship was driven by the commitment and generosity of private Canadians.

At the outset, private resettlement could be done by a "group of five" or through organizations holding "master agreements" with the government.[25] The master agreements limited the government's need to vet individual sponsoring groups and left the bulk of responsibility to the agreement holders.[26] They also encouraged resettlement by smaller groups who were unable or unwilling to take on full liability as this liability rested with the agreement holder.[27] Relatively few changes to this initial design have been made. The current sponsorship scheme permits three types of sponsorship groups: groups of five; community sponsors; and constituent groups who are members of an organization that is a sponsorship agreement holder (SAH). As of 2012, SAHs and constituent groups reportedly submitted 60 percent of private sponsorship applications, and groups of five submitted approximately 40 percent, with community sponsors only submitting a handful of applications each year.[28] There are over 100 SAHs across Canada.[29] SAHs must be incorporated organizations. These organizations represent the evolution of the original "master agreements" of the 1970s. Since 2002, organizations that have not signed a sponsorship agreement with the government and are not partnered with an SAH or a constituent group may still sponsor as a community sponsor.[30] Groups of five consist of at least five individuals who are willing and eligible to sponsor. These groups are independently formed, but each member must complete a financial profile, and the group must set out a settlement plan and financial assessment. The *Immigration and Refugee Protection Act (IRPA)* brought in the new possibility of co-sponsorships, which permit an individual to partner with an SAH, a constituent group, or a community sponsor.[31] Thus, there is a government-imposed legal framework structuring private sponsorship.

The joint assistance sponsorship (JAS) program also operates wherein private sponsors provide supplemental, non-financial support to vulnerable refugees with special needs.[32] These refugees receive government support through the resettlement assistance program.[33] Private support and government support continue for twenty-four months, and the private sponsorship can be extended for an additional year in exceptional circumstances.[34] In statistical terms, JAS cases are considered to be government-assisted refugees (GARs)[35] and are identified and referred by visa officers rather than originating through the sponsorship organizations.[36] Joint sponsorship is rooted in the ad hoc historical origins of the sponsorship model. Canadian resettlement forms used by agencies in Europe in the 1970s gave three resettlement options, which essentially equate to government, private, or shared.[37] The conceptual basis for Canadian resettlement thus began with refugees coming through public, private, or shared public-private responsibility.

Historically, refugees in the private sponsorship scheme could be either "visa office–referred" or "sponsor referred."[38] Visa office–referred refugees have already been approved by Citizenship and Immigration

Canada for sponsorship and have completed the application process. Sponsor-referred refugees are chosen by the sponsoring group and must still be reviewed by Citizenship and Immigration Canada (which is now called Immigration, Refugees and Citizenship Canada) to determine their resettlement eligibility and protection needs before the application can be accepted. The overwhelming majority of private sponsorship is of sponsor-referred refugees. In the data from 2002 to 2005, visa office–referred cases accounted for less than 2 percent of private sponsorship.[39] In 2013, the government introduced the blended visa office–referred (BVOR) program, which matches private sponsors with refugees referred for resettlement by the United Nations under a cost-sharing model where the government splits financial support with sponsors, each covering six months.[40] With the BVOR option, the likelihood of traditional visa office–referred sponsorships without the blended government support is even more reduced.[41]

The obligations of the sponsoring group to the principal refugee applicant and all family members both accompanying and non-accompanying are set out in the sponsorship application forms. They begin with the refugees' arrival in Canada and reception in the community and include lodging ("suitable accommodation, basic furniture and other household essentials") and care ("food, clothing, local transportation costs and other basic necessities of life"). Non-financial assistance is also required to assist the refugees in learning an official language and seeking employment, teaching the refugees the rights and responsibilities of permanent residence in Canada, and providing a general extension of "ongoing friendship."[42] The sponsorship obligations are for twelve months or until the refugees become self-sufficient, if this occurs before the twelve-month time frame concludes. In exceptional circumstances, the sponsorship can be extended to thirty-six months. During the sponsorship period, privately sponsored refugees are not entitled to government assistance, through either the federal or the provincial government. As is the case with refugees resettled by the government, resettled refugees pay the costs of their required medical exams and transportation to Canada, usually by way of a loan from the federal government. In a case where a visa officer feels the refugee will be unable to repay the loan, sponsoring groups may be asked to pay a portion or all of these costs.[43]

Private sponsor support parallels the support the government provides to GARs through the resettlement assistance program, which includes financial assistance for up to one year subject to self-sufficiency and a one-time household goods and furniture package.[44] The common assumption is that privately sponsored refugees are more likely to obtain self-sufficiency in the one-year period than GARs. This may be due to the personalized support and the social capital value of sponsors as network ties.[45] While the point has been acknowledged in government documents, empirical data are lacking.[46]

The objective of private sponsorship is to complement the government-assisted program.[47] In its *Guide to the Private Sponsorship of Refugees Program*, the government begins by situating private sponsorship in this complementary role. The GAR program is set out alongside Canada's continuing myth as being "[i]n keeping with [Canada's] humanitarian tradition and international obligations." Through private sponsorship, the guide continues, "Canadian citizens and permanent residents are able to provide additional opportunities for refugees."[48] These opportunities are recognized as equipping Canadians with a voice on refugee policies in order to "let interested groups express their concerns for refugees in concrete ways."[49] Elsewhere, the program has been described as an enhancement of Canada's refugee protection capacity.[50] Despite the conceptual orientation of the program, the maintenance of private sponsorship's complementary role has been a continual challenge. Both the government and sponsoring groups have pulled the program in differing directions to meet their own interests. While "additionality" is the defining mandate of private sponsors,[51] government pushback can be seen in the 2016 notation that "the principle of additionality is not part of the PSR program theory."[52] In the grip of this tug of war, the objective and ideal of additional protection are stretched and strained to the point that it risks snapping.

The Public-Private Pull

Many large church groups were initially suspicious of the legalization of private sponsorship. They feared "the government intended to use the plan as a means of dumping its responsibilities for refugees onto the private sector."[53] The Mennonite Central Committee of Canada was the first national church body to sign a master agreement in 1979.[54] While the JIAS had lobbied for the legislation, the organization itself remained hesitant to sign a master agreement with the government, content instead with the resettlement they were doing without any such agreement.[55] If anything, the JIAS imagined using the legislation to continue its small-scale resettlement of Jews from Eastern Europe as well as North Africa and the Middle East. However, two years passed between the drafting of the *Immigration Act, 1976* and its implementation in 1978.[56] The private sponsorship scheme thus merged with the Indochinese "boat people" crisis of the late 1970s. Counter to expectations, the Indochinese resettlement marked the first opportunity to test the private sponsorship scheme in practice.

The Indochinese refugee outflow followed the collapse of the government of South Vietnam in 1975. That year, Canada agreed to admit up to 3,000 Indochinese with no ties to Canada from evacuation camps in the United States and elsewhere.[57] Following this initial intake, Canada processed applications from refugee camps of those applicants with sponsoring families in Canada and began to admit small numbers of "boat people" who were attempting to escape on small vessels. An initial 176 boat people were accepted in October 1976 and another 450 in August 1977.[58] By 1978, Canada had decided upon an ongoing response of accepting fifty "boat" families per month, and, by August 1978, the government had added twenty families per month who had escaped overland to Thailand.[59]

In 1979, following the entry into force of the *Immigration Act, 1976*, Canada introduced its first global refugee plan. The plan included 5,000 refugees from Southeast Asia, a number that was later increased to 8,000.[60] Private sponsorship was considered to be outside of these numbers. In 1979, the intent was for 2,000 additional refugees to come through family sponsorship under the general immigration scheme and another 2,000 from the private sponsorship program.[61] These numbers of privately sponsored refugees had not been anticipated. Those individuals in charge of designing the program before the crisis exploded imagined there would be approximately 100 private sponsorship applications per year, and they were uncertain as to whether there would be program uptake.[62] The provision was originally regarded as being something good to have that would be used when necessary rather than depending on ad hoc arrangements.[63] By the spring of 1979, it was becoming clear to the government that the sponsorship idea was catching on.[64]

The government considered sponsorship an ideal means of enabling the settlement of the Indochinese. Howard Adelman documents a Sunday meeting organized at his home in June 1979 to petition the government to take more refugees. Two top civil servants appeared at the private meeting and proposed private sponsorship as a more proactive alternative to the petition.[65] When worsening circumstances and ever-increasing outflows made the earlier total of 12,000 refugees appear insignificant and inadequate, the government responded to public, media, and international pressure by increasing the number to 50,000.

This increase, however, came with a caveat. Using the newly legislated sponsorship scheme, the private sector would be responsible for half of this intake. The government proposed to "match" each privately sponsored refugee with a government-resettled refugee until the end of 1980.[66] With the government number already at 8,000, the matching program envisioned the government and private sponsors each resettling 21,000 additional refugees to bring the number to 50,000.[67] The matching scheme enabled the government to promote its new sponsorship program and appear responsive to both domestic and international pressure to assist the Indochinese without an excessive financial toll.[68] The matching formula further offered a "political barometer" to measure continued public support for Indochinese resettlement.[69]

Despite these clear government advantages, descriptions of the matching program suggest the government presented the program as a concession to the Canadian public. James Hathaway writes: "The government *agreed to permit* Canadian organizations and groups of individuals to privately sponsor the admission of Convention refugees and designated class members from abroad."[70] At the time the matching system was announced, private and family sponsorship was at 4,000 per year, and government numbers were set at 8,000. Sponsoring groups saw private sponsorship as providing additional resettlement "over and above" government support.[71] Doubling these numbers to cover both 1979 and 1980, the original resettlement numbers stood at 16,000 for the government and 8,000 for sponsors. The increase to 50,000 by way of a matching scheme therefore meant an increase of 13,000 more refugees for the government and private sponsors each to resettle over the two years. The government was thus expecting sponsors to almost double their numbers.[72]

To facilitate and expedite the resettlement, the Indochinese refugees were made a "designated class." The *Immigration Act, 1976* set out the potential to establish a "designated class" that "includes persons oppressed in their own country or displaced by emergency situations such as war or revolution."[73] Designating the Indochinese as a class, which foreshadows the more recent group-processing methodology that will be discussed in Chapter 7, avoided the need for individualized assessments of refugee status. As well as reducing processing time, the designated class structure reduced the requisite knowledge necessary for facilitating resettlement. Protection need and refugee status were presumed. These designations opened the door for the more broadly based sponsorships that now occur.

Although church groups were initially reluctant to support the program, private sponsorship support for the Indochinese was immediate and overwhelming. Church groups and private citizens embraced sponsorship for the protection and increased refugee resettlement numbers it offered. Fewer than 100 private sponsorships had taken place under the new act by the spring of 1979.[74] Remarkably, numbers reached 29,269 by the end of that year. The supplementary support of sponsors became the foundational core of Canadian resettlement. The Liberal opposition critic, Member of Parliament Robert Kaplan, observed: "If anything, it has been the government of Canada that has been challenged by the Canadian people."[75] With the private sector exceeding its quota, the program was extended to an additional 10,000 refugees in 1980.[76] Of the 60,000 Indochinese refugees admitted to Canada between 1979 and 1980, approximately 26,000 were government assisted, and 34,000 were privately sponsored.[77] Over 7,000 Canadian sponsoring groups took part in the resettlement.[78]

The story, however, is not quite so simple. The Indochinese resettlement weaves through two federal elections in Canada and three different political parties in power. The Liberal government of Pierre Trudeau made the original pledge in 1979 to accept 5,000 refugees. It was Joe Clark's minority Conservative government that increased the number to 8,000 and made the later promise of 50,000 through the matching formula by the end of 1980.[79] While private sponsors easily exceeded their quota, the government was in need of funds. Canada had pledged $15 million in food and medical aid to Cambodia.[80] The government was over-extended. With sponsorships soaring, the government was concerned that it could not keep up. It lacked the capacity to process the sponsorship applications and continue with its own resettlement obligations.

An internal government proposal in 1979 addressed the idea of extending the matching timeline into 1981 and prioritizing the processing of private sponsor applications over government-assisted refugees.[81] The government feared losing sponsors due to frustration if sponsored refugees were slow to arrive in Canada. Seemingly without having read the internal proposal,[82] the government opted to shift more of the Indochinese resettlement numbers to the clearly capable private sponsors.[83] The strategic decision was made to maintain the 50,000 resettlement figure for the year by substituting government-sponsored refugees with privately sponsored refugees.[84]

At the time of the government's decision on 5 December 1979, it was reported that private sponsorship exceeded its portion and was at 26,196 refugees, whereas the government had only resettled approximately 12,000 refugees. This left a further 11,800 refugees to be resettled – now by private citizens – to meet the promise of 50,000 individuals by the end of 1980.[85] This felt like a betrayal to many private sponsors. The matching formula was compromised whether interpreted as matching merely the target quota of 50,000 or more generously matching every privately sponsored refugee with a government-sponsored refugee. Members of the Standing Conference of Canadian Organizations Concerned for Refugees sent a letter on 13 December 1979 to Prime Minister Joe Clark, Minister of External Affairs Flora MacDonald, Secretary of State David MacDonald, and Immigration Minister Ronald Atkey, expressing their discontent with the government's reversal of its July 1979 commitment to match sponsored refugees on a one-to-one basis and allow private sponsorship to continue unrestricted.[86] They wrote: "We are not prepared to release the government from its obligations."[87] Having moved beyond its initial reluctance to support sponsorship to now taking full advantage of the scheme, the sponsorship community was quickly reminded of the danger that an over-reliance on sponsorship support would release the government from its own obligations.

The timing of events could not have been more dramatic or less consequential. Politics again came into play. That same day, the minority government failed to pass a motion of confidence. Parliament was dissolved on the following day, 14 December 1979. The majority Liberal government of Pierre Trudeau assumed power in April 1980. While a return to the matching formula did not occur, the new immigration minister, Lloyd Axworthy, announced the government's renewed commitment to resettlement and made the commitment for an additional 10,000 resettlement spots for a total of 60,000 on 2 April 1980.[88] The 60,000 number essentially, but not formally, rebalanced the matching formula between sponsorship and government resettlement. The announcement and the swift changes marked the line between politics and law and the role each was playing. Shortly after the announcement, Gerald Dirks observed: "Any contentiousness associated with refugee admission to Canada in recent years has not arisen due to inadequacies in the legislation but rather has resulted from policy preferences and day-to-day administrative procedures determined by the cabinet and officials of the Employment and Immigration Commission."[89] The law was broad, and the policy was malleable.

Such policies could easily manipulate the complementary design of private sponsorship. Private sponsorship was originally conceived as being limited only by the generosity and willingness of private Canadians. While the government released annual immigration quotas that included refugees, only federally assisted refugees were originally included.[90] Sponsorship's role was complementary, as the government itself explained, "because sponsored refugees are admitted to Canada over and above those accepted into the government's annual resettlement plan."[91] By the mid-1980s, the fault line of this numeric division was identified. The government tied its failure to meet its GAR quota to the requirement that visa officers also process private sponsorship applications.[92] Sponsorship groups conversely accused the government of preferentially processing sponsorship applications over GARs to the extent that privately sponsored refugees made up close to one-half of the government's annual quota.[93]

While not as overt an action as the Conservative government's abandonment of the matching formula, the result was practically the same. Only a few years into the program, the Inter-Church Committee for Refugees expressed concern that the government had endorsed a policy shift that placed most of the responsibility for refugee resettlement on the private sector.[94] This shifting of resettlement responsibility led to the first major challenge for private sponsorship. Initial hesitations had proven true, but, already, the protection potential of the program was too much for private sponsors to now abandon the scheme.

Reining in Family Reunification

Following the surge of Indochinese resettlement in 1979–80, private sponsorship settled at 4,000–6,000 arrivals per year. By the end of 1981, the crisis had subsided, and the government felt it could not fill its Southeast Asian quota of 8,000. The quota was reduced to 4,000 for the following year, and the government announced a more regionally balanced resettlement.[95] Even as the numbers diminished, the international community honoured the Canadian public for its contribution to the refugee cause.[96] Perhaps as a result of this recognition, the late 1980s brought a jump in private sponsorship, with numbers growing from 7,437 in 1987 to 21,631 in 1989.[97] The height of sponsorship, however, also marked a significant downturn in Canadian receptiveness to refugees. A numeric increase of this measure raised suspicions and strained relations between the government and sponsors.[98] Public opinion polls showed that Canadian resistance to resettlement went from 31 percent in 1989 to 49 percent by 1991.[99]

The government initiated a review of the private sponsorship program in 1990. At the time, financial overextension by sponsorship groups and mutual mistrust between government and sponsors plagued the program.[100] The review commenced with a steering committee involving representatives from private sponsorship groups, non-governmental organizations (NGOs), academia, and the federal government. Initial research and consultations led to a report that guided discussion at a national consultation. Following the consultation, a comprehensive report was compiled, reviewed, and forwarded to the minister.[101] The review points to the second major challenge of private sponsorship: maintaining the focus on refugee protection in the drive for family reunification through sponsorship. The first challenge – the shifting of responsibility – was driven by the government. The second challenge was equally the responsibility of the sponsorship community and the government, and it threatened the refugee concept. In the midst of declining sympathy for refugees, visa officers worried that the program was turning into a tool of family reunification.

The extension of Canada's government resettlement program beyond the protection of convention refugees is closely tied to sponsor influence and the desire for greater leeway in meeting the protection need. The consultations pointed to the sponsor interest in setting eligibility and admissibility criteria for resettlement.[102] The sponsorship community was also involved in the development of the humanitarian class, which consisted of the country of asylum and source country classes.[103] The expansion provided increased scope to use the program for family reunification. It also threatened to stretch protection to its breaking point: "Among the refugee-sponsoring community, the demand for family-linked sponsorships is seen as being effectively without limit, because for every refugee who arrives sponsors estimate that at least two more sponsorship requests are generated."[104] Family sponsorship generates sustainable sponsorship, but it also continually replenishes the need.

By this time, the nature of sponsorship had shifted significantly from the Indochinese. The Indochinese sponsorship was primarily a sponsorship of strangers. There was no real Indochinese base in Canada. Canadian willingness to sponsor resulted from extensive media coverage of the protection need.[105] Referrals were through the government.[106] Overseas offices originally sent refugee lists to Ottawa, where pre-matching with sponsors was done by a matching centre. By September 1979, a computer system was introduced that matched passenger lists for incoming refugees with sponsors.[107] The sponsorship that followed after the Indochinese crisis reverted back to what was envisioned by the original sponsorship lobbyists, with sponsors naming the refugees to be resettled.[108] By 2003, some estimates put nominations of family or close friends at 95–99 percent of sponsorship referrals.[109]

Sponsor-based referrals mean that the program is conceptually global and flexible. Sponsors may draw their referrals from anywhere in the world. What this means though is that sponsored referrals need not be, and often are not, recognized by the UNHCR as refugees or, if recognized, are not among the refugees referred by the UNHCR for resettlement. Canada's resettlement classes reach beyond the refugee definition to a broader consideration of individuals in need of protection. In reality, as recognized in the comprehensive review, social capital tends to guide sponsor selections. Ethnic and religious groups already settled in Canada understandably focus on sponsoring others from their families, communities, and countries. Thomas Denton, co-chair of the Manitoba Refugee Sponsors and executive director of administration and refugee sponsorship at the Hospitality House Refugee Ministry, describes this as "relational migration" to differentiate this sponsorship from the defined family class sponsorship permitted as an immigrant class.[110] In this manner, however, the private sponsorship program serves to better complement and expand the narrowly structured family reunification system in the immigration stream than it does the objective of refugee protection.[111] As Denton himself argues, "[t]hey may not be refugees, but they are still 'family,' yet unwelcome in Canada."[112] The idea of, and argument for, refugee protection are lost in the push for family reunification through any means possible.

Both overexpansion and the extension of coverage risk missing those most in need of protection. The review recognized the legitimate reasons for the familial link. Sponsors are in closer contact with refugees from their family or country and find it easier to offer support and transfer knowledge to refugees from the same cultural background.[113] It concluded: "Experience indicates that 'naming' refugees from within Canada is a legitimate and worthwhile means of accessing persons who are in need of protection."[114]

Family reunification does have a positive settlement influence. The UNHCR acknowledges that "the family unit has a better chance of successfully ... integrating in a new country rather than individual refugees. In this respect, protection of the family is not only in the best interests of the refugees themselves but is also in the best interests of States."[115]

The assessment of protection need, however, must remain central; otherwise, family reunification risks corrupting the refugee concept. As was the concern with the expansion of protection through the broader recognition of human rights violations, family reunification poses the same expansion dangers.

As Table 4 highlights, resettlement numbers continued to drop in the 1990s, tied to processing delays, the end of the Cold War, recession, and a significant increase of in-Canada claims.[116] Numbers dropped from 17,433 in 1991 to 2,838 in 1994 and sat somewhere in the range between 2,000 and 4,000 privately sponsored refugees each year until 2008. Since that time, private sponsorship ranges have been on the rise, with actual landings

TABLE 4
Private sponsorship ranges and landings, 1979–2021

Year	Planned range	Actual landings
1979		13,893
1980		21,244
1981		4,405
1982		5,863
1983		4,161
1984		3,976
1985		3,881
1986		5,222
1987		7,437
1988		12,387
1989		21,631
1990		19,307
1991		17,433
1992		8,960
1993		4,768
1994		2,838
1995		3,244
1996		3,063
1997		2,580
1998	2,800–4,000	2,148
1999	2,800–4,000	2,331
2000	2,800–4,000	2,905
2001	2,800–4,000	3,576
2002	2,900–4,200	3,041
2003	2,900–4,200	3,252
2004	3,400–4,000	3,116
2005	3,000–4,000	2,976
2006	3,000–4,000	3,337
2007	3,000–4,500	3,588
2008	3,300–4,500	3,512
2009	3,300–4,500	5,036
2010	3,300–6,000	4,833
2011	3,300–6,000	5,584
2012	4,000–6,000	4,225
2013	4,500–6,500	6,269
2014	4,500–6,500	4,560
2015	4,500–6,500	9,350
2016	15,000–18,000	18,362

Year	Planned range	Actual landings
2017	14,000–19,000	16.873
2018	16,000–19,000	
2019	17,000–21,000	
2020	18,000–23,000	
2021	18,000–23,000	

Source: Table compiled using statistics from (1979–93) Barbara Treviranus & Michael Casasola, "Canada's Private Sponsorship of Refugees Program: A Practitioner's Perspective of Its Past and Future" (2003) 4 Journal of International Migration and Integration 177; (1994–2006) Citizenship and Immigration Canada, *Summative Evaluation of the Private Sponsorship of Refugees Program* (2007), 3.2.4, online: <www.cic.gc.ca/english/resources/evaluation/psrp/psrp-summary.asp>; (2007–17) Citizenship and Immigration Canada/Immigration, Refugees and Citizenship Canada, *Annual Reports to Parliament on Immigration* (2002–18); Immigration, Refugees and Citizenship Canada, "Notice: Supplementary Information 2019–2021 Immigration Levels Plan" (31 October 2018), online: Government of Canada <www.canada.ca/en/immigration-refugees-citizenship/news/notices/supplementary-immigration-levels-2019.html>.

amounting to over 9,000 in 2015 with the change in government. In 2016 and 2017, the numbers essentially doubled, reflecting the surge in the early 1990s, and are projected to expand further. As was the case earlier, the question is whether these numbers will be maintained.

In the midst of sponsorship's diminishing numbers, the Canadian government appeared to re-embrace the program. Since 1994, the NGO–Government Committee on the Private Sponsorship of Refugees has been closely involved in the policy and legislative developments of the private sponsorship program.[117] Ninette Kelley and Michael Trebilcock suggest that the committee's creation marked a fiscal decision by the government to shift the focus away from GARs and towards private sponsorship.[118] Arguably, this shift is a simple reality that has existed since the creation of the program or at least since the Inter-Church Committee for Refugees complained that the government's use of private sponsorships to fill its annual quota represented a policy shift that placed the majority of responsibility for refugee resettlement on the private sector. Kelley and Trebilcock's observation is accurate in that the government's immigration planning for 1995–2000 listed the improvement of private sponsorship at the top of its refugee planning priorities.[119] In 2010, Jason Kenney, then minister of immigration, went on a summer tour to promote refugee resettlement and encouraged private groups that were not historically involved as SAHs to become involved in the resettlement process.[120] The 2012 federal budget more concretely moved government attention from GARs to private sponsorship with the announced shift of 1,000 resettlement spaces by decreasing the GAR target range and increasing the private sponsorship target range over the next few years.[121] By 2017, the PSR target of 16,000 was more than double the 7,500 GAR target, with the plan to move this doubling forward to over 10,000 GARs and 20,000 PSRs by 2021.

Blended Pilot Projects

Part of the government reorientation occurred through a greater intersection of government and private resettlement. The resettlement of 1,800 Afghan Ismaili refugees to Canada between 1994 and 1998 was the first example of "blending" government and private support. Blended projects are distinct from joint assistance sponsorship (JAS) and involve a sharing of financial responsibility between the government and a sponsoring group. Project FOCUS Afghanistan was a partnership between Citizenship and Immigration Canada, the Ismaili Council for Canada, and FOCUS Humanitarian Canada, a Canadian NGO. Citizenship and Immigration Canada provided the first three months of resettlement support through the adjustment assistance program, which enabled the community to fundraise and organize support for the remaining nine months of the refugees' first year.[122] Referrals came from the sponsors, but the cases were counted as GARs. The project was hailed by Citizenship and Immigration Canada as a key point in its "chronological history of the private sponsorship of refugee program" and listed as a "cost effective use of government resources."[123] A special 3/9 sponsorship pilot program for refugees from the former Yugoslavia, with the government financing the first three months and the community responsible for the next nine months, was similarly designed but with the referrals coming from the government. The government conceived of the program as a "catalyst to increase private sponsorship and stretch the benefits of the private sector funds."[124]

Blending encourages private sponsorship by groups unable to take on complete financial responsibility.[125] Denton suggests that, had private sponsorship not moved beyond its charitable origins of bringing in strangers to a more family- or relational incentive-based program, it would likely not have survived. He notes that the church organizations that spearheaded the initial push now lacked the financial resources to continue to bear the financial burden and, instead, were contracting the financial responsibility for the refugee to the familial link.[126] The increasing use of blended projects indicates a changing financial reality that leaves sponsors dependent on the government and thereby grants the government renewed control of the program.

A further program with the Sierra Leonean community was based on a 4/8 sponsorship scheme with the government financing the first four months and the community responsible for the next eight months. The program was family oriented and is discussed in more detail later in this chapter. A program between Citizenship and Immigration Canada and the Anglican primate initiated in 2009 and running until March 2011 likewise followed this model.[127] This time, however, approximately 150 refugees from diverse parts of the world, including Afghanistan, Burma, Colombia, Democratic Republic of Congo, Eritrea, Ethiopia, Iran, Iraq, Liberia, Somalia, Sri Lanka, and Sudan, were resettled.[128] Each project arose as an ad hoc negotiation between the government and a community or organization. This activity marked a movement away from the regulated legal framework for sponsorship. Law is lessened.

On 18 March 2011, Citizenship and Immigration Canada announced a new blended program for Iraqi refugees.[129] The program followed the announcement in Citizenship and Immigration Canada's 2009 annual report to Parliament, highlighting a doubling of privately sponsored Iraqi refugees accepted from the Middle East over the next five years.[130] The commencement of a blended program over a year later speaks to the government's inability to control private sponsorship by simply announcing a willingness to increase numbers. Additional governmental support is required to direct sponsorship.[131] The blended program was once again a "pilot project" with the Armenian Community Centre of Toronto and the Asmaro Chaldean Society in Windsor.[132] The program mirrored the 3/9 model used for the pilot projects with the Ismaili Council of Canada for Project FOCUS Afghanistan and the special 3/9 sponsorship pilot program for refugees from the former Yugoslavia. With this project, both the Armenian

Community Centre and the Asmaro Society received up to $100,000 in assistance in the form of three months of income support for each sponsored Iraqi refugee.[133]

Another blended pilot project was revealed less than a week later. On 24 March 2011, Citizenship and Immigration Canada announced that it would partner with the Rainbow Refugee Committee to sponsor lesbian, gay, bisexual, transgendered, and queer/questioning (LGBTQ) refugees.[134] The program followed a 3/9 support model with $100,000 of government assistance available over a three-year term, with the possibility of an extension.[135] The project is interesting as it marks the first example of a non-ethnic/religious-based blended agreement. Instead, it moves closer to the core of refugee protection by focusing the sponsorship not on a country of origin but, rather, on a specific persecution nexus – refugees fleeing persecution because of their sexual orientation or gender identity. While the agreement is with the Vancouver-based Rainbow Refugee Committee, the project is considered national in scope, with the organization connecting with other groups interested in sponsoring LGBTQ refugees.[136]

In some ways, these blending programs reflect the era of resettlement before it was formally brought under the law when organizations like the JIAS negotiated sponsorship arrangements with the government. The blended model was formalized through the BVOR program, which was introduced in 2013.[137] The BVOR program increases the amount of government support from earlier pilot projects with a 6/6 model, where the government and private sponsors each take financial responsibility for six months. With the BVOR program, however, the government took back the control over naming that many of the earlier blended models left with sponsors. This program is examined in more detail later in this book.

Another form of "blending" that involves the municipal and provincial levels of government can be seen in Winnipeg, Manitoba, where refugee sponsorship has been encouraged as part of a population-building strategy. In 2002, $250,000 of municipal funds was set aside by the city to establish the Winnipeg private refugee assistance program, an assurance fund to encourage private sponsorship.[138] The program was proposed by the Manitoba Interfaith Immigration Council (MIIC) in response to the homegrown economic development strategy approved by Winnipeg City Council in June 2002, which stated that the city must "play a leadership role in supporting enhanced immigration sponsorship programs."[139] The program commenced 13 January 2004 for a five-year period.[140] The city of Winnipeg essentially guaranteed the sponsorship by supporting groups in the event of a breakdown in the sponsorship to ensure that there would be no dependency on the federal government.[141] The agreement between the city and the Manitoba refugee sponsors group begins with "Guiding Principles" that set out the vision of the program as a population-building strategy:

1. The City desires to support private family-linked or community-linked refugee sponsorships as one effective mechanism for increasing the city's population ...
3. The parties wish to collaborate with each other and with the Government of Canada and the Province of Manitoba in increasing Winnipeg's population while meeting the humanitarian need for refugee resettlement.[142]

The original agreement was only between the city of Winnipeg and the Manitoba refugee sponsors group. The city of Winnipeg contributed the total amount for the assurance fund and $30,000 yearly for the first five years to cover the administrative support of the program.[143] From the outset, however, the intention was for a tri-level agreement involving the city of Winnipeg, the province of Manitoba, and the federal government.[144] It was Citizenship and Immigration Canada that requested the program encompass not only family-sponsored refugees but also "community-linked" sponsorship so that Citizenship and Immigration Canada could identify "unnamed" refugees from its missions abroad for sponsorship.[145] An additional five-year wind-up period was built into the agreement to ensure that all in-process sponsorships could be finalized. Extensions were granted in 2009 and 2011, thereby extending the five-year wind-up period to 31 December 2016, at which point the remaining funds were given to the Manitoba Interfaith Immigration Council and the Manitoba Refugee Sponsors to administer, and an endowment fund overseen by the Winnipeg Foundation was established.[146] Not all sponsored refugees to Winnipeg fell under the assurance fund. The intent of the fund was to enable additional sponsorship. The administrative operation of the program overseen by the

MIIC involved developing the qualifying criteria and identifying the sponsorships that would receive the assurance.[147]

As of March 2011, the fund had only been drawn upon twice – once for $400 because the sponsoring family moved to Edmonton and once for $5,000 when an emergency required the sponsored family return to Ethiopia.[148] The value of the fund was therefore growing and sat at over $300,000.[149] By June 2015, sixteen payments had been made between 2007 and 2015, and the fund's balance was $227,571.62.[150] In a 2015 report to city council, it is noted that the program "may be unique among municipalities in Canada, and has made Winnipeg the largest refugee sponsoring centre in the country: fifty percent of all refugees being sponsored each year into Canada through the federal government are being sponsored by Winnipeg sponsors."[151] Winnipeg is often considered the hub of Canadian private sponsorship. According to one report, 60–70 percent of SAH cases initiated across Canada come from the city.[152] The program speaks to the value the city of Winnipeg and the province of Manitoba see in family refugee sponsorship and the potential for this sponsorship to bring in contributing and valued members of the population. The fact that the assurance fund was barely drawn upon is attributed further to the strength of this family support.[153] Notably, Immigrant Settlement and Integration Services, a community organization in Nova Scotia, developed an assurance fund and became an SAH in 2011 to facilitate private sponsorship, based on the Manitoba model.[154]

The most recognized example of sponsor-government cooperation is the case of the Kosovar resettlement in 1999. In terms of the public face of private sponsorship between the Indochinese and Syrian resettlement programs, the Kosovar resettlement stands out in Canada as a period of pride and momentum. Yet, as with the Indochinese, the Kosovar resettlement was in no way representative of the private sponsorship program as a whole. In fact, it was not private sponsorship. The resettlement was entirely government assisted. The Kosovars were determined to be special needs refugees, and their sponsorship fell into the JAS program's non-financial scheme of support. But neither were the Kosovars typical refugees. Their movement was an emergency evacuation through a NATO operation. Serbian atrocities in Kosovo and the NATO bombing of 24 March 1999 triggered a mass exodus of displaced ethnic Albanian Kosovars into

Macedonia. Macedonia, itself a fragilely balanced ethnic state with one-quarter of its population Albanian, risked destabilization with the inflow of ethnic Albanians from Kosovo.[155] The UNHCR requested that the international community provide asylum for some 750,000 Albanian Kosovars in Macedonian and Albanian refugee camps. Canada, among other countries, responded and committed to accept 5,000 Albanian Kosovars "over and above" the annual resettlement target.[156]

While the Kosovar resettlement was unique, so was Canada's response in relation to that of other states. Elsewhere, the Kosovars were taken in on a temporary basis. Canada linked their reception to fast-tracked family reunification and offered the option of permanent residence.[157] In addition to the 7,367 GARs resettled in 2000, 3,258 Kosovars obtained permanent residence.[158] This explains why Citizenship and Immigration Canada's numbers for 2000 show that Canada resettled 10,666 GARs – 41 percent more than the average yearly number between 1995 and 2005.[159] Despite the unusual circumstances of the Kosovars' movement and the lack of individual status determinations, the UNHCR was explicit in its acknowledgment that the Kosovars were refugees. On 30 April 1999, the UNHCR published the *Protection Framework Guidance* on Kosovo that began thus:

> [T]he majority of those displaced outside the Federal Republic of Yugoslavia in the current circumstances are properly considered refugees – they are displaced because of conflict or on account of well-founded fear of persecution based on their ethnicity, imputed political opinion and/or religion. The deportation of important numbers was one means by which the forced flight was effected. It does not change their refugee character as persons unable to return to their country for refugee relevant reasons.[160]

The footnote to this quotation further clarified that "[t]his is the case for the Kosovo Albanians." The resettlement of the Kosovars is thus exemplary as it served a clear protection need and brought together efficient government support and generosity in collaboration with sponsorship assistance.

The timing of the evacuation, like the Indochinese crisis, coincided with massive changes to Canada's immigration legislation. While the Indochinese flow occurred just as refugees were being recognized as an immigrant group in the *Immigration Act, 1976*, the Kosovars' arrival occurred alongside the *IRPA*'s reorientation towards an increased emphasis on protection, family reunification, and NGO cooperation. This reorientation has been hailed as being part of the development of a more flexible and global resettlement program in Canada.[161] Government and public reaction to the Kosovars also sits in stark contrast to the Canadian reaction to the Chinese migrants that arrived by boat that same summer – the controlled and generous welcome of one group by way of resettlement compared to the resistant push against migrants seeking asylum.[162] The Kosovar resettlement is considered to have generated a new community of sponsors, a fact that may be tied to the reality that sponsors were not required to make a financial contribution.[163] However, by demonstrating the ability of the government to act so quickly in response to a massive movement of people, sponsoring groups became more forceful in their demands for the resettlement of other groups and their focus on other regions.[164] This is a reality that has been repeated with the swift resettlement of Syrian refugees to Canada in 2015–16 and with the Yazidi resettlement push that followed.[165]

Refusal Rates and Protection Concerns

Both the Kosovar resettlement and the pilot blending projects present examples of cooperative partnerships in which the government retained significant control. This control has been lost in traditional private sponsorship despite the government's ultimate discretion and oversight role. Government attempts to move the sponsorship program back to its visa officer–referral origins have met with resistance from the sponsorship community.[166] A consequence of the sponsor-referred model is that there tends to be a high refusal rate of sponsor-referred names (averaging 49 percent between 1998 and 2007), which then drains government resources without achieving resettlement and leaves sponsors frustrated.[167] From 2006 to 2010, the PSR approval rate was 57 percent.[168] The refusal rate is linked to a stated concern that the protection need is lacking in many of these cases.[169] The absence of protection need in a program premised on protection is a critical challenge. One response by sponsorship groups has been to note the difficulty in assessing refugee cases and protection needs from within Canada.[170] The practical difficulty of privatized responsibility for protection challenges the easy shifting of such responsibility.

The Canadian Council for Refugees has countered that sponsors play an important role in identifying refugees who are in need of resettlement:

> For example, sponsors work with partners such as the overseas arms of Canadian NGOs with presence in the field, NGOs' overseas implementing partners, and formal and informal connections with other NGOs in the field or engaged in refugee protection. Sponsors also work closely with refugee networks who have sources of information about refugees in need that may not be available to the government or UNHCR.[171]

As an example, they cite Iraqi resettlement and note: "While SAHs responded quickly to the crisis of displaced persons from Iraq ... the UNHCR was until quite recently considering the displacement of Iraqis as a temporary problem."[172] The Canadian Council for Refugees has further challenged the assumed accuracy and fairness of the refusals and the assumption that refusals signify ineligibility rather than a change in country conditions or circumstances unknown at the time the sponsor submitted the application.[173] Thus, while the risk of private sponsorship is that it may blur the protection need, there is also the potential for sponsors to have a better sense of the protection need than the government. It is the art of cultivating this potential, while negating the risks, that is the challenge of an effective program.

The government has taken proactive measures to increase sponsors' protection knowledge and assessment capabilities. The Refugee Sponsorship Training Program (RSTP), commenced in 1998, serves to both educate and assist sponsors. Citizenship and Immigration Canada obtained permanent funding for the program in 2003.[174] Operated by the SAH community, it provides training, guidance, and resources as well as offering an annual forum. Since May 2008, there is also an RSTP website.[175] A community sponsorship guidebook that looks at Canada's sponsorship model and breaks it into "manageable building blocks" was released in September 2017 by the Global Refugee Sponsorship Initiative.[176] Tied to the unwillingness to relinquish referral capacity to the government, as well as to the high rejection rate, the continued reality is that the use of private sponsorship as a family reunification tool undoubtedly plays a role in the refusal rate and protection concerns. Canada's evaluation of its resettlement programs in 2016 notes that 62 percent of surveyed PSRs were sponsored by a family member.[177] Responsibility cannot be placed entirely on sponsors for this conundrum. The line is fine, and the government has sent out mixed messages as it negotiates its role in facilitating sponsorship. The government uses the scheme to complement its own government-assisted program and look responsive to the demands of the Canadian public.

As already noted, in response to pressure from the Sierra Leonean community in Canada for the government to assist in the resettlement of their relatives, Citizenship and Immigration Canada offered up private sponsorship as the main solution. A blended initiative was proposed in which the government would provide the initial four months of support followed by eight months of sponsor support. The project's intent was to "enhance the community's knowledge and understanding of Canada's refugee resettlement programs and to help the community participate in the private sponsorship program."[178] Five Sierra Leonean community groups joined the sponsorship program. To facilitate this sponsorship, Citizenship and Immigration Canada sent out a "request for assistance," calling on existing sponsorship groups to assist the Sierra Leonean sponsors.[179] The pilot project, which ended in June 2001, sponsored 250 people. Citizenship and Immigration Canada's assistance request has been interpreted as a clear message in support of family reunification: "For the first time CIC [Citizenship and Immigration Canada] was recruiting support for a community to assist their refugee relatives – an acknowledgement therefore that family reunification was a legitimate use of the Private Sponsorship Program when those overseas were refugees in need of resettlement."[180] The key clause here is the last one – namely, that the Sierra Leoneans "were refugees in need of resettlement." The argument is not that sponsorship should not be for relatives. The point is that these relatives must be refugees in need of protection – a balance that is easily recognized but difficult to achieve. Perhaps as an indicator of this distinction and its blurry line for sponsors, sponsorship undertakings had been submitted for approximately 700 Sierra Leoneans.[181] The success rate was thus less than 40 percent.

From Complementary to Consuming

As noted above, in Citizenship and Immigration Canada's 2009 annual report to Parliament, the minister highlighted a doubling of privately sponsored Iraqi refugees accepted over the following five years.[182] For the government to boast of an intended accomplishment that it had relinquished to private citizens is problematic. Similarly, the 2010 increase of 2,500 resettlement places put sponsors responsible for 80 percent of the increase.[183] The 2012 budget shift of 1,000 spaces to private sponsorship from the government program further increased private responsibility for resettlement.[184] The shift marks a further subsuming of privatized responsibility within the government's own humanitarianism. Catherine Dauvergne notes that "[p]rivate sponsorship both allows the government an easy response to domestic pressure to act more humanely and allows it to withdraw from direct responsibility for admission totals ... [T]he obligation is privatized and thus the responsibility of the nation is drastically reduced."[185] The announced increase in the annual report implies a control over the selection of privately sponsored refugees that the government clearly does not possess given the ratio of visa officer referrals to sponsorship referrals. The announcement of the blended pilot project for Iraqis in 2011 speaks to the acknowledged failure to increase these numbers solely through private sponsorship and the increasingly used solution of blending support as an alternative.[186]

The complementary role of private sponsorship has given way to the risk that it may consume the government program at the government's behest. Prior to the 2015 federal election, private sponsorship was receiving an increasing profile and attention from the government. The government, however, appeared to be claiming the program as its own humanitarianism. The 2010 range announced for private sponsorship was between 3,300 and 6,000.[187] While there was no change in the lower end of this range from the two previous years, the upper end marked an increase of 1,500 from the upper range of 4,500 of the three previous years. In 2012, the lower range was increased to 4,000.[188] These increases, along with a similar adjustment of GAR numbers, were used by the government to justify a reduction in inland refugee numbers:

> With respect to the Protected Persons Class, the Government of Canada is increasing the admission range for government-assisted and privately

sponsored refugees ... The range for protected persons in-Canada and their dependants is lower, but this will likely increase in future years when the Immigration and Refugee Board of Canada achieves its full decision-making capacity.[189]

The government then abandoned any increase to government-assisted resettlement with the shift of 1,000 places from this program to private sponsors.[190] This was not playing private sponsorship numbers against GAR numbers as was done in the past. Rather, it was playing resettlement – both private and government assisted – against the in-Canada asylum scheme. When the balancing was between GARs and privately sponsored refugees, at least the refugees were entering Canada through one scheme or the other. By balancing in-Canada asylum claims against increased ranges in resettlement numbers, there is no guarantee this upper range will be met, particularly when the lower end remains constant. In 2010 and 2011, despite increasing the potential ceiling to 6,000, private sponsorship totalled only 4,833 in 2010, 5,584 in 2011, and 4,221 in 2012.[191] Moreover, the government pitted its legal obligation to recognize refugees who arrive in Canada to claim asylum against the voluntary discretion to bring further refugees to Canada and privileged the latter.

Resettlement and in-country asylum were originally conceived as complementary schemes. Private sponsorship was conceived as a complement to government resettlement. Now resettlement is contrasted against asylum, and this resettlement is increasingly being placed on the shoulders of private sponsors. This was never the intention of the program. Ironically, it was during this same time period in 2011 and 2012 that the government imposed administrative caps on sponsorship submissions by SAHs. Prior to this point, there had never been a cap on submissions. The caps were both global and specific, targeting specific missions (Nairobi, Pretoria, Islamabad, and Cairo), thereby limiting sponsors' ability to respond to specific refugees.[192] The caps raised concerns of "geographical discrimination, prejudice or racism."[193] They also raised the ire of long-time sponsors.[194] To both quantify and highlight the extent to which the desire to sponsor surpassed the allowances, the Hospitality House Refugee Ministry in Winnipeg commenced a waitlist in October 2016 to keep track of new sponsorship applications. In a period of six weeks, the list exploded with over 30,000 names.[195] In December 2016, the mission-specific caps were removed, although a total cap on SAH applications remained.[196]

In examining private sponsorship, two key themes emerge: the shifting of responsibility for refugee protection from the government to private citizens and the compromising of the international refugee definition through the use of private sponsorship for family reunification. At times, the government has played resettlement against the in-Canada asylum scheme. Until the 2015 change in government, the majority of recent resettlement increases was directed towards private sponsorship and timed alongside proposals for more restrictive legislation concerning asylum. As will be seen in the following chapter, even with the 2015 change in government, this relationship and reliance on sponsorship over government resettlement and in lieu of openness to asylum continue. These moves not only shift resettlement responsibility to private sponsors but also reorient Canada's refugee protection away from in-Canada asylum and its legal obligations towards refugees. Private sponsors, in their commitment to refugees and their desire for increased sponsorship, enable the government's aversion to the law.

While sponsors risk becoming pawns in government responsibility shifting, they are more active participants in the dilution of protection through the push for family reunification under the private sponsorship scheme. Where family members are refugees, particularly those in prioritized need of protection by the UNHCR, there is no issue and much value in using private sponsorship to bring over these refugees. The challenge lies in ensuring protection remains the core criterion for sponsorship. The sponsorship community has played a powerful role in influencing the expansion of Canada's protection criteria. The expansion of protection, however, does risk losing sight of the refugee definition. Particularly in resettlement, where action is not hinged to a legal obligation that is tied to the refugee definition, there is nothing that necessitates continued reference to refugees. Resettlement and, in particular, sponsorship are vulnerable to morphing into more of a familial migration scheme than a true complement to Canada's international refugee protection obligations.

6

The State of Sponsorship

Private sponsorship intertwines Canadians in a personal refugee experience.[1] It is often credited with creating and sustaining the refugee advocacy community in Canada[2] and hailed as a "leading mechanism for providing the kind of direct contact between newcomers and members of the host society that is essential for promoting widespread acceptance that newcomers constitute an asset to society."[3] It also serves as a continual reminder to the government of public support for the refugee cause. James Hathaway has noted, "[o]n balance, however, private sponsorship is an important vehicle for the direct injection by Canadians of humanitarianism into refugee resettlement priorities."[4] The government of Canada has itself acknowledged that "[t]he willingness of so many Canadians to give so generously of their time to assist refugees is a visible demonstration of their commitment to continuing Canada's humanitarian tradition."[5] Beyond the practical positive infusions, Donald Galloway argues that individual members of a state who want "to go beyond the call of duty to help others" should not be prevented from doing so by the state authority. He reasons that, while there is no overarching moral duty to permit free migration, "[i]t may be the case that some members of a community rightly identify it to be their moral duty to render assistance to an alien in need, not by giving that person money or other resources, but by providing shelter and a human support network."[6] For the state to prevent the admission of people under these circumstances, Galloway argues, would hinder the fulfillment of an individual member's personal moral duty. An alternative twist on this argument is that this was the twentieth century liberal-conservative vision – government legislation to facilitate non-governmental action.[7]

As the writing of this book has progressed, private sponsorship in Canada has moved from understated and undiscussed to a celebrated model hailed as a solution to global refugee flows. Whether trudging along or heralded as a trending tool, private sponsorship is now in a moment of exploratory change, and it is essential to explore Canada's newest form of "blended" private sponsorship as well as Canada's global promotion of sponsorship.

Blending and Bargaining

In between government and private sponsorship, the blended visa office–referred (BVOR) program was introduced in 2013.[8] BVOR is a cost-sharing model that has been built from previous pilot projects where the government splits the one-year financial support with sponsors, each covering six months. It is a means both to promote private sponsorship and to bring the program back within the government's power to name those refugees to be sponsored by way of visa officer referrals. As well, the government promised that the referred refugees would be "travel ready," which means that, rather than waiting years for processing, refugees arrive in Canada within one to four months.[9] Yet, in the program's first years, targets were not reached. Even with a modest target of only 200–300 refugees to be resettled through the program in 2013, only 153 BVOR refugees arrived. While the target increased to 400–500 refugees in 2014, admissions only increased to 177 arrivals.[10] In 2015, the intent was to raise BVOR admission to the desired 800–1,000 refugees. Given the lack of uptake in the preceding two years, these numbers seemed highly unlikely at the start of the year.[11]

The challenge is that the program is an affront to the two principles that private sponsors hold close – naming and additionality. The BVOR program requires sponsors to give up the power to name in exchange for a reduced financial obligation and faster processing. Nor does this blended support enable additional sponsorship. As noted in earlier chapters, a budgetary decision in 2012 shifted 1,000 government-assisted refugee (GAR) spots to the BVOR program.[12] The Canadian Council for Refugees stated emphatically that "Canadians who stepped up to sponsor BVORs were not adding to the number of refugees resettled: they were rather saving the government money."[13] Meanwhile, from the government's perspective, it has been noted that "some SAHs [sponsorship agreement holders] perceive this program as a branch of the PSR [private sponsorship of refugees] program and as a result, they interpret the BVOR program as contravening the Principles of Naming and Additionality."[14] While the government may perceive the program to be a facet of government resettlement, as with traditional private sponsorship, the failure of private citizens to act would leave the spaces unfilled. A newspaper article that was written when the program was announced accurately noted: "A thousand more refugees could be coming to Canada, if sponsors are willing to welcome them."[15]

What the BVOR program created, however, was a new possibility in a moment of crisis when Canadians were looking to "do" something. With parallels to the uptake of the newly established PSR program during the Indochinese crisis, the BVOR program created a new space for assistance just as the Syrian crisis was seeping into Canadian consciousness. In the first days of September 2015, the body of a small Syrian boy, Alan Kurdi, was found and photographed dead on a Turkish beach. The moment brought the realities of the Syrian crisis to the world's attention in a way that months of reports and statistics on drownings in the Mediterranean had failed to trigger.[16] The accessibility, relative immediacy, and lesser financial responsibility of a BVOR sponsorship made sense to Canadians with no ties to refugees but wanting to immediately help for the first time. The numbers for 2015 reached 810, just within the 800–1,000 target.[17]

By the start of 2017, BVOR numbers for Syrians alone sat at 3,931.[18] The planned BVOR admissions for 2017 were within a range of 1,000–3,000 with a target of 1,500.[19] Actual admissions only reached 1,284.[20] The uncertainty of the program is evident in the targets moving forward into 2020 and 2021, with a wide range of possible admissions from 500 to 2,500.[21] As the program gained momentum, it also picked up the traditional baggage that tends to pull private sponsorship down. While interested sponsors selected (visa office–referred) "profiles" from the government's Matching Centre, the sponsorship enthusiasm sparked by the Syrian crisis meant, in crude terms, that supply could not meet the (processing) demand.[22] One sponsorship group acutely summarized both the commodification concern of the program and the unbalanced targeting of some refugee groups over others that is drawn out in a moment of swelling public humanitarianism:

> Our group – I think like many – started because we were moved to action by the continued terrible desperation in Syria ... But there are no Syrians "available" on the lists of government-approved refugees awaiting settlement, despite that many other groups are waiting and willing to help them settle. There is a bureaucratic bottleneck somewhere ... We've decided that there are many people in great need, so we will not insist on Syrians. Indeed, there are many hidden conflicts and forgotten human rights issues. The lists include Eritreans, Congolese, Burmese, and others.[23]

Syrian refugees were in the periscopic view of many Canadians, while the broader refugee crisis raged on.

After mobilizing and securing housing, social support, and finances, newly formed BVOR sponsorship groups found themselves waiting for eligible families to sponsor, waiting for applications to be processed, or waiting for refugees to arrive.[24] In an effort to fast-track Syrian referrals, sponsors and refugees were matched before the refugee files were finalized.[25] This process left sponsors impatiently waiting for the arrival of sponsored refugees. In August 2016, the government wrote to sponsors to explain "delays were in large part due to the fact that cases were made available to sponsors prior to the finalization of eligibility, medical, and security decisions to meet the demand from sponsors at that time and to have them included in the initiative to resettle 25,000 Syrians by the end of February 2016."[26] The sponsoring groups impacted by the delay were offered "replacement cases":

> By accepting a replacement profile, sponsors will be canceling the sponsorship for the previous case that is currently delayed. We understand that sponsors may have already been in contact with the refugee(s) whose case [sic] are delayed, and IRCC [Immigration, Refugees and Citizenship Canada] will contact these refugees to inform them that their case is still in process. Should any of the cases where a sponsor has cancelled to accept a replacement case ultimately be approved, they will

be resettled to Canada as Government Assisted Refugees (GARs) with full support from the Government of Canada.

If sponsors choose to continue waiting for the original family they sponsored, rather than accepting a replacement case, they will be doing so knowing that IRCC is unable to provide timelines as to when that case will be finalized and there are no guarantees that the family will ultimately be approved for resettlement to Canada.[27]

The news was both "discouraging"[28] and "agonizing"[29] as sponsors were left to decide whether to wait for an original family or resettle a different family.[30] The specificity of the selection, even within the Syrian refugee population, was acute.

The quandary points to the quick connection between sponsors and their intended resettlement refugees' pre-arrival even in the absence of naming or pre-existing relationships. It also forces the recognition that, while processing slows referral capacity, there remains a continual need for resettlement beyond the singular selected family. The pull of "relational migration"[31] means that BVOR families bring reminders that more refugees, including extended family members, wait in need of protection.[32] Regardless of the route that is taken by the refugee, be it through a refugee claim or any resettlement stream, the echo effect points to more refugees in need. Yet it is only through traditional private sponsorship that sponsors can name the refugee to be resettled.[33]

The government's own program evaluation for the first two years of BVOR resettlement recommends that to improve the BVOR program there must be an "engagement strategy or SAHs to increase uptake of the BVOR program.[34] The government's response points to Syrian resettlement and notes that, "since the implementation of the 2015–16 Syrian refugee initiative, significant advances have been made ... [S]ponsor interest and uptake in the program ha[ve] grown to such a degree that demand now significantly exceeds supply, which makes an engagement strategy to increase uptake unnecessary."[35] This may be optimistic. As the BVOR program moves forward, its longevity is in question due to attrition, delay, frustration, or moves by the newly minted sponsors to the naming potential of pure private sponsorship. It remains to be seen whether BVOR is just a blip or a sustainable program.

The Export Experiment

After over a decade of pilot programs, shifting numbers, narrowed criteria, submission caps, and the introduction of a new sponsorship model, the change in government in 2015 came with a strong promise of resettlement, both governmental and private. Filipo Grandi, United Nations High Commissioner for Refugees (UNHCR), declared that "Canada has taken the mantle of humanitarian leadership in the world,"[36] as talk grew of sponsorship as a means to "take some of the pressure off European states teeming with asylum-seekers."[37] In September 2016, the United Nations Summit for Refugees and Migrants marked the first time that the United Nations General Assembly gathered heads of state to address the large movements of refugees as part of the seventy-first annual high-level meetings.[38] At this time, and in partnership with the UNHCR and the Open Society Foundations, Canada announced a joint initiative aimed at increasing the private sponsorship of refugees around the world.[39] This was followed by the launch of the Global Refugee Sponsorship Initiative (GRSI) in December 2016 to promote Canada's sponsorship model.[40]

The GRSI's goals are to increase overall resettlement by engaging private citizens, communities, and businesses; strengthening local host communities; and improving the political narrative on refugees and newcomers.[41] In developing training and education, technical assistance, and capacity building, the GRSI plans to both aid other states and develop Canadian expertise that will be foundational to the Canadian private sponsorship program. Media headlines hailed an "[e]xtraordinary initiative"[42] and the export of a "Canadian success story."[43] Whereas, in the past, the Canadian government has turned to private sponsorship as evidence of its own humanitarianism at home, the newly elected government was embracing not just the numbers but also the resettlement model itself on a global stage. In April 2017, the GRSI met with "over 30 European stakeholders" and in May met with representatives from Chile, Brazil, and Argentina.[44]

An uptake in interest in private sponsorship was already building prior to Canada's promotion plans. Australia initiated a pilot program in 2012 that was formalized in 2015.[45] In June 2015, Theresa May, speaking as home secretary, announced plans for the United Kingdom to "develop a community sponsorship scheme, like those in Canada and Australia, to allow individuals, charities, faith groups, churches and businesses to support refugees directly."[46] Looking at various loosely labelled sponsorship mechanisms operating as of 2015 in Argentina, Australia, Germany, Ireland, and New Zealand, as well as in Canada, Judith Kumin summarizes that there is no "one-size-fits-all" model, with differences "not only with respect to the status granted to the refugee, but also in such important aspects such as who is eligible to sponsor and be sponsored, the nature of the sponsor's obligations, and whether privately sponsored refugees are *within* or *in addition* to the government financed resettlement quota."[47] In Australia, where the Refugee Council of Australia had long lobbied for a program that would align with the Canadian model,[48] the council was left with numerous concerns with the Australian implementation.[49] Kumin's 2015 report explores the potential for private sponsorship in the European Union. Kumin raises ten key questions concerning program objectives, eligibility to sponsor, sponsor responsibilities, scope of a safety net for sponsors, sponsorship eligibility, selection process, service entitlements and temporary or permanent status, relationship to resettlement quotas, potential partners, and mechanisms for monitoring and evaluation.[50] Sponsorship is not simple.

Private sponsorship undoubtedly builds community connections between citizens and refugees, engages citizens in refugee advocacy, and creates an atmosphere of welcome for newcomers. Daniel Hiebert identifies how the decentralized, multi-stakeholder selection approach of Canada's immigration policy creates a "wider sense of ownership" and "also greatly facilitates the legitimacy of policy and provides a kind of insulation against the potential demands of populist groups."[51] However, as the argument of this book illustrates, the history of sponsorship has not been without challenges. Even the formal export announcement raised some eyebrows for its lack of prior consultation with private sponsors. Between the September announcement and the December meeting, Citizens for Public Justice (CPJ) noted that "Canada's interest in sharing best practices with other countries will be worthwhile only when the resettlement process at home is overhauled to reflect more equity and efficiency."[52] For the CPJ, two major concerns involved the narrow focus of the Syrian resettlement and the burden of transportation loans that had been lifted for certain Syrian refugees but not for other resettlement refugees. A policy brief from the Refugee Research Network/Centre for Refugee Studies, which was released shortly after, raised "gaps in knowledge" and noted the importance of history in Canada's program, the "luxury of cold ocean geography," and the reality of hidden sponsorship costs absorbed by government coverage of education, health, and social services.[53] My own concerns, which echo throughout this work and elsewhere,[54] are anchored in the relationship between resettlement and asylum. Canada embraced resettlement because geography meant it was not a country of first asylum. New state interest results conversely from the reality of an influx of asylum seekers. Concerns with the privatization of state responsibility and the power of selection that resettlement offers over uncontrolled asylum raise questions about who will benefit from additional sponsorship places and who will face increased obstacles to access.

Goodwill, Generosity, and Government Responsibility

As the uptake on private sponsorship increases, it is important to reflect on the theoretical and protection shifts that the model encompasses. Private sponsorship adds a layer to the charity-rights dichotomy. The distinction between the legal right to *non-refoulement* and the humanitarianism that premises the charitable act of resettlement was addressed earlier in this book. The benefit of a rights-based stance in law is that it adds a concrete assertion of legal obligation and accountability to refugee protection. It further adds dignity to the demand. There is an entitlement to rights. There is equality between the parties. Stuart Scheingold defines this as "the call of the law."[55] He suggests that the assertion of a right implies a legitimate and dignified reciprocal relationship that is societal and not personal.[56] The current alternative calls in refugee protection are for compassion, humanitarianism, and morality.[57] Such claims lack reciprocity and are founded on personal need. As Catherine Dauvergne explains, "[a] claim for compassion does not effectively function as a right because rights are grounded in equality but compassion is grounded in generosity and inequality."[58] As long as refugees seek only compassion, they remain dependent, often invisible, outsiders in the realm between persecuting and protecting countries. Resettlement depends upon this charity.

Yet, to probe this further, GARs have been designated as being entitled to assistance from the government, whereas PSRs depend on the additional generosity of private citizens.[59] It is this charitable aspect that partially grounds the traditional resistance to privately supported resettlement in

Europe. Nordic countries, in particular, are known for their generous acceptance and support of the neediest refugees.[60] And, yet, this action is firmly seen as a government responsibility.[61] The nature of the state as a provider of public welfare assistance can be seen as a determining factor of the extent to which private actors play a role in resettlement. Stronger welfare states may take a greater role in assisting refugees, whereas other states might leave assistance to the private sector, meaning that greater private sector involvement increases the promotion of private-public partnerships.[62] Citizens of social welfare states tend to find the idea of private sponsorship distasteful as it suggests a discontent with government services and also threatens to undermine the stability of the social welfare state.[63]

From the outset, the concern about private sponsorship in Canada has been the privatization of a responsibility that is considered to rest with the state as a whole. There is no clear consensus on the basis of this responsibility, be it moral, humanitarian, or burden sharing and demonstrative of international solidarity. Since the *Immigration Act, 1976*, the vague allusion to "Canada's international legal obligations with respect to refugees and ... its humanitarian tradition with respect to the displaced and the persecuted" has defined the government's sense of its refugee responsibility.[64] Thus, with the Indochinese resettlement, church groups expressed concern that the government was shifting its international burden onto Canadian citizens. As Hathaway observes, "[m]oreover it may be argued that the government should not be permitted to make the implementation of its international burden-sharing obligation largely dependent on the goodwill of the private sector."[65] But why is it that this burden is perceived to be governmental? The assistance of private citizens enabled Canada to offer more resettlement places per capita than any other state during the Indochinese crisis[66] and has reinvigorated generosity with the Syrian crisis to the extent that Canada and the UNHCR are promoting the program more globally.[67]

But there are practical reasons to resist the attractions of private sponsorship. While the benefits of sponsorship support for refugees, be they sponsored, government assisted, or asylum seekers, are continually hailed, there is a risk in hinging refugee advocacy on a group working in a specific refugee niche. In bringing the compelling faces of refugees to Canada, private sponsors see a very particular need. Private sponsors are continually frustrated by long processing delays and outright rejections of the refugees they are seeking to protect.[68] In following these cases – both during the processing in camps and the slow work of integration – sponsors are acutely aware of the immense suffering and the challenges that refugees face. Often, by their very ability to arrive independently, the stories and situations of asylum seekers who claim protection in Canada are markedly different from those who have been resettled from overseas. These distinctions and the visible desperation of sponsored refugees can lead to an assessment of deservingness. Private sponsors are susceptible to see truth in the rhetorical divisions between genuine refugees "over there" and false refugees abusing the in-Canada system.[69]

One interesting consequence of this pronounced rhetoric on genuineness is a consequent shift in the resettlement focus. Mary Crock, Ben Saul, and Azadeh Dastyari argued in 2006 that the heightened awareness of camp-based refugees and the rejection of asylum seekers as genuine refugees led to a shift in the regions where Australia was selecting refugees for resettlement:

> At the height of the influx of boat people at the end of the 1990s, complaints were made repeatedly that the unauthorized arrivals were taking the place of "genuine refugees" who were languishing in UNHCR refugee camps. The rhetoric heightened awareness of the neglect of long-term refugees in African and Middle Eastern camps. In response, the intervening years have seen a dramatic rise in the intake of UNHCR recognized refugees from Africa.[70]

This awareness of camp-based refugees, while a positive move towards visibility, remains troubling when parcelled with the complete rejection of the genuine plight of asylum seekers.

This spectrum of reception is again playing out in Canada as resettlement sits in a privileged position both politically and publicly with targeted programs for Syrian and Yazidi refugees.[71] At the same time, asylum flows at the border with the United States have met with public resistance and political reluctance. A poll marking Canada's 150th birthday in 2017 noted that 57 percent of Canadians were open to welcoming more Syrian refugees (through resettlement), but 70 percent felt security along the Canada-US border should increase.[72] In March 2017, Conservative leadership candidate Maxime Bernier suggested that "[w]e should close the loophole in the Third Safe Country agreement with U.S. and sent [sic] them back. They are unfairly getting ahead of real refugees."[73] Bernier's insinuation of the unreal, bogus nature of these claims aligns with Conservative immigration critic Michelle Rempel's assertion of legality that "[p]ersons coming from a safe country and not directly fleeing persecution should not be able to ignore our laws and enter Canada illegally ... If they do, they should be charged."[74] These political statements misunderstand or misstate the law as it is not illegal for a refugee or refugee claimant to enter Canada without authorization, but the irregularity of their entrance sits in stark contrast to the controlled and orderly admission of resettlement refugees.[75]

If private sponsorship serves as a "political barometer,"[76] it may be a tainted and biased barometer jeopardizing one aspect of the protection scheme in justification of another. While this concern speaks to the heightened protection focus of sponsors, the alternative risk of overly focusing on family reunification over protection equally risks the program's complementary objective. The argument has been made in the US context that, "[i]n some sense, however, the use of family ties in refugee resettlement can be seen as an admission of defeat in efforts to protect the vulnerable – a reversion to traditional immigration predilections when more need-based policies are too troublesome to implement."[77] A correlated concern is that, where family reunification and protection do properly intersect, continued sponsorship may not be sustainable since either the willingness or the ability to sponsor may be quickly strained.

Further, a protection scheme dependent on private support works well for singular appeals but lacks the sustainability of a government program. The first comprehensive review of the private sponsorship program in the 1990s cautiously acknowledged this dilemma: "It remains to be seen whether the resource is renewable, like forests, or whether it more closely resembles gold and, once again mined, is depleted."[78] These concerns point to the slippery slope between a complementary program of private sponsorship and the government's reliance on such a scheme. Government resettlement results from a combination of factors that includes the sense that, as a geographic outlier to refugee flows, Canada's international obligation includes resettlement and the burden-sharing role in resettlement that Canada not only has played but also has led since the outset of the modern regime. There is also the scope that the government values resettlement as a means of controlling entrance to Canada and creating increasing obstacles to asylum while still maintaining a strong commitment to refugee protection through resettlement.

Private sponsorship is conversely driven by a different incentive basis. With outsider strangers such as the Indochinese, and, now, the Syrians, the support is driven by a more pure humanitarian desire to ameliorate human suffering than can likely ever be present in government actions tied to political interests. But, with the continued dominance of sponsor-based referrals, the incentives behind private sponsorship are much more personal.

At Law's Border

The place of law in refugee resettlement becomes further blurred when examined in the context of citizen-guided private and blended sponsorship. Beyond the state's choice to voluntarily resettle refugees is the additionally required voluntariness of private citizens who take on the responsibility for this resettlement. Despite these layers of choice, independence, and discretion, law is still present. Private sponsorship has been legislated in Canada since refugees were first recognized in the *Immigration Act, 1976*. As was the case with government resettlement, the law was a formalization of a process already taking place in an ad hoc manner. The move from pilot projects to the BVOR program is a more recent formalization. The law provides predictability and structure, but sponsorship is not dependent on the law.

A benefit of the law over the ad hoc responses of the past is the ability to expedite resettlement, as was done through the use of designated classes for the Indochinese, and this subject will be examined again in the discussion of group processing. Similarly, as was seen with the *Immigration and Refugee Protection Act*, where the law brought in the new possibility for co-sponsorship, law can also grant individual Canadians greater flexibility in participating in sponsorship applications.[79] The law is thus the facilitator of change in resettlement, although it can also be an inhibitor that delays processing times and prevents sponsorship at the numeric levels desired by sponsors.

While, prior to legalization, the government possessed absolute discretion to allow or deny sponsorship, the law further structures the government's oversight role. The regulatory framework of private sponsorship, permitting sponsorship but only under certain conditions such as the requirement that groups be composed of five or more people, places the program within the government's control. Most significantly, all sponsor-referred refugees must be reviewed by the government for eligibility and protection need, giving the government ultimate discretion on sponsored resettlement. The high refusal rate of sponsorship applications is indeed one of the greatest tensions between the government and private sponsors.

As the controller of the law, the government permits private action and thereby takes a degree of credit for the private choice. This can be seen in the interpretation of events that suggests that the government "agreed to permit" the private sponsorship of the Indochinese at the outset of private sponsorship[80] and in more recent examples wherein former Minister of Citizenship and Immigration Jason Kenney announced numeric increases to resettlement primarily based on private sponsorship and the Trudeau government's announced global export of private sponsorship without first consulting sponsorship groups. Not only is the government assuming acknowledgment of the actions of its citizens, but it is also simultaneously shifting responsibility further away from itself to its citizens for this protection responsibility. Even the Syrian resettlement pushed by the Trudeau government's election promises leaned more heavily on private sponsors than was intended and ultimately placed the numeric BVOR credit on the government side of resettlement.[81] The initial suspicion of private sponsorship was based on this feared shifting of responsibility.

At the same time, the willingness of private Canadians to partner with the government to complement and increase the government's resettlement program, and the increasing interest in this model of resettlement in other states, should arguably remind the government of its own obligations and of the strength of public support for resettlement. Sponsors, as active partners with the government on refugee protection, also feel a vested interest in the resettlement program and, thereby, both desire and feel entitled to influence the law as the bearers of the financial responsibility for a significant portion of Canadian resettlement.

Alternatively, then, rather than shifting responsibility, private sponsorship can be seen as both an indicator of support for the resettlement program and a crucial means of advocacy for the refugee cause. As such, private sponsorship reminds the government that its voluntary commitment to refugees is supported by the public and should be maintained. And, yet, it is partially the strength of this support and the dominance of sponsorship support for refugee resettlement that can permit the government to rhetorically privilege this manner of protection over its legal obligation of *non-refoulement*.

Despite the law, there is thus an interpretative malleability to the government-sponsor relationship that can lead in different directions depending on the predilections of the government in power. While the legal framework for private sponsorship has experienced only subtle revisions since it was introduced over forty years ago, the application of the provisions has differed significantly, fluctuating from numeric highs to lows and now creeping back up, shifting from the sponsorship of strangers to that of family and now seemingly re-embracing strangers through the BVOR process and from complaints that the government favours the processing of sponsorship applications over GARs to the reverse complaints of excessive delays in processing time. The legal framework and use of quotas and thresholds make resettlement a flexible program that can prioritize or ignore certain refugee groups and issues. As was seen with the 2012 federal budget, this numeric shift of responsibility can occur as a fiscal change absent any law. Private sponsorship particularly brings to the fore the intersection of politics and law in resettlement. Legislation can remain unchanged, while the policies that underlie the legislation drastically differ. Both the Indochinese and the Syrian resettlements, which took place during changing governments, encapsulate this reality. The listing of source country resettlement countries, as will be discussed shortly, further confirms this point.

While the private sponsorship program's objective is to complement the government program and resettle additional refugees, the reality is that the program has the potential to, and is often used for the purpose of, shifting resettlement responsibility to the private sector and compromising the in-Canada asylum program. By both enabling the government's restrictive actions towards asylum through the justification of continued refugee support by way of resettlement and, increasingly, private sponsorship, and pushing for sponsorship that is more family oriented than protection focused, the earlier discussion has demonstrated how sponsorship risks moving Canada further away from its international obligations rather than complementing these commitments. This is not to say that sponsorship necessitates such a shift. There are, indeed, many positive aspects to sponsorship that promote refugee protection, increase Canada's protection capacity, and speak to the positive benefits of sharing this model with other states. Many of the recommendations in Chapter 8 will focus on re-orientating Canada's refugee program to ensure that it is these aspects of private sponsorship that are cultivated.

Canada's government resettlement program and private sponsorship – the two components of Canada's resettlement program – as well as their blending through BVOR have been examined. Yet, within these two streams, other modes of resettlement also occur. The next chapter focuses on Canada's use of source country and group resettlement, looking back at the demise of the former program while recognizing how the latter gained momentum. As programs that interweave both government and private support, group resettlement and source country resettlement permit the program to be examined in another light. They are, moreover, the clearest abandonments of the refugee definition that requires an assessment of an individual outside his or her home country.

7

Beyond the Convention

At this point, the book has looked at resettlement from the governmental and private citizen perspectives. While this discussion has provided the framework of resettlement in Canada, it is the smaller programs within this framework that often define and direct Canadian resettlement. To an extent, this was seen in the examination of the recurring use of blended pilot projects that combined government and private support. This chapter moves to examine two further forms of resettlement in Canada. The first is a resettlement class that previously existed within the regulations, the source country class. This class allowed individuals who remained in their home country to seek resettlement. The second is an administrative processing method that enables the recognition of a group of refugees for resettlement rather than the traditional individual process. Despite their differences, both programs fundamentally shift away from the refugee definition in the scope of protection they offer: the former by the exemption from the definition's requirement of having fled across an international border; the latter by circumventing the individual assessment required by the definition.

Canada appears to be drawn to the appeal of the concept of group resettlement. Meanwhile, source country class resettlement, which had been a component of the Canadian resettlement program in some form from the outset, has fallen from favour. The Canadian government in 2011 repealed the source country class from the *Immigration and Refugee Protection Regulations (IRPR)*.[1] Understanding both of these programs, their use of discretion, and their relationship to protection at a time when they are expanding and shrinking respectively completes and clarifies the picture of Canadian resettlement.

Going to the Source

Asylum in Canada expands beyond those individuals within the international convention definition of a refugee. Expansion beyond the refugee definition has been part of Canada's refugee law since the implementation of the *Immigration Act, 1976*.[2] That Act conceived of designated classes in refugee-like situations.[3] A government document explains: "Such persons may not be able to meet the strict definition of 'refugee' in the Convention for such technical reasons as that they remain in their own countries."[4] In 1979, the self-exiled designated persons class, the Indochinese designated class, and the political prisoners and oppressed persons class were established.[5] The political prisoners and oppressed persons class was accessible to nationals of enumerated countries who remained in their country of origin.[6] The class was known as the Latin American designated class until the addition of Poland in 1982.[7] Following Canada's massive Indochinese resettlement, there remained a willingness to resettle, but the United Nations High Commissioner for Refugees (UNHCR) was no longer able to provide enough referrals to meet with capacity. As was the case with private sponsorship, the Canadian government used these designated classes to fill the referral capacity gap. Originally as a response to a call from the UNHCR to address the plight of Chileans and Argentinians, the political prisoners and oppressed persons class broadened to include El Salvador, Uruguay, Guatemala, and Poland.

As with private sponsorship, the concept of source country resettlement preceded legislative recognition. In 1973, Robert Adams, the assistant deputy minister of immigration, wrote to Joseph Kage, the national executive vice-president of the Jewish Immigrant Aid Services of Canada (JIAS), acknowledging the concept of source country resettlement: "In summary, we have already recognized that there are oppressed minorities in certain countries and that these people could be refugees within the universally accepted definition, except that they are still within their country of origin."[8] This recognition was both humanitarian and strategic. It enabled the government not only to broaden the scope of recognition to offer greater protection but also to have greater selective control in the granting of that protection.

The political prisoners and oppressed persons class and the predecessor Latin American class were also largely influenced by visa considerations. A surge in inland asylum claims from Latin American countries was met with the imposition of visa requirements. Source country resettlement through the designated classes served as a "safety valve" for the acknowledged real refugees requiring an escape.[9] It also equipped the government with the humanitarian base from which to justify the tightening of borders.

From the beginning, Canada's resettlement of refugees was further tied to "invisible conscription" as refugee plans and allotments combined designated classes and convention refugees.[10] Analysis from the early 1980s indicates that 70 percent of government resettlement fell within the designated classes with resettlement of convention refugees at only 30 percent.[11] Here then is a clear indication of law creating enhanced discretion. Rather than imposing on the government any obligation to resettle refugees, the law enabled the government to structure a politically discretionary settlement program with a label of refugee and humanitarian protection, while increasingly controlling the border. At the same time, this discretion moved this program further from the ambit of refugee law. As Bill Frelick notes,

> [a] discretionary refugee admissions program, therefore, does not come close to meeting international legal requirements to protect refugees. In-country programs are even more problematic. Since the applicant is already inside his or her home country, he cannot actually be a refugee at all at the time of applying for refugee status, and, logically, his denial cannot be called *refoulement* since he or she cannot be returned to a place where he or she is already present.[12]

This is protection, but it is not refugee protection or protection obligated by law.

In its final form prior to the repeal of the source country class, the umbrella humanitarian protected persons abroad class set out in the *IRPR* included those individuals who did not meet the refugee definition either because they did not meet the definition's requirement of a nexus to persecution or because they had not fled across an international border. Those in the humanitarian protected persons abroad class fell within two subclasses: the country of asylum class and the source country class.[13] Until 2011, when the latter source country class was repealed, these classes had existed in their same forms since May 1997.[14]

The source country class was defined in the *IRPR*.[15] Source country resettlement could be achieved through the government-assisted refugee (GAR) program, through private sponsorship, or by the individual coming as a self-supporting refugee.[16] The class applied to individuals who had not crossed an international border and remained in their home country of nationality or permanent residence. Schedule 2 of the *IRPR* listed the eligible countries for source country resettlement. Table 5 sets out the four iterations of the schedule. In its final form, six countries were listed: Colombia, the Democratic Republic of the Congo, El Salvador, Guatemala, Sierra Leone, and Sudan.[17] Applicants had to be "residing in their country of nationality or habitual residence," and the country had to be a country on the list when a visa for Canada was issued.[18] The schedule was generally reviewed annually and could be amended by Citizenship and Immigration Canada. That said, the list had not been amended since 29 June 2001.[19] In evidence given before the House of Commons Subcommittee on International Human Rights in 2010, Debra Pressé, as acting director general of the Refugee Affairs Branch at Citizenship and Immigration Canada, stated: "The source country list as a tool, we will acknowledge, is not particularly flexible."[20] Ultimately, it seems

TABLE 5
Designated source countries by year, 1997–2011

Year	Designated source countries
1997	Bosnia-Herzegovina, Croatia, El Salvador, Guatemala, Sudan
1998	Bosnia-Herzegovina, Croatia, El Salvador, Guatemala, Sudan, *Colombia, Cambodia, Liberia*
1999–2000	Bosnia-Herzegovina, Croatia, El Salvador, Guatemala, Sudan, Colombia, *Democratic Republic of Congo* (Cambodia and Liberia removed)
2001–11	El Salvador, Guatemala, Sudan, Colombia, Democratic Republic of Congo, *Sierra Leone* (Bosnia-Herzegovina and Croatia removed)

Note: Newly added states are in italics.
Source: Citizenship and Immigration Canada, "Regulatory Impact Analysis Statement" 145:12 Canada Gazette Part 1 (19 March 2011) 1002.

that the government had determined that the source country class was not a tool worthy of continued use.

The source country class, however, did not seem that inflexible or difficult to change through the annual review. Beyond being from a listed country on the schedule, individuals in this class had to be "seriously and personally affected by civil war or armed conflict," "been or are being detained or imprisoned with or without charges, or subjected to some other form of penal control, as a direct result of an act committed outside Canada that would, in Canada, be a legitimate expression of freedom of thought or a legitimate exercise of civil rights pertaining to dissent or trade union activity," or meet the refugee definition aside from the out-of-country requirement.[21]

Those in the source country class, therefore, had to meet the same requirements of either the convention refugee abroad class or the country of asylum class aside from not crossing an international border. To be on the list, it was required that the country also be safe enough for Canadian officials to work. The regulations required that a source country be a country "where an officer works or makes routine working visits and is able to process visa applications without endangering their own safety, the safety of applicants or the safety of Canadian embassy staff."[22] From an administrative perspective, source country class resettlement resolved some of the issues that tended to make resettlement difficult. A cooperative government offered a safe environment for visa officers and a relatively stable location for an office to be established. However, it was the combined requirements that there not only be civil war or armed conflict but also safe working conditions that limited both the list and the use of source country resettlement.[23] Thus, despite six listed potential source countries in the schedule, by the program's end, operative source country resettlement was only occurring out of Colombia. Prior to the repeal, Pressé stated:

> Quite frankly, there are countries on the list now that we know could come off, but we don't want to waste the valuable time of members of parliament by taking countries off when we couldn't add any new countries to the list because the countries that people would want to add today are not countries that we can operate in.[24]

The class therefore failed to act with the intended reactive flexibility for which it was conceived.

Applications to the class, however, were high. Between 2005 and 2009, the Canadian embassy in Colombia received an average of 4,700 applications annually.[25] In Bosnia, from 1998 to 2001, there were approximately 6,236 applications.[26] These applications, when considered to include family members, amounted to potential refugee numbers far outweighing the upper range for resettled refugees in the annual immigration plan. At the time of repeal, the government reported low success rates amounting to less than 10 percent in Colombia.[27] The government conducted a review of the source country class in 2009 to evaluate its continued effectiveness.[28] The review identified three issues with the program: (1) limited eligibility and lack of flexibility; (2) lack of referral capacity and necessity for direct access that encompasses foreign nationals; and (3) lack of access or awareness by vulnerable persons.[29] In a news release on 18 March 2011, Minister of Citizenship and Immigration Jason Kenney announced the government's intent to repeal the source country class.[30] Notice was given in the *Canada Gazette* on 19 March 2011 of the proposal to remove the source country class from *IRPR*.[31] The news release came the same day as the announcement of blended support for Iraqi refugees.[32] In fact, the news release announcing the source country class repeal oddly included multiple references to the unrelated Iraqi resettlement and the group resettlement of the Bhutanese from Nepal.[33] This rhetorical interlacing of resettlement models, positioning both blended private sponsorship and group resettlement in contrast to source country resettlement, clearly signalled the direction of the government's interests.

The proposed repeal emphasized the government's desire to return the resettlement program closer to the original intentions of refugee protection for those meeting the convention refugee definition. It was couched in two major justifications: better management by eliminating direct access and the ability for Canada to work more closely with its partner organizations, including the UNHCR, other resettlement countries, and private Canadian sponsors.[34] The regulatory impact analysis statement that accompanied the announcement noted: "Consultations with the UNHCR have suggested that repealing the class could benefit the organization and persons in need of humanitarian protection by making available more resettlement spaces for UNHCR-referred refugees."[35] The report indicated that "[t]he proposed repeal of the class and the transfer of resettlement spaces to UNHCR-referred refugees would be consistent with UNHCR's appeals for more resettlement spaces for Convention refugees."[36] The analysis went on, however, to note that the greatest impact and consequences of the repeal would be felt by private sponsorship groups:

> Additional pressure may be put on the private sponsorship community and certain ethnic communities in Canada ... to sponsor refugees who would have previously applied for resettlement through direct access and been eligible for government assistance ... Colombians in Canada may also face pressure to sponsor relatives abroad through the family class, or the PSR program, in the case of refugees who have fled across the border.[37]

This recognition seemingly contradicts the renewed focus on protection by returning to a more family-centric resettlement approach that tends not to support UNHCR-referred refugees.

The anticipated pressure that the repeal could cause on private sponsors signified a further shifting of the burden from government to private responsibility. Moreover, the resettlement of these individuals following the repeal required the often dangerous and illegal or irregular crossing of an international border in order to access non-source country resettlement. This amounted to a shifting of the burden to host countries neighbouring the source country. Estimates in 2011 suggested that approximately 500,000 Colombians had already fled to the neighbouring countries of Ecuador, Panama, and Venezuela.[38] Contrary to Canada's aggressively voiced concern about human smuggling set out in the government's Bill C-4's *Preventing Human Smugglers from Abusing Canada's Immigration System Act*,[39] the repeal of the source country provisions presumably led to more people turning to smugglers to escape their country of origin.[40] Essentially, despite the government's stated intent to return to UNHCR-referred refugees, the repeal of the source country class had increased dependence on private sponsors and increased the usage of human smugglers, leading to increased burdens in neighbouring countries. The commitment to international protection did not appear to be at the forefront of this decision.

The repeal further demonstrates the fragility of the legal framework that regulates resettlement. Any component of Canada's resettlement program could likewise be repealed. Earlier discussion in this book has illustrated that resettlement has never been a smooth or uncomplicated process. Here the government was opting to deal with the program's difficulties by abandonment rather than by reform. There is no legal basis to prevent a future government from doing the same with any or all of the components of its voluntary resettlement program, regardless of how unlikely this may seem at a particular moment.

In an apparent acknowledgment of the underlying rationale for the creation and benefit of the source country class and the predecessor designated classes, the government noted that the discretionary power of the minister in section 25 of the *Immigration and Refugee Protection Act (IRPA)* could still be used to grant admission to those who did not meet the refugee definition.[41] Commonly referred to as a "humanitarian and compassionate application," it provides the minister of citizenship and immigration with the discretionary power under section 25 to grant a foreign national permanent resident status or an exemption from any applicable criteria or obligations of the *IRPA* to a foreign national either in Canada or outside of Canada who is inadmissible or who does not meet the requirements of the act, if justified by humanitarian and compassionate considerations.

While legally accurate that a humanitarian and compassionate application could be made, it is unlikely that this discretionary power better enables the identification of the most vulnerable individuals in need of protection. Section 25 was changed significantly by the *Balanced Refugee Reform Act*[42] and by the *Protecting Canada's Immigration System Act*.[43] Previously, the section gave the minister discretionary power to grant permanent residence to a foreign national either inside or outside of Canada on the basis of humanitarian and compassionate grounds, the best interests of the child, or public policy considerations.[44] The amendments limit the circumstances in which public policy can be considered by the minister, ensure the payment of fees before the application is considered, and also make persons that may pose a security risk or be involved in serious criminality inadmissible to apply. It is specifically noted that the minister may not consider factors taken into account during refugee determination. Key aspects of section 25 are set out in the following quotation:

> 25. (1) Subject to subsection (1.2), the Minister must, on request of a foreign national in Canada who applies for permanent resident status and who is inadmissible – other than under section 34, 35 or 37 – or who does not meet the requirements of this Act, and may, on request of a foreign national outside Canada – other than a foreign national who is inadmissible under section 34, 35 or 37 – who applies for a permanent resident visa, examine the circumstances concerning the foreign national and may grant the foreign national permanent resident status or an exemption from any applicable criteria or obligations of this Act if the Minister is of the opinion that it is justified by humanitarian and compassionate considerations relating to the foreign national, taking into account the best interests of a child directly affected ...
>
> (1.1) The Minister is seized of a request referred to in subsection (1) only if the applicable fees in respect of that request have been paid.
> ...
>
> (1.3) In examining the request of a foreign national in Canada, the Minister may not consider the factors that are taken into account in the determination of whether a person is a Convention refugee under section 96 or a person in need of protection under subsection 97(1) but must consider elements related to the hardships that affect the foreign national.
>
> 25.1 (1) The Minister may, on the Minister's own initiative, examine the circumstances concerning a foreign national who is inadmissible – other than under section 34, 35 or 37 – or who does not meet the requirements of this Act and may grant the foreign national permanent resident status or an exemption from any applicable criteria or obligations of this Act if the Minister is of the opinion that it is justified by humanitarian and compassionate considerations relating to the foreign national, taking into account the best interests of a child directly affected.

(2) The Minister may exempt the foreign national from the payment of any applicable fees in respect of the examination of their circumstances under subsection (1).

...

25.2 (1) The Minister may, in examining the circumstances concerning a foreign national who is inadmissible or who does not meet the requirements of this Act, grant that person permanent resident status or an exemption from any applicable criteria or obligations of this Act if the Minister is of the opinion that it is justified by public policy considerations.

(2) The Minister may exempt the foreign national from the payment of any applicable fees in respect of the examination of their circumstances under subsection (1).

From the *IRPA*'s introduction in 2002 to 2010 when the source country class repeal was being considered, a total of 6,506 visas were issued on humanitarian and compassionate grounds to foreign nationals outside of Canada. The approval rating of applications ranged from a high of 92 percent in 2003 to a low of 44 percent in 2005 (see Table 6). These numbers, however, do not differentiate between asylum seekers and other foreign nationals with strong ties to Canada.[45] It is difficult to assess what the addition of asylum applicants from previous source countries has done to these numbers in the years since. While applications may have increased, the narrowed scope of section 25 prohibiting consideration of refugee factors means any increase in admissions is highly unlikely.

The regulatory impact analysis indicates that consultations preceding the repeal of the source country class were undertaken with the UNHCR, the Canadian Council for Refugees, the Province of Quebec, and the Department of Foreign Affairs and International Trade.[46] The Canadian Council for Refugees alleges that any suggestion that there were consultations is a misrepresentation. The organization asserts that it was never consulted on the elimination of the program, only on its improvement.[47] The Canadian Council for Refugees details meetings with Citizenship and Immigration Canada in 2009 and 2010 and claims that, in 2010, Citizenship and Immigration Canada indicated the purpose of the regulatory impact analysis was to determine how to make the class flexible and responsive.[48]

TABLE 6
Humanitarian and compassionate applications outside Canada, 2002–10

Year	Passed	Refused	Withdrawn	Approval rate (%)*
2002	7	3	0	70
2003	445	41	8	92
2004	456	61	24	88
2005	856	1,079	390	44
2006	1,450	1,733	197	46
2007	1,009	273	309	79
2008	1,029	155	278	87
2009	738	151	256	83
2010	596	219	323	73

* excluding withdrawn applications.
Source: Obtained through ATI Request A-2011-02100/bm. Response prepared by IR Statistics Unit.

This apparent failure by the government to honestly consult the largest umbrella organization representing refugee issues in Canada in advance of proposing the repeal further confirms the vulnerability of discretionary resettlement.[49]

Interestingly, while practically no academic attention has been devoted to this form of resettlement, a short piece by Judith Kumin addresses source country resettlement in an edited collection from 2007 entitled *Innovative Concepts for Alternative Migration Policies*.[50] Kumin starts from the reality of increasingly restrictive measures by states to deter illegal entry and argues that "there is at least a moral responsibility for states to offset control measures with other means to allow persons in need of protection to find it."[51] Recognizing the traditional concerns associated with resettlement – a pull factor that discourages voluntary repatriation, the potential for fraud, and camp security concerns when demand exceeds availability – Kumin proposes source country processing as a potentially better alternative.[52] A convincing list of benefits of this approach, including the reduction of irregular and dangerous movements; the use of a burden-sharing mechanism to reduce spontaneous arrivals in the region of origin; the ability of states to manage and control intake; the reduced time spent in limbo; and the required dialogue between the country of resettlement and the country of origin, supports Kumin's argument.⁵³ Conversely, her acknowledged disadvantages seem no less daunting than those attached to traditional resettlement and include the potential risk to the applicant while the process is under way if the application is denied, as he or she remains in the country where persecution is feared; the risk that source country processing will serve as an excuse for states to prevent access to asylum; and the realities that the process lacks transparency, is subject to discretion, and is likely to benefit only a small number of individuals.⁵⁴ These latter two listed disadvantages are in fact identical to those attached to traditional resettlement. The article suggests that source country processing may be an appealing option in Europe and something that the UNHCR should consider as a complement to the strategic use of resettlement.⁵⁵ Canada, noted as the clear leader in this form of resettlement for over thirty years and an example to the world, ended its program less than five years after the article's publication.

In her 2015 report exploring the potential for private sponsorship in the European Union, Kumin again notes the value of source country resettlement as a component: "If one of the objectives of private sponsorship is to discourage irregular movement, it would make sense to extend eligibility to persons still in their countries of origin."⁵⁶ She notes that this was the underlying rationale for the US program of in-country processing for minors in El Salvador, Guatemala, and Honduras and for the UNHCR's Program for Orderly Departure from Vietnam in 1979.

A case study of Colombia offers a better understanding of the operation of Canada's source country class, the justifications for its removal, and the consequences of the repeal.

Colombia

In November 2010, prior to the repeal of the source country class, I represented the Canadian Council for Refugees as a delegate on a fact-finding mission to Colombia. The objective of the delegation was to gather information on the human rights situation within the country in the face of declining acceptance rates of Colombian refugees at the Canadian Immigration and Refugee Board as well as significantly reduced source country class resettlement from Colombia to Canada. Interviews were conducted with twelve organizations in Bogota.⁵⁷ Through the assistance of the Jesuit Refugee Service, we visited an internally displaced persons (IDP) camp in Soacha, south of Bogota, and met with several IDPs. At the time, Colombia had one of the largest populations of internally displaced persons in the world with over three million displaced persons within Colombia and hundreds of thousands seeking refuge in other countries in the region.[58] By 2017, the UNHCR had noted that IDP numbers were on the increase and reaching 7.5 million.[59] Figures were expected to rise to 7.56 million by 1 January 2018 and to 7.7 million by the end of 2019.[60]

Resettlement requires cooperation between the host and resettlement countries. With so few resettlement places available, the Canadian government can afford to be selective in terms of where it focuses its resettlement. For a long time, Citizenship and Immigration Canada perceived source country resettlement from Colombia as being extremely workable. Colombia is a developed country with a cooperative government that wanted the persecutory agents out.[61] Colombians can also be seen as "desirable" refugees since they are well educated and easily integrated: "One of the representations that was most frequently put forward was that of Colombian refugees as self-sufficient, independent and committed to their goals in Canada."[62]

The ease of resettlement from Colombia is matched with the foreign policy, burden-sharing argument it provides.[63] At the time of the repeal, Colombians represented the largest human displacement in the Western hemisphere and the world.[64] Canada was the only country to resettle directly from Colombia, while both Canada and the United States took Colombians from neighbouring countries through resettlement or as refugees who reached their territories. The UNHCR had likewise increasingly focused on IDPs in Colombia. In its 2010 global appeal, the agency noted: "UNHCR's financial requirements in Latin America have increased steadily in recent years. This is mostly due to the Office's greater involvement with IDPs in Colombia and the reinforcement of protection for unregistered individuals in refugee-like situations in the neighbouring countries."[65] With little assistance from the rest of the world for the plight of the Colombians, a policy argument could have been made in Canada for regional burden sharing and a justifiable reduction of responsibility for the arguably more complicated and less desirable refugee flows in other parts of the world that are closer to other states. And, for a long time, Canada operated a successful source country resettlement program out of Colombia.

Yet, despite these incentives and the attractions of resettlement from Colombia, Canada steadily decreased its resettlement targets in the region. In 2008, the Bogota target was 1,960. It dropped to 1,350 in 2009 and was halved to 700 in 2010.[66] In 2011, the target was set for less than 400.[67] Previously, the Canadian embassy in Bogota had agreements with humanitarian organizations to refer persons in need of protection for source country class resettlement.[68] In the final few years of the program, the government eliminated the referral capacity. The protection coordinator for the International Committee of the Red Cross (ICRC) in Colombia indicated in November 2010 that the ICRC had previously supported requests from the Canadian embassy for resettlement but was told that Canadian resettlement was reduced and that the available numbers were already filled for 2010–11 through the backlog of applications at the embassy.[69] At that time, the ICRC signalled that it was able and willing to recommence with referrals if requested.[70] A non-governmental organization (NGO) representative interviewed during the Canadian Council for Refugees delegation to Bogota indicated that she had previously worked for a different NGO that made referrals to the Canadian embassy and had enjoyed an open, trusting relationship with the visa officers but that that relationship no longer existed.[71] One organization did confirm to the delegation, prior to the repeal of the class, that, while the referral program no longer officially existed, this organization was still able to communicate with the embassy on a number of cases, including about ten groups comprising a total of sixty people over the year.[72] In a few of the cases, the embassy had recommended finding a private sponsor, and the resettlement was successful.[73] This organization also reinforced, however, that, while they previously enjoyed a fluid and privileged relationship with the Canadian visa officers in Bogota, this was no longer the case, and they had been given the impression that the source country class program was being shut down.[74]

Indeed, four months after these interviews took place in Bogota, the Canadian government announced its intention to not only close down the source country program in Colombia but also to repeal the source country class regulations altogether.[75] A key justification underlying the repeal was the arguable necessity for direct access applications for source country resettlement. The difficulties identified with direct access were the inundation of claims it created while, at the same time, failing to grant access to the most vulnerable people. Citizenship and Immigration Canada's regulatory impact analysis statement indicated that "there were no organizations willing to refer Source Country Class applicants without funding and no funding was available."[76] This assessment contradicts the information received from organizations interviewed in Bogota that expressed both a willingness to provide referrals and a concern for the vulnerable persons identified by them with diminishing protection options. Pastor Peter Stucky of the Colombian Mennonite Church in Bogota called the program "a lifesaver for many people in Colombia" and noted that the repeal of the legislation "closes the last option."[77]

Impressions gained from interviews in Bogota suggest a different rationale for the Canadian government's desire to shut down the program, at least in Colombia. The conflict in Colombia fundamentally shifted under government crackdowns, and the lines blurred between ideological revolutionaries and those engaged in generalized crime and drug trafficking.[78] Within this new environment, the political counsellor at the Canadian embassy in Bogota acknowledged that alliances were being made between paramilitaries and guerrillas who would have previously been enemies.[79] Both the messaging from the Colombian government that there was no longer a persecution risk in Colombia[80] and the increasing inability to establish an individual's alliances complicated Canada's ability to credibly identify those in need of resettlement.

In addition, fraudulent applications plagued the program while the referral system was still in operation. There were instances in Quebec of refugees identifying paramilitaries among those resettled.[81] The ICRC indicated that individuals used fraudulent referrals allegedly from the ICRC at the Canadian embassy.[82] In 2004, a scheme was discovered by Colombian authorities in which substantial bribes were being paid to civil servants employed by the Colombian National Senate for documents identifying individuals as victims of death or abduction threats from either the guerrillas or the paramilitaries. The documents were reportedly used at the Canadian embassy in Bogota to achieve source country class resettlement for at least fifty people.[83] Having consequently eliminated referrals, the Canadian embassy was inundated with direct access applications and inquiries, with an average of approximately 4,700 applications per year between 2005 and 2009.[84] The headaches and processing costs of source country resettlement seemed to outweigh the benefits, even while the need still existed.

Group Resettlement

As source country resettlement dwindled and ultimately came to an end, group resettlement gained in momentum and support. Advocacy for the resettlement of refugee groups in Canada dates back to the consultations that preceded the *Immigration Act, 1976*. Commenting on the white paper on immigration in 1967, Joseph Kage of the JIAS pushed not only for private sponsorship but also for the "sponsorship of groups, who may not necessarily come within the outlined provisions for admission."[85] Despite this early push, group processing is a relatively new form of resettlement recognized by the international community. The "group processing methodology" came out of Goal 5 of the *Agenda for Protection* in which the fifth objective was "[e]xpansion of resettlement opportunities."[86] The methodology is thus a component of the strategic use of resettlement. The international *Multilateral Framework of Understandings on Resettlement*, which resulted from a United Nations process co-chaired by Canada in 2004 following the *Agenda for Protection*, likewise encouraged states to pursue the use of group resettlement.[87]

Whereas refugee status is, by definition, an individual status, group processing challenges this through a simplified referral and processing system. Group processing allows the UNHCR to expand its resettlement submissions through the use of a "group profile and proposal" for thousands of refugees at one time with a uniform refugee claim, clearly defined membership, and particular vulnerabilities or protection needs rather than an individual case-by-case processing with a resettlement referral form for each refugee.[88] While source country resettlement was a refugee "class," meaning those resettled under this program were required to meet the specified definition set out in the regulations,[89] group resettlement is considered an "administrative arrangement" to efficiently move refugees from a particular camp.[90] Group processing, tied with funding increases, enabled the UNHCR to raise submission levels above the number of available places made by resettlement states.[91] Within the first two years of the implementation of the group processing methodology by the UNHCR, thirteen refugee groups, totalling approximately 43,000 refugees, were submitted for consideration globally.[92] The UNHCR considers group processing to be one of the factors responsible for an overall increase in resettlement between 2005 and 2014.[93] By 2010, the UNHCR stopped increasing referrals as states could not meet the demand.[94]

As the program commenced in Canada, the Canadian government described it as a "fundamental shift in our policy approach to refugee identification and selection."[95] The 2005 annual report to Parliament on immigration placed Canada "at the forefront of using group resettlement strategically."[96] Group resettlement enabled Canada to address protracted situations in a strategic manner by removing a large and cohesive group from the protraction. The first three group resettlement projects in Canada were the Somali-Sudanese, the Karen, and the Bhutanese.[97]

Whereas individualized state resettlement still struggles to achieve international cooperation, group processing appears to offer more simplified and successful cooperation between states by virtue of the ability to concentrate on a large group and achieve visible success. The first Canadian pilot project in 2003 involved group processing of Sudanese and Somali refugees in Kenya. Canada and Australia, in cooperation, decided to jointly resettle the two smallest minority groups being persecuted in the Dadaab refugee camps.[98] To overcome the domestic legislative requirement for individual refugee assessments, the minister's discretion in section 25 of the *IRPA* to grant an exemption from the act was used to declare the Sudanese and Somalis as *prima facie* refugees and vulnerable.[99] This permitted Citizenship and Immigration Canada to use a singular claim for each group and to exempt the refugees from the "ability-to-establish" requirement.[100] The efficiency of the group process thus played out in both the United Nations and domestic spheres.

Canada next requested that the UNHCR identify a group of Burmese refugees in Thailand for 2006–07, which led to the resettlement of 806 Karen refugees.[101] A second wave of resettlement for the Karen group was announced in 2007 with the intention of bringing over 2,000 refugees.[102] In total, 3,900 Karen were ultimately resettled in Canada.[103] Other countries to resettle Karen refugees using the group methodology included the United

States, Australia, the United Kingdom, Finland, the Netherlands, New Zealand, Sweden, Norway, and Ireland.[104]

In 2007, Canada also committed to the resettlement of 5,000 Bhutanese from Nepal over three to five years. The refugees are Bhutanese of Nepalese origin who were stripped of their Bhutanese citizenship in the 1990s and fled to Nepal. Canadian officials travelled to Nepal in September 2008, October 2009, October 2010, and April 2011.[105] As of October 2011, all 5,000 Bhutanese had been selected, and almost 4,500 had arrived in Canada; in June 2012, the government announced the resettlement of an additional 500 Bhutanese refugees whose only family connections were in Canada.[106] In March 2013, the government announced that it would resettle 1,000 more Bhutanese, and, by the next year, 5,760 Bhutanese refugees had arrived in Canada.[107] Resettlement occurred in more than twenty-one communities across Canada, including Charlottetown, Fredericton, St. John's, Saint-Jérôme, Ottawa, London, Windsor, Hamilton, Winnipeg, Saskatoon, Lethbridge, and Vancouver, with large numbers being resettled in Quebec.[108] The resettlement was part of an operation with other countries to address the protraction of Bhutanese in Nepal dating back almost two decades.[109] Originally, nine countries, including the United States, Australia, New Zealand, Finland, Denmark, Norway, Sweden, the United Kingdom, and the Netherlands, were involved,[110] with resettlement ultimately occurring in all but Finland.[111] An agreement was entered into between the eight countries and the UNHCR to resettle approximately 70,000 of the 100,000 Bhutanese refugees in Nepal.[112] By December 2010, 40,000 Bhutanese refugees had been resettled across the eight countries.[113]

In Canada, the Bhutanese resettlement process differed from the Somali-Sudanese resettlement. Unlike the singular form used with the Somali and Sudanese refugees, shortened forms for each applicant were used, and interviews were organized so that large numbers could be completed during the same visit:

> Rather than asking them to give us 5,000 forms of 30 pages each, because we knew the 5,000 were part of a complete, comprehensive census and we had received the complete census, we asked for a shorter form.
>
> Instead of going to the camps in Nepal two to four times a year to do a few at a time, Canada goes in once a year to interview 1,000 people at a

time with these shorter forms. The arrivals are staggered. It's not faster; it's just a way to use our resources more effectively. Eight countries are in the camp, and we can't all use the generators at the same time, so we take turns going in.[114]

The Bhutanese resettlement also represented a more multilateral endeavour, with agreement and sharing between the numerous states involved. A health centre was also built in Nepal to be used as a cultural orientation and transit centre. Costs for the centre were shared between Canada, Australia, and the United States.[115] A common protocol, as well as the use of doctors, was shared between states for tuberculosis testing, and seven states joined in a diplomatic démarche to the Nepali government to obtain exit permits from Nepal and development assistance for the residual population.[116] As a global whole, the Bhutanese resettlement has had the highest success rate in the world, with an acceptance rate of 99 percent of submissions.[117] Similar to Colombians, the Bhutanese can be regarded as "desirable" refugees. Citizenship and Immigration Canada's website describes them as speaking a "variety of languages" and possessing a "range of employment skills."[118] More importantly, the government points out, "many speak English and it is not uncommon for the young adults to have secondary, and even post-secondary education."[119]

The resettlement of Karen refugees from Burma and of Bhutanese refugees from Nepal both involved international cooperation among Australia, the United States, and Canada, which also worked with additional countries on the resettlement. What is interesting given the close alignment between the states on this form of resettlement is the divergence in their public promotion of group processing. While Canada publicly promoted its use of the group resettlement methodology, with updates on the Citizenship and Immigration Canada website,[120] information on the use of the methodology in refugee selection was much less publicly available in the United States or Australia.[121] At the time, one resettlement worker in Australia commented that she could not imagine the Australian government ever promoting resettlement as it is "very taboo politically."[122] In the United States and Australia, the group processing system appears to be absorbed into their resettlement programs, whereas Canada appears keen to promote its efforts on this front.

Promotion may be linked to the growing trend in all of Canada's resettlement initiatives to encourage private sponsors to take part in the group resettlement. An information update on the Bhutanese resettlement concluded with the link that "[i]nterested parties can sponsor and help integrate Bhutanese refugees into our communities through the Private Sponsorship of Refugees Program."[123] Citizens for Public Justice noted that group resettlement is an ideal partnership between government and sponsoring groups: "Sponsoring groups have the resources and motivation to help resettle and integrate newcomers that the public sector finds hard to gather. As was the case with the Indochinese in the 1970s, there is tremendous potential for a meeting of mutual need from either side in the group processing exercise."[124] In this way, a program that shows growing potential for international cooperation while meeting the UNHCR's needs is also conducive to public-private partnerships, which is again a move towards encouraging the private sponsorship of strangers.

Demonstrating the increasing Canadian public awareness of group resettlement in Canada, Pride Uganda Alliance International approached the House of Commons Subcommittee on International Human Rights in 2010 with a proposal that the government use group processing to address the persecution of homosexual Ugandans.[125] The request was in fact a request for both source country and group resettlement for the Ugandans. The Rainbow Refugee Committee then contacted Pride Uganda to participate in its blended private sponsorship project to sponsor lesbian, gay, bisexual, transgendered, and queer/questioning refugees.[126]

Group resettlement offers many benefits over traditional individualized resettlement. It is more efficient and less costly to process groups over individuals. The transplanting of families and social networks eases integration in a new community: "Relationships with people in the receiving society are difficult to establish because of the feelings of strangeness they produce. This is related to cultural differences, but also to distrust around relationships with unknown people that refugees bring with them."[127] At the same time, the populations selected for group resettlement tend to be "new and few," meaning that they are small ethnic groups with little or no established community in Canada.[128] This, in turn, raises other settlement challenges. While refugees undoubtedly benefit from the collective support group resettlement offers, bringing over significant numbers of refugees from a specific population to a Canadian community requires that community to be receptive and prepared for the group. In anticipation of the arrival of the first group of Bhutanese refugees in British Columbia, the Immigrant Services Society of British Columbia (ISSBC) launched a comprehensive community-based pre-arrival planning process in Coquitlam, where close to one thousand Bhutanese were to be settled.[129] The ISSBC contacted a reporter from the *Globe and Mail* and convinced her to travel to Nepal to cover the resettlement.[130] As a result, on 18 July 2009, the front page of the *Globe and Mail* featured large photographs of a Bhutanese family both in the Nepalese refugee camp and after arriving in Vancouver on 16 July 2009.[131] Two articles in the paper covered the tragic fate of the Bhutanese of ethnic Nepalese descent who were driven into Nepal in the early 1990s and languished in refugee camps for almost two decades. The reporters detailed the immense challenges of coming to Canada and transitioning from a primitive rural existence to life in a large city with limited English. The articles were sympathetic and understanding, designed to promote the welcoming of the refugees into the community. While necessary to the successful integration of the Bhutanese refugees, this promotion of the image of needy camp-based refugees fuels the rhetorical divide between these refugees and others who come to Canada to claim asylum on their own. At the same time the Bhutanese began their journey to Canada, the Canadian government reintroduced visa requirements for Czech and Mexican citizens entering Canada in reaction to rising refugee claim numbers from these countries.[132] The day before the profiled family arrived, the *Globe and Mail* quoted then Minister of Citizenship and Immigration Jason Kenney:

> It's not lost on economic migrants who want to jump the queue that we have a system that's fairly easy to abuse. And where people can settle in Canada, sometimes for several years, with a mixture of a work permit and/or social benefits, and if they're determined to, they can game our system and abuse our generosity.[133]

The welcomed arrival of the Bhutanese in British Columbia also preceded the very unwelcomed arrival three months later of the first of two boatloads of Tamil migrants off the coast of British Columbia in October 2009. In the midst of the government's queue-jumping rhetoric and the repeated assertions that respectable refugees wait patiently in camps for resettlement, group resettlement further skews the invalidity of this image. The necessity to ensure that the incoming group is welcomed and integrated incidentally fuels the perceived divide between the deservingness of these camp-origin refugees and those who independently claim asylum.

Group resettlement may also affect the global reach of resettlement. Canada's resettlement program has traditionally been global in its application. In 2010, visa officers travelled to more than forty countries and interviewed refugees from over sixty nationalities.[134] Until 2003, when the United States initiated a global program, Canada had the only global resettlement program in the world.[135] In contrast, group resettlement means that refugees from specific groups in identified camps will be targeted for resettlement. This selection seems to focus on small, resolvable situations of protraction that garner international attention and agreement. Refugees in other camps, or not in camps, may be increasingly excluded from the resettlement program if group resettlement gains momentum. For these refugees, waiting patiently will get them nowhere. They are left with no option but to claim asylum on their own.

There are also criticisms of group resettlement that counter not only the selection of group refugees but also the benefits of efficiency and increased settlement success. An internal UNHCR report on the group resettlement of the Somali-Sudanese minority out of the Dadaab camps noted the tensions created among groups in the camp:

> [T]he resettlement process for Somali-Sudanese has created a lot of bad blood, misunderstanding and false expectations amongst the refugee population. These reactions are neither a surprise, nor difficult to comprehend ... Many fail to understand how this group was selected for group resettlement ... They believe that this group has the least right for consideration as they spent only a little time in Dadaab ... The rest of the community is restricted to the option of individual screening, which is a slow process and benefits a few. We have started receiving many letters from different communities in the refugee camp, including some groups of whom nobody has ever heard, claiming persecution and hoping for consideration for group resettlement.[136]

From the perspective of the UNHCR's staff working on resettlement in the camps, the group resettlement was problematic:

> Although the Somali-Sudanese have faced problems, presently it is not of such a nature that mere membership of the Somali-Sudanese community warrants resettlement. Our attempts to develop the resettlement referral system at the camp level into a credible and transparent procedure are jeopardized by these disruptive initiatives.[137]

The reality is that resettlement of any kind involves the selection of some refugees but never the selection of all. Tensions arise, often with competition and desperation for the limited spaces. Protection, from the perspective on the ground, sometimes appears to be more compromised than it is affected through resettlement programs. Group resettlement simply multiplies these issues by the high profile that comes with resettling large groups from a camp over a distinct period of time.

The Bhutanese resettlement likewise faced criticism that this refugee population was not the most in need.[138] Moreover, it was not a refugee group entirely, or necessarily, wanting resettlement. Citizenship and Immigration Canada's website promoting the program boasted: "The Bhutanese refugees are very enthusiastic and optimistic about resettling in Canada."[139] The reality was that the Bhutanese were ethnic Nepali, and many wished to remain in Nepal and were still hoping for a solution permitting their return to Bhutan. In 2009, a repatriation campaign was commenced by a senior citizens group resistant to resettlement and wishing only to return to Bhutan. The group registered over 8,000 refugees.[140] In April 2011, talks resumed between Bhutan and Nepal on the repatriation of the remaining refugees following the resettlement program.[141]

Citizenship and Immigration Canada's information bulletins distributed to the Bhutanese in advance of resettlement further betrayed the reality of rumours and hesitations surrounding the resettlement. The second bulletin directly addressed the misinformation: "Rumours that you will be 'sold' for slave labour or forced to fight in Iraq are false. It is also false that you will be forced to live in a refugee camp. There are no refugee camps in Canada."[142] The third information bulletin contained a heading: "Stories that Are False."[143] In addition to again dismissing the above rumours more forcefully, it added: "Cold weather does NOT prevent people in Canada from having children. There are families of all sizes in Canada. It is up to individuals to decide how many children they will have."[144] This was not a group uncomplicatedly keen on resettlement. Counter to the images of refugees waiting in long queues, hoping to win the resettlement lottery, or sneaking in through a back door, Canada was actively pursuing and convincing the Bhutanese to resettle.

The critiques of group resettlement speak to the fear that the benefits of efficiency, lessened expense, cooperative international burden sharing, and potential resolution of certain camp populations get privileged in the strategic use of resettlement over protection of the neediest refugees. The Bhutanese were considered a small, forgotten, and growing refugee population for which no other resolution was possible. With their resettlement, the international community could congratulate itself on the effective achievement of a durable solution for a refugee population. By 2010, Canada began a shift from global resettlement to multi-year commitments focused primarily on protection needs.[145] Potential advantages of the commitments included "enhanced collaboration and coordination with other countries, coordinated referral requests with UNHCR, and efficiency savings in terms of better meeting the needs of large groups and potential improvements in processing time."[146] Evaluating the commitments between 2010 and 2014, Immigration, Refugees and Citizenship Canada noted: "A few key informants noted that the multi-year commitments did not eliminate or reduce the resettlement program's overall flexibility to respond to international priorities, as the proportion of refugees to be resettled as part of multi-year commitments accounted for about half of GARs level."[147]

Law and Discretion

With these resettlement models, the law is far away and moving further afield. Both the source country class and group resettlement are intentional manoeuvres away from law. They move beyond the refugee definition and Canada's protection commitments and, therefore, distance the program from the law. Canada's international legal obligations are expanded through voluntary and discretionary routes to protection. This has been the case since the first refugee legislation was introduced in the 1970s. As with the original willingness by states to legalize asylum, humanitarianism clearly underlies this expansion, but so does the consequent ability to blend law and discretion. Refugee numbers set out in government statistics combine convention refugees and other protection classes. A politically discretionary settlement program is thus established with the label of refugee and humanitarian protection. The law itself, through expanded classes, is able to create enhanced discretion.

Discretion is particularly primary with source and group resettlement. General discretion influences the decision-making on which countries were placed within the source country class schedule and the choice of where to target group resettlement. These decisions often determine what "type" of refugee is resettled. With both the Bhutanese and the Colombians, this has tended to mean educated, English-speaking refugees. Refugee lawyer David Matas long ago lamented:

> Refugee policy, generally, in the Government of Canada suffers from its coming out of the Immigration Department. No element of refugee admission is examined solely from the angle of protection. Because it is the Immigration Department that decides on refugee admission, immigration and refugee policy become inextricably intertwined.[148]

With the move to eliminate the source country class and the designation of groups for group processing, there is also a shift to broaden the discretionary power set out in section 25 of the *IRPA*. This power has been described as "a concession to the fact that no system of migration rules could possibly account for all the variables, all the exigencies, and all the mitigating circumstances that would render the operation of the rules harsh, unjust, or even contrary to Canada's own interests."[149] It is thus created for the benefit of the applicant. The exemption component of section 25 has been used in group resettlement to bypass individual assessments, and the government has indicated that permanent resident visas through section 25 could be granted to individuals who would otherwise have received protection through the shut-down source country class.

While potentially broad in scope, section 25 is more likely of limited practical application in replacing the source country class. The guidance and structure of the regulatory framework of the source country route to admission is lost in the non-protection-specific power of section 25. It is a move from specific access set out in the regulatory scheme by the creation of a class to the broad discretion of section 25 that lacks any direction. Section 25's discretion is dually vague in its optional application by the minister and the vagueness of the meaning behind the "humanitarian and compassionate" terminology.[150] Moreover, the government manual of policy and procedural guidance for processing humanitarian and compassionate applications notes at the outset the limited intended use of the discretion:

> The humanitarian and compassionate decision-making process is a highly discretionary one that considers whether a special grant of an exemption from a requirement of the Act is warranted. It is widely understood that invoking Subsection 25(1) is an exceptional measure and not simply an alternate means of applying for permanent resident status in Canada.[151]

In no way can this discretionary power be perceived as having replaced the source country class. A further consequence of this transition is that those attaining permanent residence status through section 25, rather than through the source country class provisions, will not be tied to the refugee scheme or the resulting rights and benefits that attach to entrance through this route, including transportation loans, resettlement services, and revenue support.[152] Applicants must also now pay fees to have their claims considered.[153]

This shift in the legislation, even from one form of voluntary action to a discretionary scheme, highlights the fragility of the legal framework. While the legalized framework of resettlement classes implies concrete obligation, with the repeal of the source country class, it is shown to be a fragile regulation that can be easily discarded with little real consultation and minimum uproar. Within the month that the proposed repeal was announced, during which there was a thirty-day opportunity to submit comments on the proposal to Citizenship and Immigration Canada, only two Canadian journalists covered the story, with their articles appearing in only a handful of papers.[154] Neither national Canadian newspaper, the *Globe and Mail* or the *National Post*, covered the story.

Opting to repeal the source country class as a solution to the problems that were evident also challenges the government's stated commitment to bring resettlement closer to the law and the legal refugee definition. The reality is that the repeal likely caused increased human smuggling. While the government's convoluted melding of laws has led to allegations of queue jumping and so forth, in this case the government was turning a blind eye to the immigration law consequences of its intended repeal. In countries such as Colombia, where the need for protection continues, and, as noted by Pastor Peter Stucky, Canadian source country resettlement was the "last option," the removal of this option leaves the illegal/irregular crossing of borders, often through the assistance of smugglers, as the ultimate last option.[155]

Beyond the increasing use of broad, generalized discretion, there are the administrative and management influences on resettlement decisions that operate outside of the law. These considerations determine in which countries the source country class operated, the decision to eliminate referrals for the source country class, and the repeal of the class when the subsequent direct access approach overwhelmed the program. Similarly, with the resettlement of groups, considerations of efficiency, lessened expense, and the resolution of certain camp populations played a parallel role with protection when the focus was on the strategic use of resettlement. The government's justification for the repeal of the source country class was couched in many references to returning resettlement to its legal origins. Statements emphasize placing resettlement selection more in line with the UNHCR's referrals and the international refugee definition. This is a move, at least rhetorically, towards the firm notion of law. The proposal emphasized Citizenship and Immigration Canada's expressed desire to return resettlement to the original protection intentions set out in international law. At the same time, however, the stated desire to work with private sponsors and increase private sponsorship has achieved the opposite result. This was a move away from these very laws towards more family-centric resettlement with less resemblance to refugee law. Law may be invoked to achieve other political objectives, narrowing the government's protection obligations.

Turning, however, to the increased use of group resettlement, the emphasis on private sponsorship can be seen through a different lens. While not stated anywhere as the government's intention, the use of private sponsorship for group resettlement does suggest the potential to move private sponsorship away from named sponsorship and reconnection to the UNHCR's referrals. Since these groups tend to represent the "new and few," there is not a strong familial sponsorship base in Canada. The group sponsorship encourages private sponsorship similar to the Indochinese resettlement. It is a sponsorship of strangers. Here, then, the government can be seen to be attempting to regain control of sponsorship by redirecting its focus through group resettlement, as it has similarly done with blended projects and the blended visa office–referred program.

It is not clear whether the shifts that are occurring will bring Canadian resettlement closer to law or deeper into a discretionary realm of decision-making that has as much to do with international cooperation, management, and efficiency as it does with humanitarian protection. Syrian and Yazidi resettlement to Canada currently highlights not only a high protection focus but also a selective focus. What does seem clear is that private Canadian citizens are being granted an increasing role in protection. But, as their role shifts through the increased use of both blended initiatives and the resettlement of larger groups alongside the loss of source country resettlement, the question, again, is whether sponsors will continue with the level of support they currently are offering to named referrals, often with familial links. The continuance of resettlement as a mechanism of protection is vulnerable in this foundational shifting, even if the underlying intent does prove to be a return to international origins and definitions.

This chapter, in both the novelty of group resettlement and the fate of the source country class, ends with more hesitant conclusions. It does conclude, however, with a clear awareness of a changing and vulnerable resettlement program – a program that is often guided by decision-making that is as focused on efficiency as it is on protection; that is turning more to discretion than to a regulated selection process; that is increasingly turning to private sponsors to carry the responsibility; and that can easily be repealed or simply fall into disuse without any legal change whatsoever. Despite its issues and the foundational shifts afoot, Canada remains one of the leading resettlement countries in the world, while other countries slowly, yet increasingly, are taking on small numbers of resettlement refugees or, in the case of the United States, drastically decreasing their commitments.

The book has shown law's presence, influence, and power in resettlement. The task now is to take the inevitable intersections of law and the categorizations of legality and, seeing them clearly, use them to regain complementarity between asylum and resettlement. Understanding law's role in this program, and its positive potential rather than its use as collusion, is key to this recovery. The concluding chapter thus returns the apocryphal to the forefront of the discussion.

8

Unsettling Refugee Resettlement

The idea of resettlement is simple. States voluntarily bring refugees to their territories who have fled elsewhere but not received adequate protection. Resettlement is complicated by its multiple purposes, not only offering a solution but also working as a tool of protection and expression of international burden sharing. Both as protection and solution, resettlement is meant as a complement to the laws of asylum and the obligation of *non-refoulement*. Too often and too easily, it has served as the opposite – a justification for limiting access to asylum and a challenge to the right of refugees to seek asylum. Rather than acting as a means of burden sharing, it has become a means of burden trading and burden evasion. The legality of the controlled entrance of refugees across an international border that resettlement offers is at the forefront of this convolution.

This places resettlement at the nexus of issues of rights, responsibility, and obligation. While the discussion occurs in the absence of a legal scheme for refugee resettlement, the law is nonetheless present. Resettlement is not simply a voluntary act that states may or may not opt to pursue. The analytical work on the place of law within resettlement has shown that resettlement is more legally influenced and influential to the legal scheme than assumed. It is an act of international protection and burden sharing that is influenced by law and that, through its voluntary nature, influences the international refugee law of *non-refoulement*.

While there has been a recent reorientation of the refugee regime and resurgence in resettlement discourse over the past decade at the national and the international levels, it has often been stuck at the "strategic" policy level and has lacked a comprehensive examination or in-depth consideration, particularly of the legal consequences. Canada has taken the lead on much of the resettlement reform internationally, leading the core group that drafted the *Multilateral Framework of Understandings on Resettlement*,[1] prefacing the recent reform of Canadian refugee law with announcements of increased resettlement numbers, taking a leadership role on the Syrian resettlement, and now working to promote the private sponsorship model globally. At the same time, there is an outstanding gap between action and knowledge and a growing sense of need among refugee advocates, Canadian policy-makers, and the United Nations High Commissioner for Refugees (UNHCR) for work on this issue.[2]

In some ways, this book begins to fill the gap. Its argument has been that law is relevant to resettlement. While the idea proposed at the outset in Chapter 1 is that law is intertwined and ever-present and cannot be examined in isolation, the aim of this book has been, to the extent that it is possible, to distill the law from the politics, policies, and rhetoric attached to resettlement. Seeing the law more clearly enables a better understanding of its use and intentional misuse. It also enables a better understanding of resettlement, an understanding that could not be approached from the position that resettlement is voluntary and that law is irrelevant.

In examining the basic models of resettlement used by Canada, this book has traversed decades and regions looking at the origins and reworkings of resettlement policies, the resettlement of specific refugee groups, and the rare instances of judicial intervention. In doing so, a basic program has exploded in multiple directions, extracting a clearer, yet more complicated, appreciation of the power of both law and resettlement outside the constraints of their own defined terms and beyond a temporal moment. In closing, it is useful to review the key realizations from each chapter and reflect on the understanding of law. From there, recommendations will be made, using the revelations gained, to move resettlement forward in a manner that is better aligned to its complementary intent to provide for the protection of refugees.

Law Distilled, Resettlement Unsettled

Resettlement is movement, and Chapter 2 explored the idea of movement to demonstrate the significant distinction between acquiring international legal status as a convention refugee and actually acquiring refuge and protection. The dichotomous relationship between refugee protection and resettlement and early tensions between protection and immigration incentives that resettlement brings to the fore were laid out. Claudena Skran has noted that "[t]he notion that the contemporary refugee crisis is unique lacks a historical perspective," which sets the stage for an understanding of the Canadian resettlement that followed.[3] The "myth of difference" articulated by B.S. Chimni to explain the paradigm shift in protection that occurred at the end of the Cold War has been repeated with the arrival of boat people in the 1990s and 2000s and policies justifying restrictive measures.[4]

This discussion framed the recent resurgence of resettlement in the context of restatements of state interest. The historical review illustrated that, while states appear to change their approaches to refugees, it is arguably the refugee realities that change, and state approaches only alter to remain consistently state centred. Convention Plus and the strategic use of resettlement clearly signalled the abandonment of humanitarian rhetoric and a focus on state enticements. At the same time, access to asylum was challenged, and status determinations have been met with varying success. International law, in itself, has been shown to be inadequate to achieve refugee protection, and the law is increasingly replaced with incentive-based arguments for resettlement. The failing and abandonment of law are contrasted to its increasing presence in the rhetoric of Canada's resettlement policies.

Canadian resettlement, which is tugged at both by its parallels to immigrant selection and by in-Canada asylum and is reflective of both programs by combining compassion and strategic interests, was the focus of Chapter 3. This is reinforced by the maintenance of a single piece of legislation, the *Immigration and Refugee Protection Act (IRPA)*, which addresses both immigration and refugee protection.[5] The discussion zeroes in on the move from refugee policy to refugee law in Canada and the evolving nature of that law through legal reform targeting the unwanted, the irregular, the presumed threats, and the assumed bogus claims. As suspicions circling asylum grow, so does the enticement towards the controlled entry that resettlement offers. Situated between undesired and uncontrolled asylum entrants and the desired and controlled selection of immigrants, resettlement's position is precarious and vulnerable to actual and rhetorical manipulation within a humanitarian framing.

Chapter 4 placed resettlement within Canada's immigration pie of numeric admissions that can be seen as both minute and globally generous. The framework and criteria for resettlement focus on the reality that resettlement is a selection process. The review of resettlement cases before the Federal Court hinted at the difficulty of access to the court system and a high degree of concern about visa officer decision-making in resettlement. These cases further highlighted the tenuous connection between the UNHCR's determination of refugee status and visa officer decisions on resettlement applications, which often fail to even mention this mandate refugee status. Law's role in resettlement means little more than controlled entry. The Canadian government exercises a selective assertion of law, and resettlement is legally framed rather than legally imposed.

The idea of legal layering and discretion was raised here. It is discretion that is at the core of resettlement. The discretionary basis of resettlement distinguishes it from the state's legal obligations to refugees. The intentional arguments for interchangeability between resettlement refugees and inland refugee claimants is based on this divide. There is no discretion with *non-refoulement,* and the law is strong. Yet the international legal obligation of *non-refoulement* has no application in resettlement, and Canadian courts have made clear that an asylum seeker present in Canada possesses greater rights than a refugee seeking resettlement. Resettlement, with weak law and high discretion, is much more amenable to the state's interests.

Chapter 5 considered how the private sponsorship of refugees has influenced both the resettlement program and refugee protection. In addition to the government interests covered earlier in the book, this examination introduces the interests of private citizens. Private interests are often in conflict with state interests even as private sponsorship is meant to complement government resettlement. This is yet another level of failed complementarity, just as the resettlement program in general is meant as a complement to the grant of asylum but, instead, sits in contrast. The history of the development of private sponsorship within the context of the ever-growing promise of Indochinese resettlement demonstrated the line between politics and law when faced with broad laws and malleable policy. Private sponsorship moved from a complementary addition to the government's program to the private sector taking on primary responsibility for the resettlement. This shift began to repeat itself with announcements curtailing asylum access, enabling broader sponsorship at greater rates of increase than the government program, and the shift of 1,000 spaces from the government program to private sponsorship. Yet, with sponsors' growing responsibility for resettlement came a change in the nature of that resettlement with less and less resettlement of strangers and the increasing use of the program as a tool for family reunification.

At the same time, however, more than ever before, the actions of private sponsors are being celebrated by the Canadian government under the rubric of its own humanitarianism. Just as the earlier discussion reveals the contrast between government resettlement and in-country asylum, the additional division between resettlement by the government and resettlement by private citizens is also highlighted. Each layer of complementarity is replaced with competition. Refugees lose out, and private sponsors bear the majority of the burden. Their commitment to refugees and facilitating resettlement can trap private sponsors into enabling the government's aversion to the law with increasingly restrictive legislation limiting asylum and increased resettlement through the sponsors. Meanwhile, a reliance on private sponsors leaves the government struggling against the movement of the program into family reunification.

The intersection of law and politics was at its height particularly as the narrative of sponsorship was hailed as humanitarianism by two distinct federal governments – Conservative and then Liberal. Chapter 6 moved from the Conservative government's reliance on sponsorship to the Liberal government's celebration and international promotion of sponsorship. It also examined the embrace of the blended visa office–referred (BVOR) program by a new community of engaged Canadians and the remaining challenges with this model. These programs challenge notions of goodwill and generosity and the dependency on charity over a reliance on law.

The issues of the previous chapters were brought to the fore in Chapter 7 by demonstrating the complete fragility of the resettlement program and its legal framing through the repeal of the source country class and the enhanced focus on discretion that led to the replacement of this program and the move towards increased group resettlement. The repeal of the source country class further indicated greater dependency on private sponsorship but with greater government control. Intentional manoeuvres away from the law and the blending of law and discretion were reinforced in this discussion.

Law in the Fields Beyond

For those questioning law's relevance to resettlement, the chapters sought to move their gaze from law's resting place at the border to its reach beyond. The intent has been to look differently at law, approaching it from outside of itself, beyond the state's border and in the act of resettlement. This perspective reveals a mingling of contradictory laws and the fictional force of doors, queues, and a sense of legal order directed by state interests. Rather than the typical canonical controversy between a legal system of rules and one swayed by politics, the understanding of law here has used the system of rules as a springboard to analyze law's influence and abilities. This is not a moment of law but, rather, the movement of law. This movement reveals what is absent in the traditional stagnant debate. It challenges the traditional understanding of law's ordering ability.[6] The argument is not that law does not possess this categorizing potential. Rather, while law's power is typically thought to lie in its authoritative labelling of legal and illegal, right and wrong, this analysis reveals law's hidden power – the representation of authoritative pronouncements obscuring an underlying flexibility, discretion, and contradiction. The obscuration results from more than law's shadow[7] or impact,[8] as there is often intention attached, although the influence of both are also there. While this has been the argument throughout, a final example will secure the point.

Layers of myth have guided the Canadian resettlement approach. Historically, and still entrenched in the legislative recital, this approach is mythically grounded in humanitarianism.[9] Increasingly, however, this myth is being layered with a myth of legal worship.[10] Law that is definitive; law as an absolute; and law imbued with an uncompromising morality. In a single news release on increases to Canada's resettlement program in 2011, the government emphasized the legality of resettlement in four of the seven paragraphs. The first paragraph sets the scene that "refugees often spend many years – sometimes decades – in squalid refugee camps or urban slums. They wait patiently for the chance to immigrate to Canada or other countries *legally*." The second paragraph indicates that "Canada's program for refugees to resettle here *legally* went from being one of the most generous in the world, to being even more generous." The sixth paragraph repeats again that "[a]ll of these individuals who immigrated to Canada through our resettlement programs waited patiently in the queue for the chance to come to Canada *legally*. They followed the *rules*." The seventh and final paragraph of the document is a single sentence that makes clear that "[t]he Government will stand up for these refugees' *rights* to be processed in a *fair* and *orderly* fashion, consistent with our *laws* and *values* – and not allow human smuggling operations to result in people jumping to the front of our immigration queue."[11] In one page and in just over 500 words, the mythical legal layering inundates the reader with a story of the benevolent and generous Canadian state and the patient, law-respecting, nearly martyred refugee battling against the depraved human smugglers who enable undeserving others to cut the queue like naughty schoolchildren.

It is not incorrect to indicate that resettled refugees enter Canada legally. It verges on the absurd, however, to imagine these refugees are waiting "patiently" in squalid camps and slums for decades for their unlikely chance at resettlement. It is misleading to suggest that there is a queue for asylum in Canada, particularly when the systems regulating resettlement and processing inland claims for asylum are independent from each other. And while human smuggling can be a nasty, dangerous, and exploitative criminal enterprise, the implication that those using human smugglers to access asylum are undeserving of protection fails to appreciate the fear and desperation of those fleeing persecution. Moreover, the statement completely ignores the rights of refugees who enter Canada as asylum claimants on their own, particularly their right to *non-refoulement*.

Despite the government of Canada's firm commitment to law that oozes out of the news release, the above announcement was simply an increase to resettlement ranges, predominantly on the private sponsorship side. Since that time, the government shifted even more of its resettlement to the private sponsorship side. This is the mythical force of law in its ability to silence and exclude. It mutes the voice of the very refugees who have been resettled by celebrating a patience and respect for the law that more realistically was desperation and inability to do anything other than wait and hope. It mutes the voices of the refugees who remain in the camps and slums by leaving them with this same law that is meaningless to them unless resettlement is chanced upon and this legal right of entry bestowed upon them. And it unfairly places this law as a fictional, but convincing, blockade against refugees seeking asylum who by necessity may enter irregularly but who cannot be penalized for this entry and possess the right to *non-refoulement* in both Canadian and international law.

Stepping beyond legal doctrine contributes to this greater understanding of law's actual power of exclusion beyond mere categorization. Even the resettlement refugees who fit within this vision of fairness, order, rules, and law – who land on the correct side of the legal/illegal dichotomy in the above narrative – are marginalized and excluded by this false descriptive. It is an example of Margaret Davies's argument that legal categorization creates an "artificial distinction between law and non-law."[12] The reality is that resettlement refugees possess no legal right to resettlement and remain dependent on the benevolent generosity of the state, a generosity that the news release is not shy to highlight.

For all refugees then – both those who enter on their own to claim asylum and those who enter through resettlement – the law blurs and challenges their access to protection. For asylum-seeking refugees, one layer of law – that of "illegal" entrance – is used to counter their legal right to *non-refoulement*, access to which is further challenged by layered legality preventing initial access to asylum. For resettlement refugees, law offers them no access to the state and, in Canada, limited ability to challenge an eligibility determination through judicial review. The fact that the government permits their controlled and legal entry is an exercise of law that has been bequeathed by the state. There is no right to entry prior to the state's determination of eligibility for resettlement. The celebration of this respect for the law in the news release is merely self-congratulation by the Canadian government on the successful management of its border.

This example helps to illustrate law's power. The examination of resettlement demonstrates a singular instance of law's fluidity. Rather than what, the chapters have examined where the law is and offered a multitude of answers. What comes out of the analysis is a deeper understanding of law's power to silence, exclude, and marginalize, and a recognition of how the intersections of layered legality determine the operation and circumvention of refugee protection.

Recommendations

The dual intentions of this book were to look at law's role in the non-legal act of resettlement and, using this newfound awareness, gain an understanding of resettlement to not only encourage resettlement but also maintain a commitment to the notion of refugee protection and access to asylum. The body of the chapters has taken up the former task and demonstrated the multitude of legal influences in resettlement and how refugees are influenced by the law and from outside of the law, often to the detriment or dismantlement of inland protection. The following recommendations take up the latter task of rebalancing resettlement and asylum through the restructuring of the resettlement program.

This restructuring is not grounded in law. The canvassing of law's intersections with resettlement and the layered legality of this analysis make clear that law in itself is not an adequate answer to the challenges of resettlement and, too often, is the cause of resettlement's tangled positioning. For the same reasons that this book as a whole required reaching beyond law to grasp the relationship between law and resettlement, the recommendations exist outside of the law to seek out the means to rein in law's silencing power. These recommendations were first drafted at a time of unlikely receptiveness – a time when the veil of humanitarianism that cloaks Canada's actions towards refugees was virtually transparent and there was an increasingly clear taint of meanness to the almost constant flow of new legislation and policies affecting refugees. The tides have changed with a new government, a commitment to government-assisted resettlement and the promotion of private sponsorship, and an increase in humanitarian admissions, although as a federal election again nears commitment is once again wavering. Beyond this, there is global interest in resettlement and Canadian attention devoted to the promotion of the private sponsorship model. But what remains at the time of writing is an uncertainty of where Canadian resettlement will move beyond the flurry of attention and concern devoted to Syrian refugees and the international uptake on private sponsorship.

The recommendations that follow align with neither the interests of the state nor necessarily the interests of resettlement advocates or private sponsors. Indeed, at points where the analysis has noted the corruption of the legal status of "refugeehood" through the use of resettlement, this work may be considered counterproductive by those advocating for increased resettlement numbers.[13] The recommendations reflect the interests of refugees, respect for the refugee definition, and the legal obligation of *non-refoulement* as well as a desire to preserve and increase refugee protection through both inland asylum and resettlement.

Recommendation 1: End Divisive Discourse

The first recommendation is a call for the return of complementarity between the law of asylum and resettlement. For this to occur, the divisive discourse employed by states, which is prevalent in the media and public opinion and even used in reference to the refugees divided by the discourse, must end. There is no refugee queue and only one door. Images of and allusions to queue cutting and entrance through the back door are misleading and detrimental to responsible protection. The divide between resettlement and asylum is one of entry, not legality. Both resettlement and *non-refoulement* are imperfect, but necessary, protection tools. Any increased focus on resettlement must not be in exchange for reduced access to asylum or an abandonment of the commitment to *non-refoulement*.

Recommendation 2: Better Align Resettlement and Refugee Status

While resettlement refugees are continually presented as "genuine" or "real" refugees in comparison to those seeking asylum, particularly in the present moment when claimants are entering irregularly to avoid the *Safe Third Country Agreement*,[14] Canadian resettlement tends to pay inconsistent attention to an individual's actual status as a refugee. Proof of refugee status is currently a requirement for some sponsorship applications, yet this same status is not presumptive of resettlement eligibility in visa officer decision-making. While it is important to ensure protection for those who cannot access status by not extending the requirement to all sponsorships, greater deference to a grant of refugee status by the UNHCR or a foreign state would better ensure that protection concerns remain at the forefront of resettlement decisions. Indeed, this is the purpose of the BVOR program and the model of private sponsorship that the UNHCR is encouraging other states to adopt, but its sustainability in Canada remains uncertain.

Recommendation 3: Limit Discretionary Decision-Making

Discretion is inherent and unavoidable in resettlement selection. Its presence should not be enhanced or relied upon by legislating broad discretionary powers into the resettlement program. The above recommendation for refugee status to be presumptive of resettlement eligibility is an example of limiting discretion. With each increase of discretion, the commitment to protection becomes more tenuous. Discretion can act as a safety valve when the application of law would lead to an injustice. This is where section 25's humanitarian and compassionate exemption in the *IRPA* is at its best. The repeal of the source country class with the justification that section 25 can assume a protection role when necessary pushes discretion to an extreme where it is more likely to create injustice than remedy it. Legislating discretion does not infuse it with legal strength or obligation. It moves the resettlement program further from the law.

Recommendation 4: Connect Private Sponsorship and Government-Assisted Resettlement

Two key issues face the private sponsorship program: the shifting of resettlement responsibility onto private sponsors and the movement of the program away from stranger sponsorship to a form of family reunification. In their willingness to bring in the greatest number of resettlement cases, sponsors unwittingly permit the government's manoeuvres to have private sponsorship supplant government-assisted resettlement. This challenge is heightened when private sponsorship tends towards family reunification. Yet, if such sponsorship is curtailed, the counter-risk is that the willingness of private sponsors to continue resettlement will diminish.

The issue of family reunification will be addressed separately in Recommendation 5. Here the recommendation addresses remedying the shifting of responsibility while maintaining incentives for private sponsors. As was a motivating force with the Indochinese resettlement, private sponsorship is at its best when the principle of additionality operates to ensure that it is a true complement to government resettlement. While tying the numbers one to one, similar to what was done with the Indochinese matching program, risks putting too much pressure on sponsors and ultimately reducing government numbers, my proposal is to link successful private sponsorship to future increases in government resettlement. For each private sponsorship beyond the lower numeric range, the government should promise an increase in its admissions of at least half that number the following year. This is preferable to current range increases that carry with them no actual guarantee of increased resettlement numbers and that have resulted in sponsorship numbers greatly outweighing government commitments yet again.

As an example in 2017, the lower range for private sponsorship was 14,000, and actual sponsorship reached 16,873. This amounted to 2,873 sponsorships beyond the lower range. Under the proposed linkage, this would have required the government to increase its 2018 resettlement by at least 1,436 admissions. Sponsors would thus be motivated to both continue and increase their resettlement activities, but these increases would not come in exchange for continued government resettlement and would instead also ensure government increases in resettlement. Such a linkage would also realign private sponsors and the government in a shared pursuit that would bring additional cooperative benefits. For example, long-term sponsors are well connected to refugee communities in Canada who, in turn, maintain ties to their home communities. Sponsors tend to have a good pulse on protection needs. As such, they are an untapped resource for the government. In terms of returning the program to its complementary origins, finding other means of complementarity such as sharing protection knowledge could be a helpful start.

Recommendation 5: Clarify Place of Family Reunification

The use of private sponsorship as a tool for family reunification has been one of the major generators and challenges of the sponsorship program. While the government attempts to curtail this use and return the program to stranger-based protection, it must be cognizant of the effect this could have on support for the program and the willingness of sponsors to continue their sponsorships. And, as the joint assistance sponsorship of refugees from Sierra Leone has demonstrated, family reunification and refugee protection can overlap, and the former does not preclude the latter. It is also clear, however, that family networks and social capital are beneficial to successful integration in a resettlement state. Both the United States and Australia have a specific family reunification stream within their resettlement programs.[15]

Rather than curtailing this mode of sponsorship, the recommendation is to separate it out as a form of private sponsorship. The stream could complement the general family class provisions in the *IRPA* that permit the sponsorship of immediate family by enabling sponsoring groups to assist with this process.[16] Preferably, it would reach more broadly than the family class limit of immediate family with the addition of the sponsorship support. By clarifying this stream of sponsorship and separating it from the sponsorship of refugees in need of protection, the reality of Canada's protection offerings would be more transparent. This recommendation speaks to the recognition that resettlement need not be limited to refugee protection and that such a program would enable private citizens to provide assistance as they see fit – essentially, the original premise of private sponsorship. While such a program would likely diminish some sponsorship support for refugees, it is not recommended that the family stream be connected to the government obligation in Recommendation 4. Thus, the incentive for refugee protection by private sponsors would still exist.

Recommendation 6: Re-Establish Some Level of Protection for Internally Displaced Persons (IDPs)

The repeal of the source country class was a broad and capricious solution to a troubled program that required reform, not erasure. This book repeatedly asserts the importance of commitment to the refugee definition for the maintenance of refugee protection. Source country resettlement of IDPs, however, recognizes that offering protection before an international border is crossed alleviates the heightened dangers of such crossings and the reliance on human smugglers. Such programs thus align in reducing both refugee numbers and smuggling operations. These programs should not be as static as the previous unchanging list in Canada. Rather, just as the Canadian government has done with the group-processing methodology, particular source country groups could be identified for focused resettlement attention where necessary and feasible.

Recommendation 7: Ensure Sponsorship Is Not a Solution for Asylum Flows

In September 2017, the Global Refugee Sponsorship Initiative launched its guidebook on the building blocks of community sponsorship.[17] State interest in the Canadian model is growing. While the excitement and effort of creating additional resettlement spots are to be commended, the initiative does not address the factors underlying increased interest globally after four decades of Canada's relative isolation in private sponsorship. Understanding and addressing state interests are no easy tasks, and the recommendation here, tied to Recommendation 2, is merely to ensure more proactively that resettlement and private or community sponsorship are considered in relation to asylum and the overarching concern with protection.

Open Doors

"A thousand windows and a thousand doors: Not one of them was ours, my dear, not one of them was ours."[18] In the end, it must be remembered that refugee resettlement is a small piece in a complicated puzzle, a failing regime where protraction grows and hope wanes. Nor does resettlement alone offer settlement and solution. It is but the start and the chance of a life free from fear and full of possibility. This book has shed new light on resettlement and brought it forward for examination on its own rather than as a secondary consideration or trade-off. It has shown that resettlement is complicated, malleable, and easily manipulated. It is also an incredibly important, yet fragile, door to protection that is too small to begin with and can too easily close. At its best, it is a complement to the promise of asylum and recognition that not all refugees can integrate locally, repatriate, or seek asylum on their own. At its worst, it is offered to obscure the cruel intent of restrictions to asylum access and used as a tool of selection for those who are often not the most in need.

Law, meanwhile, is a powerful concept that instills a sense of authority and justice that belies its underlying nuances and layered reality. There is no legal obligation on a state to resettle refugees. Nothing about resettlement necessitates reference to refugees whatsoever. And, yet, law is there, present and powerful in resettlement. Resettlement cannot be fully understood without acknowledging this legal influence. The book has concerned itself with the selection of resettlement refugees. While touched upon, their arrival and integration into the resettlement state have been of secondary concern. Upon arrival, law's role in terms of the resettlement refugee's rights and access becomes clearer. The law still differs, however, from the rights of in-Canada asylum seekers and recognized refugees and between sponsored refugees and government-assisted refugees. A comparison of law's presence upon arrival would be a fitting starting point for future research building on this work. With the shifting of political preference towards resettlement, research systematically separating these refugee groups would provide a documented response to the increasing tendency to conflate these protection categories and present them as interchangeable.

This book is also reaching its conclusion in the midst of significant scholarship in Canada on the Syrian resettlement and on Canadian sponsorship programs. Much of this research is the result of targeted research on the Syrian resettlement funded by the Social Sciences and Humanities Research Council in July 2016.[19] While I have touched on the Syrian resettlement to a degree, the hope is that this book will provide a framework and broader context in which to understand particularized Syrian studies. The success of a sponsorship cannot be measured outside of considerations of government resettlement and inland refugee protection.

More globally, the final draft of the *Global Compact for Refugees* was released in June 2018. The compact recognizes that "[t]he need to foster a positive atmosphere for resettlement, and to enhance capacity for doing so, as well as to expand its base, cannot be overstated."[20] In addition, the compact notes "complementary pathways for admission" that include "clear referral pathways for family reunification, or ... private or community sponsorship programmes that are additional to regular resettlement."[21] Again, it is hoped that this book will contribute to an understanding of the relationship between resettlement, sponsorship, and asylum as states work towards the compact's objectives.

Seeking refuge is a journey that no one pursues willingly or if there is any alternative option. Whether a refugee walks across a border, boards a boat, or flies across the world is more a matter of circumstance than choice. It is not a marker of legitimacy or genuine fear. No one willingly leaves her home, her family, her friends, her country for an uncertain and often dangerous journey to start with nothing in a different country with an unfamiliar language and culture where her skills, education, and training may be worthless. In Franz Kafka's parable, the man from the country "forgets the other doorkeepers, and this first one seems to him the sole obstacle preventing access."[22] Resettlement is only the first door, the beginning of the journey. Refuge is not the golden ticket that it is often considered to be by those casting suspicion and judgment from the comfort and familiarity of home. Both the law of asylum and the law of resettlement have arisen out of a disgust with the horrors of humankind and an international desire to be and to do better and to protect those in need. Since the signing of the *Convention Relating to the Status of Refugees*, the horror of the world, or at least our awareness of it, has only increased, and refugee numbers continue to grow.[23] The immensity of the problem should not lead to the barracking of borders and the closing of doors. At law's border, asylum and resettlement should be doors that remain open.

Appendix

FEDERAL COURT OF CANADA RESETTLEMENT CASES

2016

Barat v Canada (Minister of Citizenship and Immigration), [2016] FCJ No 504 (application for judicial review allowed; Afghan applicant, visa application in Pakistan).

Krikor v Canada (Minister of Citizenship and Immigration), [2016] FCJ No 458 (application for judicial review allowed; Iraqi applicant, visa application in Jordan).

Hosaini v Canada (Minister of Citizenship and Immigration), [2016] FCJ No 337 (application for judicial review allowed; Afghan applicant, visa application in Pakistan).

Hossain v Canada (Minister of Citizenship and Immigration), [2016] FCJ No 293 (application for judicial review allowed; Afghan applicant, visa application in Pakistan; identified as sponsorship).

Al-Anbagi v Canada (Minister of Citizenship and Immigration), [2016] FCJ No 258 (application for judicial review allowed; Iraqi applicant, visa application in Jordan).

Haidari v Canada (Minister of Citizenship and Immigration), [2016] FCJ No 234 (application for judicial review allowed; Afghan applicant, visa application in Pakistan).

Ameni v Canada (Minister of Citizenship and Immigration), [2016] FCJ No 142 (application for judicial review allowed; Afghan applicant, visa application in Pakistan; identified as sponsorship).

2015

Sahar v Canada (Minister of Citizenship and Immigration), [2015] FCJ No 1500 (application for judicial review allowed; Afghan applicant, visa application in Pakistan).

Nshogoza v Canada (Minister of Citizenship and Immigration), [2015] FCJ No 1236 (application for judicial review dismissed; Rwandan applicant, visa application in Kenya).

Pushparasa v Canada (Minister of Citizenship and Immigration), [2015] FCJ No 812 (application for judicial review dismissed; Sri Lankan applicant, visa application in Malaysia; identified as sponsorship).

Mariyadas v Canada (Minister of Citizenship and Immigration), [2015] FCJ No 765 (application for judicial review dismissed; Sri Lankan applicant, visa application in India; identified as sponsorship).

Wardak v Canada (Minister of Citizenship and Immigration), [2015] FCJ No 684 (application for judicial review allowed; Afghan applicant, visa application in Pakistan).

Ravichandran v Canada (Minister of Citizenship and Immigration), [2015] FCJ No 677 (application for judicial review allowed; Sri Lankan applicant, visa application in India).

Sakthivel v Canada (Minister of Citizenship and Immigration), [2015] FCJ No 251 (application for judicial review allowed; Sri Lankan applicant, visa application in Malaysia).

Janvier v Canada (Minister of Citizenship and Immigration), [2015] FCJ No 222 (application for judicial review dismissed; Haitian applicant, visa application in Dominican Republic; identified as sponsorship).

2014

Mohamed v Canada (Minister of Citizenship and Immigration), [2014] FCJ No 193 (application for judicial review dismissed; Somalian applicant, visa application in Saudi Arabia).

Hashi v Canada (Minister of Citizenship and Immigration), [2014] FCJ No 167 (application for judicial review allowed; Somalian applicant, visa application in Kenya).

Muthui v Canada (Minister of Citizenship and Immigration), [2014] FCJ No 134 (application for judicial review dismissed; Kenyan applicant, visa application in United States).

2013

Bakhtiari v Canada (Minister of Citizenship and Immigration), [2013] FCJ No 1330 (application for judicial review dismissed; Afghan applicant, visa application in Pakistan; identified as sponsorship).

Adel v Canada (Minister of Citizenship and Immigration), [2013] FCJ No 1421 (application for judicial review dismissed; Afghan applicant, visa application in Pakistan).

Hasi v Canada (Minister of Citizenship and Immigration), [2013] FCJ No 1223 (application for judicial review dismissed; Somalian applicant, visa application in Kenya).

Lukavica v Canada (Minister of Citizenship and Immigration), [2013] FCJ No 98 (application for judicial review allowed; Bosnian applicant, visa application in Austria; identified as sponsorship).

Ismailzada v Canada (Minister of Citizenship and Immigration), [2013] FCJ No 49 (application for judicial review allowed; Afghan applicant, visa application in Pakistan; identified as sponsorship).

2012

Benhmuda v Canada (Minister of Citizenship and Immigration), [2012] FCJ No 1321 (application for judicial review allowed; Libyan applicant, visa application in Malta).

Mezbani v Canada (Minister of Citizenship and Immigration), [2012] FCJ No 1199 (application for judicial review allowed; Iranian applicant, visa application in Pakistan; identified as sponsorship).

Atahi v Canada (Minister of Citizenship and Immigration), [2012] FCJ No 746 (application for judicial review dismissed; Afghan applicant, visa application in Pakistan).

Teweldbrhan v Canada (Minister of Citizenship and Immigration), [2012] FCJ No 408 (application for judicial review allowed; Eritrean applicant, visa application in Uganda; identified as sponsorship).

Kumarasamy v Canada (Minister of Citizenship and Immigration), [2012] FCJ No 314 (application for judicial review allowed; Sri Lankan applicant, visa application in India).

Karimzada v Canada (Minister of Citizenship and Immigration), [2012] FCJ No 204 (application for judicial review dismissed; Afghan applicant, visa application in Pakistan; identified as sponsorship).

2011

Sellappha v Canada (Minister of Citizenship and Immigration), [2011] FCJ No 1690 (application for judicial review dismissed; Sri Lankan applicant, visa application in Sri Lanka; identified as sponsorship).

Dusabimana v Canada (Minister of Citizenship and Immigration), [2011] FCJ No 1521 (application for judicial review dismissed; Rwandan applicant, visa application in South Africa; identified as sponsorship).

Adan v Canada (Minister of Citizenship and Immigration), [2011] FCJ No 830 (application for judicial review allowed; Somalian applicant, visa application in Kenya; identified as sponsorship).

Sivakumaran v Canada (Minister of Citizenship and Immigration), [2011] FCJ No 788 (application for judicial review dismissed; Sri Lankan applicant, visa application in India; identified as sponsorship).

Woldesellasie v Canada (Minister of Citizenship and Immigration), [2011] FCJ No 653 (application for judicial review allowed; Eritrean applicant, visa application in Egypt).

Kidane v Canada (Minister of Citizenship and Immigration), [2011] FCJ No 651 (application for judicial review allowed; Eritrean applicant, visa application in Egypt).

Weldesilassie v Canada (Minister of Citizenship and Immigration), [2011] FCJ No 652 (application for judicial review allowed; Eritrean applicant, visa application in Egypt).

Ghirmatsion v Canada (Minister of Citizenship and Immigration), [2011] FCJ No 650 (application for judicial review allowed; Eritrean applicant, visa application in Egypt).

Hakimi v Canada (Minister of Citizenship and Immigration), [2011] FCJ No 69 (application for judicial review dismissed; Afghan applicant, visa application in Pakistan; identified as sponsorship).

2010

Alharazim v Canada (Minister of Citizenship and Immigration), [2010] FCJ No 1519 (application for judicial review dismissed; Sierra Leonean applicant, visa application in Senegal).

Adil v Canada (Minister of Citizenship and Immigration), [2010] FCJ No 1228 (application for judicial review allowed; Afghan applicant, visa application in Tajikistan; identified as sponsorship).

Saifee v Canada (Minister of Citizenship and Immigration), [2010] FCJ No 693 (TD) (application for judicial review allowed; Afghan applicant, visa application in Tajikistan).

Shokohi v Canada (Minister of Citizenship and Immigration), [2010] FCJ No 514 (TD) (application for judicial review allowed; unidentified applicant, identified as sponsorship).

Kumarasamy v Canada (Minister of Citizenship and Immigration), [2010] FCJ No 239 (TD) (application for judicial review allowed; Sri Lankan applicant, visa application in Ghana).

Sribalaganeshamoorthy v Canada (Minister of Citizenship and Immigration), [2010] FCJ No 6 (TD) (application for judicial review dismissed; Sri Lankan applicant, visa application in Malaysia; identified as sponsorship).

2009

Besadh v. Canada (Minister of Citizenship and Immigration), [2009] FCJ No 847 (TD) (application for judicial review dismissed; Sudanese Christian applicant, visa application in Egypt).

Alakozai v Canada (Minister of Citizenship and Immigration), [2009] FCJ No 374 (TD) (application for judicial review dismissed; Afghan applicant, visa application in Pakistan; identified as sponsorship).

Qurbani v Canada (Minister of Citizenship and Immigration), [2009] FCJ No 152 (TD) (application for judicial review dismissed; Afghan applicant, visa application in Pakistan; identified as sponsorship).

Latif v Canada (Minister of Citizenship and Immigration), [2009] FCJ No 93 (TD) (application for judicial review allowed; Afghan applicant, visa application in Pakistan; identified as sponsorship).

2008

Nassima v Canada (Minister of Citizenship and Immigration), [2008] FCJ No 881 (TD) (application for judicial review dismissed; Afghan applicant, visa application in Pakistan).

Azali v Canada (Minister of Citizenship and Immigration), [2008] FCJ No 674 (TD) (application for judicial review dismissed; Iranian applicant, visa application in Turkey).
Nasir v Canada (Minister of Citizenship and Immigration), [2008] FCJ No 634 (TD) (application for judicial review allowed; Afghan applicant, visa application in Pakistan; identified as sponsorship).
Qarizada v Canada (Minister of Citizenship and Immigration), [2008] FCJ No 1662 (TD) (application for judicial review dismissed; Afghan applicant, visa application in Pakistan; identified as sponsorship).
Kamara v Canada (Minister of Citizenship and Immigration), [2008] FCJ No 986 (TD) (application for judicial review dismissed; Sierra Leonean applicant, visa application in Guinea; identified as sponsorship).

2007

Sutharsan v Canada (Minister of Citizenship and Immigration), [2007] FCJ No 294 (TD) (application for judicial review allowed; Sri Lankan applicant, visa application in England; identified as sponsorship).
Salimi v Canada (Minister of Citizenship and Immigration), [2007] FCJ No 1126 (TD) (application for judicial review dismissed; Afghan applicant, visa application in Pakistan; identified as sponsorship).
Anton v Canada (Minister of Citizenship and Immigration), [2007] FCJ No 798 (TD) (application for judicial review allowed; Sri Lankan applicant, visa application in England).
Asl v Canada (Minister of Citizenship and Immigration), [2007] FCJ No 632 (TD) (application for judicial review allowed; Iranian applicant, visa application in Japan; identified as sponsorship).

2006

Khwaja v Canada (Minister of Citizenship and Immigration), [2006] FCJ No 703 (TD) (application for judicial review dismissed; Afghan applicant, visa application in Russia).
El Karm v Canada (Minister of Citizenship and Immigration), [2006] FCJ No 1225 (TD) (application for judicial review dismissed; Palestinian applicant, visa application in Egypt; identified as sponsorship).

Abdulle v Canada (Minister of Citizenship and Immigration), [2006] FCJ No 1898 (TD) (application for judicial review allowed; Somalian applicant, visa application in Yemen).

2005

Jimenez v Canada (Minister of Citizenship and Immigration), [2005] FCJ No 1312 (TD) (application for judicial review dismissed; Colombian applicant, visa application in Colombia; identified as sponsorship).

Velautham v Canada (Minister of Citizenship and Immigration), [2005] FCJ No 1385 (application for judicial review allowed; Sri Lankan applicant, visa application in England).

Beltran v Canada (Minister of Citizenship and Immigration), [2005] FCJ No 1007 (application for judicial review dismissed; Colombian applicant, visa application in Colombia).

Asmelash v Canada (Minister of Citizenship and Immigration), [2005] FCJ No 2145 (TD) (application for judicial review dismissed; Eritrean applicant residing in Ethiopia, visa application through Kenya).

2004

Muhazi v Canada (Minister of Citizenship and Immigration), [2004] FCJ No 1670 (TD) (application for judicial review allowed; Rwandan applicant, visa application in Kenya; identified as sponsorship).

Alemu v Canada (Minister of Citizenship and Immigration), [2004] FCJ No 1210 (TD) (application for judicial review allowed; Ethiopian applicant, visa application in South Africa; identified as sponsorship).

Beganovic v Canada (Minister of Citizenship and Immigration), [2004] FCJ No 406 (TD) (application for judicial review dismissed; former Yugoslavian applicant, visa application in Germany).

2003

Rudi v Canada (Minister of Citizenship and Immigration), [2003] FCJ No 1220 (TD) (application for judicial review allowed; Afghan applicant, visa application in Sri Lanka; identified as sponsorship).

Abdi v Canada (Minister of Citizenship and Immigration), [2003] FCJ No 219 (TD) (application for judicial review allowed; Somalian applicant residing in Ethiopia, visa application through Kenya; identified as sponsorship).

Horvat v Canada (Minister of Citizenship and Immigration), [2003] FCJ No 354 (TD) (application for judicial review dismissed; Bosnian applicant, visa application in Germany).

Sarkissian v Canada (Minister of Citizenship and Immigration), [2003] FCJ No 489 (TD) (application for judicial review dismissed; Iranian applicant, visa application in Germany).

Atputharajah v Canada (Minister of Citizenship and Immigration), [2003] FCJ No 332 (TD) (application for judicial review dismissed; Sri Lankan applicant, visa application in England).

2002

Dang v Canada (Minister of Citizenship and Immigration), [2002] FCJ No 910 (TD) (application for judicial review allowed; Cambodian applicant, visa application in Vietnam; identified as sponsorship).

Ha v Canada (Minister of Citizenship and Immigration), [2002] FCJ No 1788 (TD), revised [2004] FCJ No 174 (CA) (original application for judicial review dismissed; Cambodian applicant residing in Vietnam, visa application through Singapore; identified as sponsorship).

Mahzooz v Canada (Minister of Citizenship and Immigration), [2002] FCJ No 1203 (TD) (application for judicial review dismissed; Afghan applicant, visa application in Pakistan; identified as sponsorship).

2001

Haljiti v Canada (Minister of Citizenship and Immigration), [2001] FCJ No 500 (TD) (application for judicial review allowed; unidentified applicant, visa application in Germany).

Mujezinovic v Canada (Minister of Citizenship and Immigration), [2001] FCJ No 1487 (TD) (application for judicial review dismissed; Serbian applicant, visa application in Austria).

Bahtijari v Canada (Minister of Citizenship and Immigration), [2001] FCJ No 976 (TD) (application for judicial review dismissed; former Yugoslavian applicant, visa application in Germany).

2000

Phan v Canada (Minister of Citizenship and Immigration), [2000] FCJ No 728 (TD) (application for judicial review allowed; Vietnamese applicant, visa application in Germany; identified as sponsorship).

1999

Mengesha v Canada (Minister of Citizenship and Immigration), [1999] FCJ No 1322 (TD) (application for judicial review dismissed; Ethiopian applicant, visa application in Jamaica; identified as sponsorship).

Mohamed v Canada (Minister of Citizenship and Immigration), [1999] FCJ No 1230 (TD) (application for judicial review dismissed; Ethiopian applicant, visa application in Germany; identified as sponsorship).

Smajic v Canada (Minister of Citizenship and Immigration), [1999] FCJ No 1904 (TD) (application for judicial review dismissed; Bosnian applicant, visa application in Germany).

1997

Ayubi v Canada (Minister of Citizenship and Immigration), [1997] FCJ No 777 (TD) (application for judicial review allowed; Afghan applicant, visa application in Pakistan; identified as sponsorship).

Oraha v Canada (Minister of Citizenship and Immigration), [1997] FCJ No 788 (TD) (application for judicial review dismissed; Iraqi applicant, visa application in Italy; identified as sponsorship).

Zia v Canada (Minister of Citizenship and Immigration), [1997] FCJ No 784 (TD) (application for judicial review dismissed; Iraqi applicant, visa application in Jordan; identified as sponsorship).

1996

Jallow v Canada (Minister of Citizenship and Immigration), [1996] FCJ No 1452 (TD) (application for judicial review dismissed; Iraqi applicant residing in Malta, visa application in Italy; identified as sponsorship).

1994

Knarik v Canada (Solicitor General), [1994] FCJ No 816 (TD) (application for judicial review dismissed; Iranian applicant, visa application in Germany).

Notes

Chapter 1: Law's Role in Resettlement

1 *Convention Relating to the Status of Refugees*, 28 July 1951, 189 UNTS 150 (entered into force 22 April 1954) [*Refugee Convention*].
2 United Nations High Commissioner for Refugees (UNHCR), *Resettlement Handbook* (November 2004), 1–2.
3 *Global Consultations on International Protection, Strengthening and Expanding Resettlement Today: Challenges and Opportunities*, Doc EC/GC/02/7 (25 April 2002), para 5.
4 "States Parties to the Convention and the Protocol," online: *UNHCR* <www.unhcr.org/pages/49da0e466.html>. Nauru most recently acceded to the convention on 28 June 2011.
5 Asian-African Legal Consultative Organization, *Bangkok Principles on the Status and Treatment of Refugees* (31 December 1966), art III(3); *Declaration on Territorial Asylum*, Doc A/RES/2312(XXII) (14 December 1967), art 3(1); *Resolution on Asylum to Persons in Danger of Persecution*, adopted by the Committee of Ministers of the Council of Europe (29 June 1967), 2; *Convention Governing the Specific Aspects of Refugee Problems in Africa*, 10 September 1969, 1001 UNTS 45 (entered into force 20 June 1974), art III(3); *American Convention on Human Rights*, 21 November 1969, 1144 UNTS 123 (entered into force 18 July 1978), art 22(8); *Convention against Torture and Other Cruel, Inhuman or Degrading Treatment or Punishment*, 10 December 1984, 1465 UNTS 85 (entered into force 26 June 1987), art 3(1).
6 See UNHCR, *Note on Non-Refoulement (Submitted by the High Commissioner)*, Doc EC/SCP/2 (23 August 1977), online: <www.unhcr.org/refworld/docid/3ae68ccd10.html>; Guy Goodwin-Gill & Jane McAdam, *The Refugee in International Law*, 3rd ed (Oxford: Oxford University Press, 2007), 352–53; but, for a response, see also James Hathaway, *The Rights of Refugees under International Law* (Cambridge, UK: Cambridge University Press, 2005), 363–64.

7 *Statute of the Office of the United Nations High Commissioner for Refugees*, Doc UNGA A/RES/428(V) (14 December 1950) [*UNHCR Statute*].
8 This is true even in some states like Kenya, which is a state party to the *Refugee Convention*, but where most refugees are left in camps with only the lesser designation of *prima facie* status unless they are being processed for resettlement. See Jennifer Hyndman & Bo Viktor Nylund, "UNHCR and the Status of Prima Facie Refugees in Kenya" (1998) 10 International Journal of Refugee Law 21.
9 "Global Trends: Forced Displacement in 2017," 2, 4, online: *UNHCR* <www.unhcr.org/5b27be547.pdf> ["Global Trends 2017"].
10 *Ibid*, 22–23.
11 *UNHCR Statute*, *supra* note 7, s 1.
12 There are agreed upon criteria for the UNHCR to determine its resettlement referrals endorsed by its Executive Committee in 1996, but states are in no way bound by these criteria. UNHCR Executive Committee, *Resettlement: An Instrument of Protection and a Durable Solution*, Standing Committee Doc EC/46/SC/CRP.32 (28 May 1996).
13 *Refugee Convention*, *supra* note 1.
14 "Global Trends 2017," *supra* note 9, 30.
15 While ad hoc resettlement changes the number of states each year, the UNHCR indicates thirty-five resettlement states worldwide in 2017. *Ibid*.
16 UNHCR Executive Committee, *Progress Report on Resettlement*, 60th Meeting, UN Doc EC/65/SC/CRP.11 (2014), 3.
17 *Ibid*.
18 *Ibid*.
19 UNHCR, "UNHCR Projected Global Resettlement Needs 2016," 21st Annual Tripartite Consultations on Resettlement, Geneva, 29 June–1 July 2015 (2016), 53, online: <www.unhcr.org/protection/resettlement/558019729/unhcr-projected-global-resettlement-needs-2016.html>.
20 UNHCR, "UNHCR Projected Global Resettlement Needs 2017," 22nd Annual Tripartite Consultations on Resettlement, Geneva, 13–15 June 2016 (2017), 12, online: <www.unhcr.org/protection/resettlement/575836267/unhcr-projected-global-resettlement-needs-2017.html>.
21 *Ibid*.
22 *Ibid*.
23 "How the EU Manages Migration" (25 October 2018), online: *Council of the European Union* <www.consilium.europa.eu/en/policies/migratory-pressures/managing-migration-flows/>.
24 *Ibid*.
25 "Global Trends 2017," *supra* note 9, 30.

26 See as examples James C Hathaway & Alexander Neve, "Making International Refugee Law Relevant Again: A Proposal for Collectivized and Solution-Oriented Protection" (1997) 10 Harvard Human Rights Journal 115; Peter H Schuck, "Refugee Burden-Sharing: A Modest Proposal" in Peter H Schuck, ed, *Citizens, Strangers, and In-Betweens: Essays on Immigration and Citizenship* (Boulder, CO: Westview Press, 1998) 281.

27 See Hathaway, *supra* note 6; Erika Feller, "Asylum, Migration and Refugee Protection: Realities, Myths and the Promise of Things to Come" (2006) 18 International Journal of Refugee Law 509; Michelle Foster, *International Refugee Law and Socio-Economic Rights: Refuge from Deprivation* (Cambridge, UK: Cambridge University Press, 2007); Emma Haddad, *The Refugee in International Society: Between Sovereigns* (Cambridge, UK: Cambridge University Press, 2008); Jane McAdam, *Complementary Protection in International Refugee Law* (Oxford: Oxford University Press, 2007).

28 *Balanced Refugee Reform Act*, SC 2010, c 8 (assented to on 29 June 2010; formerly Bill C-11); *Protecting Canada's Immigration System Act*, SC 2012, c 17 (assented to on 28 June 2012; formerly Bill C-31).

29 Ironically, the recent increase in Canadian resettlement numbers has been accompanied by a louder voice of criticism and demands by those involved in resettlement and private sponsorship. See Michelle Zilio, "Sponsors Frustrated by Slowing Pace of Resettling Syrian Refugees," *Globe and Mail* (24 March 2016), online: <www.theglobeandmail.com/news/politics/sponsors-frustrated-by-slowing-pace-of-resettling-syrian-refugees/article29390093/>; Bob Hepburn, "How Trudeau Ruined a Feel-Good Story: Hepburn," *Toronto Star* (15 May 2016), online: <www.thestar.com/opinion/commentary/2016/05/15/how-the-trudeau-ruined-a-feel-good-story-hepburn.html>; Michelle Zilio, "Ottawa Lacks 'Precise' Jobs Data for Syrian Refugees," *Globe and Mail* (12 May 2016), online: <www.theglobeandmail.com/news/politics/most-government-sponsored-syrian-refugees-in-permanent-homes-mccallum/article29991005/>; Wanyee Li & Bal Brach, "Syrian Refugees Not Arriving Quickly Enough Say BC Private Sponsors," *CBC News* (8 April 2016), online: <www.cbc.ca/news/canada/british-columbia/syrian-refugees-not-arriving-quickly-enough-say-b-c-private-sponsors-1.3527930>; David Irish, "Syrian Refugee Application Backlog Frustrates Nova Scotia Groups," *CBC News* (29 March 2016), online: <www.cbc.ca/news/canada/nova-scotia/syrian-refugees-backlog-1.3510663>; Justine Hunter, "After Arriving in Canada, Syrian Refugees Still Stuck in Limbo," *Globe and Mail* (13 January 2016), online: <www.theglobeandmail.com/news/british-columbia/syrian-refugees-stuck-in-limbo-of-vancouver-hotels-temporary-housing/article28177637/>; Michael Friscolanti, "Sponsors of Syrian Refugees Are Left in Limbo," *Maclean's* (7 April 2016), online: <www.macleans.ca/politics/sponsors-of-syrian-refugees-are-left-in-limbo/>.

30 Desmond Manderson, "Apocryphal Jurisprudence" (2001) 23 Studies in Law, Politics and Society 81.
31 *Ibid*, 89.
32 *Ibid*, 105.
33 See Shauna Labman & Jamie Chai Yun Liew, "Law and Moral Licensing in Canada: The Making of Illegality and Illegitimacy along the Border" International Journal of Migration and Border Studies [forthcoming].
34 Robert Mnookin & Lewis Kornhauser, "Bargaining in the Shadow of the Law: The Case of Divorce'" (1978–79) 88 Yale Law Journal 950, 951.
35 *Ibid*, 968. For Mnookin and Kornhauser, this suggests that the primary function of the legal system is to enable private ordering and dispute resolution.
36 *Ibid*, 997.
37 Margaret Davies, *Asking the Law Question*, 2nd ed (Sydney: Law Book Company, 2002).
38 *Ibid*, 5.
39 *Ibid*, 93.
40 *Ibid*, 7.
41 *Ibid*, 16.
42 *Ibid*, 6.
43 See John Rawls's discussion of a "just society" in John Rawls, *A Theory of Justice* (Cambridge, MA: Belknap Press, 2005); see Ronald Dworkin's concept of integrity within, but not among, political communities in Ronald Dworkin, *Law's Empire* (Cambridge, MA: Belknap Press, 1986), 185.
44 Catherine Dauvergne, *Making People Illegal: What Globalization Means for Migration and Law* (Cambridge, UK: Cambridge University Press, 2008), 175. Andreas Wimmer and Nina Glick-Schiller similarly suggest that a "container model of society ... developed in the social sciences and became dominant after the Second World War." They challenge the "taken-for-granted assumption of methodological nationalism" that precludes migration research. Andreas Wimmer & Nina Glick-Schiller, "Methodological Nationalism and Beyond: Nation-State Building, Migration and the Social Sciences" (2002) 2:4 Global Networks 301, 309, 310.
45 The exception to this is natural law, which offers a universal embrace. While natural law is not limited to the state, it nonetheless remains limited by beliefs and notions of authority. See Jeremy Webber, "National Sovereignty, Migration, and the Tenuous Hold of International Legality: The Resurfacing (and Resubmersion?) of Carl Schmitt" in Oliver Schmidtke & Saime Ozcurumezeds, eds, *Of States, Rights, and Social Closure* (New York: Palgrave Macmillan, 2008) 75.
46 Jutta Brunnée & Stephen Toope, *Legitimacy and Legality in International Law: An Interactional Account* (Cambridge, UK: Cambridge University Press, 2010), 9.

47 *Ibid.*
48 *Ibid*, 10.
49 Brunnée and Toope therefore present an interactional theory that considers international law as not just between states but also through the interactions of a variety of actors (elites, media, non-governmental organizations [NGOs], and citizens). Their aim is to explain the creation of and arguments for upholding international law. *Ibid*, 5.
50 Bernard Hibbitts, "Last Writes? Reassessing the Law Review in the Age of Cyberspace" (1996) 71 New York University Law Review 615, 1.3, online: <https://www.law.pitt.edu/archive/hibbitts/lastrev.htm>.
51 See Lee Epstein & Gary King, "The Rules of Inference" (2002) 69 University of Chicago Law Review 133; Howard Erlanger et al, "New Legal Realism Symposium: Is It Time for a New Legal Realism?" (2005) 2 Wisconsin Law Review 335; Paddy Hillyard, "Law's Empire: Socio-Legal Empirical Research in the Twenty-First Century" (2007) 34 Journal of Law and Society 266; Brunnée & Toope, *supra* note 46, for discussions of law's interaction with the social sciences.
52 *Immigration and Refugee Protection Act*, SC 2001, c 27 [*IRPA*]; *Immigration and Refugee Protection Regulations*, SOR/2002-227.
53 *Immigration Act*, RSC 1985, c I-2.
54 In November 2015, following the election of a new federal government, Citizenship and Immigration Canada was rebranded as Immigration, Refugees and Citizenship Canada.
55 Debra Pressé, interview with author, 18 November 2009; Chris Friesen, interview with author, 26 February 2010; Marta Kalita, interview with author, 17 March 2010; John Peters, interview with author, 17 March 2010; Howard Adelman, telephone interview with author, 8 July 2010; Rivka Augenfeld, telephone interview with author, 9 July 2010, and interview with author, 23 August 2010; Jackie Halliburton, interview with author, 11 March 2011; Mike Molloy, interview with author, 24 March 2011.
56 The Canadian Council for Refugees (CCR) began in 1978 as the Standing Conference of Canadian Organizations Concerned for Refugees. The organization changed its name to the Canadian Council for Refugees in 1986 and sought charitable status. Its mission statement, adopted in 1993, positions the CCR as "a non-profit umbrella organization committed to the rights and protection of refugees in Canada and around the world and to the settlement of refugees and immigrants in Canada." With a focus on information exchange, networking, policy analysis, and advocacy for and among its member organizations involved in protection, sponsorship, and settlement, the CCR does much to promote public and political awareness of refugee rights, interests, and protection. With connections to NGOs, academics, and government officials, the CCR is a leading Canadian voice on refugee issues and provider of information. See "Brief History of Canada's Response to Refugees" (2009), online:

Canadian Council for Refugees <ccrweb.ca/canadarefugeeshistory5.htm>; "Mission Statement," online: *Canadian Council for Refugees* <ccrweb.ca/en/about-ccr>.
57 Francisco Rico Martinez & CCR, "The Future of Colombian Refugees in Canada: Are We Being Equitable?" (2011), online: *Canadian Council for Refugees* <ccrweb.ca/files/ccr_colombia_report_2011.pdf>.
58 The Colombian National Organization of Indigenous Peoples; the Black Communities Process of Colombia; the Embassy of Canada to Colombia; the UNHCR representative in Colombia; the International Red Cross Committee in Colombia; the Defensoria del Pueblo, Colombia (National Ombudsman Office); the Centre for Research and Popular Education; the Coordinacion para los Derechos Humanos y el Desplazamiento; the Colombian Jurists Commission Jesuit Refugee Service; the Mennonite Church in Colombia; the Department of Sociology at the National University of Colombia.
59 On 10 March 2011, the Canadian government gave notice to remove the source country class from the *IRPA*'s regulations. Citizenship and Immigration Canada, "Regulatory Impact Analysis Statement" 145:12 Canada Gazette Part 1 (19 March 2011) 1001.
60 Although in indicating the central argument, I do not mean to suggest that the discussion is one-sided or dismissive of alternative views.
61 Shauna Labman, *The Invisibles: An Examination of Refugee Resettlement* (LLM Thesis, Faculty of Law, University of British Columbia, 2007).

Chapter 2: Movement

1 Leviticus 19:34; Numbers 35:6; Deuteronomy 23:15–16 (King James Version).
2 *Convention Relating to the Status of Refugees*, 28 July 1951, 189 UNTS 150 (entered into force 22 April 1954) [*Refugee Convention*].
3 *Protocol Relating to the Status of Refugees*, 31 January 1967, 606 UNTS 267 (entered into force 4 October 1967) [*1967 Protocol*].
4 *Statute of the Office of the United Nations High Commissioner for Refugees*, UNGA Doc A/RES/428(V) (14 December 1950), 5 [*UNHCR Statute*].
5 *Continuation of the Office of the United Nations High Commissioner for Refugees*, UNGA Res 57/186 C.3 104 (4 February 2003). The final five-year continuation of the office of the United Nations High Commissioner for Refugees (UNHCR) was made on 18 December 2002.
6 *Implementing Actions Proposed by the UNHCR to Strengthen the Capacity of His Office to Carry Out Its Mandate*, UNGA Doc A/RES/58/153 (24 February 2004).
7 *Refugee Convention*, supra note 2, art 1(A).
8 *Ibid*, art 33(1).
9 For example, Malaysia, Jordan, and Lebanon are all within the top ten countries of asylum from which the UNHCR made resettlement submissions in 2017, and none

is a state party to either the *Refugee Convention* or the *1967 Protocol*. UNHCR, "UNHCR Projected Global Resettlement Needs 2019," 24th Annual Tripartite Consultations on Resettlement, Geneva, 25–26 June 2018 (2019), 70, online: <www.unhcr.org/protection/resettlement/5b28a7df4/projected-global-resettlement-needs-2019.html>. Nor have other large refugee-hosting states, including Pakistan, Iraq, and India, become state parties to the *Refugee Convention* or the *1967 Protocol*. Pakistan hosts the second-largest refugee population in the world, with approximately 1.4 million refugees. In 2017, Iraq hosted 247,100 refugees from the Syrian Arab Republic, and, in 2016, India hosted 4,500 refugees from Afghanistan and, in 2017, hosted 18,100 refugees from Myanmar. "Global Trends: Forced Displacement in 2017," 14, 17, 42, online: *UNHCR* <www.unhcr.org/5b27be547.pdf> ["Global Trends 2017"].

10 For a discussion of the use of private actors for migration control, see Thomas Gammeltoft-Hansen, *Access to Asylum: International Refugee Law and the Globalization of Migration Control* (Cambridge, UK: Cambridge University Press, 2011).

11 For helpful discussions on engineered regionalism, the demise of protection, and moves towards containment and encampment, see Matthew Gibney, "Forced Migration, Engineered Regionalism and Justice between States" in Susan Kneebone & Felicity Rawlings-Sanei, eds, *New Regionalism and Asylum Seekers* (New York: Berghahn Books, 2007) 57, 57–77 [Gibney, "Forced Migration"]; Guglielmo Verdirame & Barbara Harrell-Bond, *Rights in Exile: Janus-Faced Humanitarianism* (New York: Berghahn Books, 2005), 289; BS Chimni, *The Geopolitics of Refugee Studies and the Practice of International Institutions: A View from the South* (Oxford: Refugee Studies Programme, 1998); Alexander Aleinikoff, "State-Centered Refugee Law: From Resettlement to Containment" in EV Daniel & JR Knudsen, eds, *Mistrusting Refugees* (Berkeley: University of California Press, 1995), 257–72.

12 Matthew J Gibney, *The Ethics and Politics of Asylum: Liberal Democracy and the Response to Refugees* (Cambridge, UK: Cambridge University Press, 2004), 195.

13 Jason Kenney, quoted in Steven Chase, "Ottawa Helps Block Another Batch of Smuggled Sri Lankans," *Globe and Mail* (14 June 2012).

14 UNHCR, *Resettlement Handbook* (November 2004), 1–2.

15 *Versailles Peace Treaty*, 26 June 1919, 225 Parry 188 (entered into force 10 January 1920), arts 1–30. Components of this section have been developed from Shauna Labman, "Looking Back, Moving Forward: The History and Future of Refugee Protection" (2010) 10 Chicago-Kent Journal of International and Comparative Law 1.

16 League of Nations, Fourteenth Council Session, Annexes 245, 245a.

17 *Ibid*. The League of Nations resolutions mentioned *non-refoulement* only briefly and in connection with repatriation: "Finally, the Conference considered that no Russian

refugee should be compelled to return to Russia (*non-refoulement*) but that it would be expedient to collect without delay particulars of the number of refugees desiring to be repatriated (*voluntary repatriation*)." Quoted in Ivor C Jackson, "Dr Fridtjof Nansen a Pioneer in the International Protection of Refugees" (2003) 22 Refugee Survey Quarterly 7, 9.

18 Fridtjof Nansen, "Russian Refugees: Report to the Council of July 20th, 1922 by Dr. Nansen," *Official Journal* (August 1922).
19 Claudena Skran, "Profiles of the First Two High Commissioners" (1988) 1 Journal of Refugee Studies 277, 284 [Skran, "Profiles"].
20 *Ibid*.
21 *Ibid*, 289.
22 Claudena Skran, *Refugees in Inter-War Europe: The Emergence of a Regime* (Oxford: Clarendon Press, 1995), 131.
23 *Convention Relating to the International Status of Refugees*, 28 October 1933, 159 LNTS 3663. Eight states ratified the convention: Belgium, Bulgaria, Czechoslovakia, Denmark, France, Great Britain, Italy, and Norway. It was signed, but not ratified, by Egypt. See Robert J Beck, "Britain and the 1933 Refugee Convention: National or State Sovereignty?" (1999) 11 International Journal of Refugee Law 697, 600, 603.
24 Skran, "Profiles," *supra* note 19, 289.
25 John Torpey, *The Invention of the Passport: Surveillance, Citizenship and the State* (Cambridge, UK: Cambridge University Press, 2000), 138.
26 *Provisional Arrangement Concerning the Status of Refugees Coming from Germany*, 4 July 1936, 3952 LNTS 77; *Convention Concerning the Status of Refugees Coming from Germany*, 10 February 1938, 4461 LNTS 61 [*1938 Convention*].
27 *1938 Convention*, *supra* note 26, art 15, stated: "With a view to facilitating the emigration of refugees to overseas countries, every facility shall be granted to the refugees and to the organizations which deal with them for the establishment of schools for professional re-adaptation and technical training."
28 Alessandra Roversi, "The Evolution of the Refugee Regime and Institutional Responses: Legacies from the Nansen Period" (2003) 22 Refugee Survey Quarterly 21, 28.
29 Torpey, *supra* note 25, 135.
30 Roversi, *supra* note 28, 29.
31 Gil Loescher, *Beyond Charity: International Cooperation and the Global Refugee Crises* (Oxford: Oxford University Press, 1993), 48–49 [Loescher, *Beyond Charity*].
32 Atle Grahl-Madsen, *The Status of Refugees in International Law* (Leyden: AW Sijthoff, 1966), 17.
33 *Question of Refugees*, UNGA Resolution 8(I) (12 February 1946).
34 *Constitution of the International Refugee Organization*, 15 December 1946, Part 1(C)(1).
35 Loescher, *Beyond Charity*, *supra* note 31, 49–50.

36 James Hathaway, "The Evolution of Refugee Status in International Law: 1920–1950" (1984) 33 International and Comparative Law Quarterly 348, 376.
37 Dennis Gallagher, "The Evolution of the International Refugee System" (1989) 23 International Migration Review 579, 579.
38 Loescher, *Beyond Charity, supra* note 31, 51.
39 *Refugees and Stateless Persons*, UNGA Resolution 319(IV) (3 December 1949).
40 *UNHCR Statute, supra* note 4.
41 Erika Feller, "The Evolution of the International Refugee Protection Regime" (2001) 5 Washington University Journal of Law and Policy 129, 131.
42 *Refugee Convention, supra* note 2.
43 Gil Loescher, "Protection and Humanitarian Action in the Post-Cold War Era" in Aristide R Zolberg & Peter Benda, eds, *Global Migrants, Global Refugees: Problems and Solutions* (New York: Berghahn Books, 2001) 171, 172.
44 James Hathaway, *The Rights of Refugees under International Law* (Cambridge, UK: Cambridge University Press, 2005), 92–93 [Hathaway, *Rights of Refugees*]. Of course, the atrocities of the Second World War also loomed large on the states supporting the *Refugee Convention*. Peter Showler suggests that the promise not to send people back to persecution is commonly viewed as the response of "nations still bruised by post-Holocaust guilt, conscious of having denied entry to pre-Holocaust Jews." Peter Showler, *Refugee Sandwich: Stories of Exile and Asylum* (Montreal and Kingston: McGill-Queen's University Press, 2006), 212.
45 Hathaway, *Rights of Refugees, supra* note 44, 964.
46 Gary Troeller, "UNHCR Resettlement: Evolution and Future Direction" (2002) 14 International Journal of Refugee Law 85, 87.
47 UNHCR Executive Committee, *Resettlement as an Instrument of Protection*, ExCom Conclusion No 67 (1991), para (g), online: <https://www.unhcr.org/excom/exconc/3ae68c4368/resettlement-instrument-protection.html>.
48 See Chimni, *supra* note 11; Stephen Castles, "The Factors that Make and Unmake Migration Policies" (2004) 38 International Migration Review 852.
49 Troeller, *supra* note 46, 85, 89.
50 Gervase Coles, "The Human Rights Approach to the Solution of the Refugee Problem: A Theoretical and Practical Inquiry" in A Nash, ed, *Human Rights and the Protection of Refugees under International Law* (Halifax: Institute for Research on Public Policy, 1988) 195, 211.
51 *Ibid.*
52 Aleinikoff, *supra* note 11, 260.
53 Coles, *supra* note 50, 199.
54 See Gil Loescher & James Milner, *Protracted Refugee Situations: Domestic and International Security Implications* (Abingdon, UK: Routledge for the International Institute of Strategic Studies, 2005).

55 See Coles, *supra* note 50; Jennifer Hyndman, *Managing Displacement: Refugees and the Politics of Humanitarianism* (Minneapolis: University of Minnesota Press, 2000) [Hyndman, *Managing Displacement*]; James Hathaway, "Reconceiving Refugee Law as Human Rights Protection" (1991) 4 Journal of Refugee Studies 113 [Hathaway, "Reconceiving Refugee Law"]; Aleinikoff, *supra* note 11, 264.
56 Chimni, *supra* note 11, 364.
57 Hyndman, *Managing Displacement*, *supra* note 55, 181.
58 WR Böhning & ML Schloeter-Paredes, eds, *Aid in Place of Migration? Selected Contributions to an ILO-UNHCR Meeting, a WEP Study* (Geneva: International Labour Office, 1994).
59 PL Martin, "Reducing Emigration Pressure: What Role Can Foreign Aid Play?" in Böhning & Schloeter-Paredes, *supra* note 58, 241, 242, 244.
60 Verdirame & Harrell-Bond, *supra* note 11, 289.
61 *Ibid*.
62 Gibney, "Forced Migration," *supra* note 11, 57–77.
63 Verdirame & Harrell-Bond, *supra* note 11, 289.
64 Loescher & Milner, *supra* note 54, 21; Chimni, *supra* note 11; Aleinikoff, *supra* note 11; Gibney, "Forced Migration," *supra* note 11.
65 Verdirame & Harrell-Bond, *supra* note 11, 289.
66 Aleinikoff, *supra* note 11, 265.
67 Loescher & Milner, *supra* note 54, 21.
68 Chimni, *supra* note 11, 351. The current rhetorical twist of presuming asylum seekers, particularly those arriving by boat, to be terrorist threats rather than refugees can be seen as the newest construction of the myth of difference.
69 *Ibid*, 369.
70. *Ibid*, 364–65.
71 Verdirame & Harrell-Bond, *supra* note 11, xiv.
72 Hyndman, *Managing Displacement*, *supra* note 55, 18.
73 *Ibid*, 4, 190.
74 Gibney, "Forced Migration," *supra* note 11, 63.
75 Aleinikoff, *supra* note 11, 266.
76 *Ibid*.
77 Hathaway, "Reconceiving Refugee Law," *supra* note 55, 117.
78 See Alexander Betts & Jean-François Durieux, *Convention Plus as a Norm-Setting Exercise* (Oxford: Oxford University Press, 2007); Jean-François Durieux, "The Role of International Law: Convention Plus" (2005) 24 Refugee Survey Quarterly 89; Marjoleine Zieck, "Doomed to Fail from the Outset? UNHCR's Convention Plus Initiative Revisited" (2009) 21 International Journal of Refugee Law 387; Debra Pressé

& Jessie Thomson, "The Resettlement Challenge: Integration of Refugees from Protracted Refugee Situations" (2007) 24 Refuge 48.
79 UNHCR, *Handbook and Guidelines on Procedures and Criteria for Determining Refugee Status* (December 2011) [*UNHCR 2011 Handbook*].
80 *New York Declaration for Refugees and Migrants,* UNGA Doc A/RES/71/1 (3 October 2016); UNHCR, *Global Compact for Refugees: Final Draft* (26 June 2018), online: <www.unhcr.org/events/conferences/5b3295167/official-version-final-draft-global-compact-refugees.html>.
81 Jennifer Hyndman, "Second-Class Immigrants or First Class Protection? Resettling Refugees to Canada" in Pieter Bevelander et al, eds, *Resettled and Included? The Employment Integration of Resettled Refugees in Sweden* (Malmö: Holmbergs, 2009) 247, 255.
82 In the introduction to the UNHCR's *Global Consultations*, the editors note that "it has been noticeable that the post-September 11 context has been used to broaden the scope of provisions of the 1951 Convention allowing refugees to be excluded from refugee status and/or to be expelled. The degree of collaboration between immigration and asylum authorities and the intelligence and criminal law enforcement branches has also been stepped up." Erika Feller et al, *Refugee Protection in International Law: UNHCR's Global Consultations on International Protection* (Cambridge, UK: Cambridge University Press, 2003), 5. Catherine Dauvergne has noted: "The worldwide fear of terror has overlapped and intertwined with the fear of illegal migration." Catherine Dauvergne, "Sovereignty, Migration and the Rule of Law in Global Times" (2004) 67 Modern Law Review 588, 588.
83 John Fredriksson, "Reinvigorating Resettlement: Changing Realities Demand Changed Approaches" (2002) 13 Forced Migration Review 28, 30; Gregor Noll & Joanne van Selm, "Rediscovering Resettlement: A Transatlantic Comparison of Refugee Protection" (2003) 3 Migration Policy Institute Insight 1, 2.
84 UNHCR Resettlement Service, *UNHCR-NGO Toolkit for Practical Cooperation on Resettlement: 1. Operational Activities – Identification and Referral of Refugees in Need of Resettlement: Definitions and FAQs* (June 2015), online: <www.unhcr.org/protection/resettlement/4cd416d79/unhcr-ngo-toolkit-practical-cooperation-resettlement-1-operational-activities.html>.
85 *UNHCR 2011 Handbook, supra* note 79, 245.
86 *Ibid.*
87 *Immigration and Refugee Protection Regulations*, SOR/2002-227, ss 144–47.
88 *Ibid.*
89 Michael Casasola, "UNHCR Updates on Resettlement Activities for 2015–2016" (18 January 2016), online: *Canadian Orientation Abroad* <www.coa-oce.ca/unhcr-updates-on-resettlement-activities-for-2015-2016>.

90 "Global Trends 2017," *supra* note 9, 8.
91 *Ibid*, 29–30.
92 *Ibid*, 30.
93 Betts & Durieux, *supra* note 78, 510.
94 "Global Trends 2017," *supra* note 9, 23–24.
95 Loescher & Milner, *supra* note 54, 14.
96 UNHCR Executive Committee, *Conclusion on Protracted Refugee Situations*, ExCom Conclusion No 109 (LXI) (8 December 2009).
97 Coles, *supra* note 50, 206.
98 See Michael Casasola, "Current Trends and New Challenges for Canada's Resettlement Program" (2001) 19 Refuge 76, 77; for discussions of pull-factor arguments, see Loescher, *Beyond Charity*, *supra* note 31, 16, 22, 59.
99 UNHCR, *Report of the UNHCR Working Group on International Protection* (Geneva: UNHCR, 1992); see also Bill Frelick, "Preventive Protection, and the Right to Seek Asylum: A Preliminary Look at Bosnia and Croatia" (1992) 4 International Journal of Refugee Law 439.
100 "Global Trends 2017," *supra* note 9, 44.
101 Art 14(2) of the *Universal Declaration of Human Rights* sets out the right to seek and to enjoy asylum. *Universal Declaration of Human Rights*, 10 December 1948, UN Doc A/810 (1948), 71.
102 Catherine Dauvergne, *Making People Illegal: What Globalization Means for Migration and Law* (Cambridge, UK: Cambridge University Press, 2008), 57.
103 Jane McAdam, *Complementary Protection in International Refugee Law* (Oxford: Oxford University Press, 2007), 15.
104 *Ibid*, 267.
105 Hathaway, "Reconceiving Refugee Law," *supra* note 55, 120.
106 James C Hathaway & Michelle Foster, *The Law of Refugee Status*, 2nd ed (Cambridge, UK: Cambridge University Press, 2014), 27.
107 Rebecca Hamlin, *Let Me Be a Refugee* (New York: Oxford University Press, 2014).
108 Sean Rehaag, "Judicial Review of Refugee Determinations: The Luck of the Draw?" (2012) 38:1 Queen's Law Journal 1; see also Sean Rehaag, "'I Simply Do Not Believe': A Case Study of Credibility Determinations in Canadian Refugee Adjudication" (2017) 38 Windsor Review of Legal and Social Issues 28.
109 "Global Trends 2017," *supra* note 9, 45.

Chapter 3: History, Humanitarianism, and Law

1 Components of this section have been developed from Shauna Labman, "Queue the Rhetoric: Refugees, Resettlement and Reform" (2011) 62 University of New Brunswick Law Journal 55.

Notes to pages 32–34 191

2 Citizenship and Immigration Canada (CIC), News Release, "Expanding Canada's Refugee Resettlement Programs" (29 March 2010) [CIC, "Expanding Canada's Refugee"].
3 SC 2010, c 8 (assented to 29 June 2010) (formerly Bill C-11) [*BRRA*].
4 Minister Jason Kenney made the announcement at an Ottawa immigration centre where it was reported that over 100 refugees gathered to hear the speech and cheered at the increases. Norma Greenaway, "Tories Tackle Refugee Backlog While Opening Door to Those in Camps Overseas," *Canwest News Service* (29 March 2010).
5 Canadian Council for Refugees (CCR), Media Release, "CCR Welcomes Opening of Door to More Privately Sponsored Refugees" (21 July 2010).
6 Canadian Bar Association, National Citizenship and Immigration Law Section, *Bill C-11, Balanced Refugee Reform Act* (May 2010).
7 CIC, "Expanding Canada's Refugee," *supra* note 2.
8 A detailed discussion of the legal reforms is set out later in this chapter in the section "Boatloads, Back Doors, Rhetoric, and Reform."
9 Susan Davis et al, *Not Just Numbers: A Canadian Framework for Future Immigration* (Ottawa: Minister of Public Works and Government Services Canada, 1997), 9.
10 CIC, *OP 5: Overseas Selection and Processing of Convention Refugees Abroad Class and Members of the Humanitarian-Protected Persons Abroad Classes*, manual (2006), 8, online: <www.canada.ca/content/dam/ircc/migration/ircc/english/resources/manuals/op/op05-eng.pdf>.
11 For a more detailed analysis of the discretionary nature of Canadian refugee law, see Catherine Dauvergne, *Humanitarianism, Identity, and Nation: Migration Laws of Australia and Canada* (Vancouver: UBC Press, 2005), 218 [Dauvergne, *Humanitarianism*].
12 KG Basavarajappa & Bali Ram, "Historical Statistics of Canada," *Population*, Series A1-247, online: *Statistics Canada* <www.statcan.gc.ca/pub/11-516-x/sectiona/4147436-eng.htm#1>. According to the 2016 Census, Canada's population stands at 35,151,728,
13 Gerald E Dirks, *Controversy and Complexity: Canadian Immigration Policy during the 1980s* (Montreal and Kingston: McGill-Queen's University Press, 1995), 61 [Dirks, *Controversy and Complexity*]. Yet, in the early part of the twentieth century, Canada overtly applied racial criteria in its immigration laws and limited other unwanted immigrants. For example, the intent of the *Immigration Act*, SC 1906, c 19 was described by the responsible minister, Frank Oliver, minister of the interior, as being "to enable the Department of Immigration to deal with undesirable migrants." The *Chinese Immigration Act* 1923, 13–14 George V, c 38, which is commonly referred to as the *Chinese Exclusion Act*, banned most forms of Chinese immigration to Canada. For an overview of the extent of Canada's exclusionary policies, see Janet

Dench, "A Hundred Years of Immigration to Canada 1900–1999: A Chronology Focusing on Refugees and Discrimination" (2000), online: *Canadian Council for Refugees* <ccrweb.ca/en/hundred-years-immigration-canada-1900-1999>; David Matas, "Racism in Canadian Immigration Policy" (1985) 5:2 Refuge 8.

14 Dirks, *Controversy and Complexity*, supra note 13.
15 *An Act Respecting Immigration and Immigrants*, SC 1896–69, c 10; *Immigration Act*, SC 1906, c 19; *Immigration Act*, SC 1909–10, c 27.
16 *Immigration Act*, SC 1952, c 42.
17 David Corbett, *Canada's Immigration Policy: A Critique* (Toronto: University of Toronto Press, 1957), 198–99 [emphasis added].
18 Gerald E Dirks, "A Policy within a Policy: The Identification and Admission of Refugees to Canada" (1984) 17 Canadian Journal of Political Science 279, 280 [Dirks, "Policy within a Policy"]; Alan G Green & David Green, "The Goals of Canada's Immigration Policy: A Historical Perspective" (2004) 13:1 Canadian Journal of Urban Research 102.
19 Joseph Kage, "Stepping Stones towards the New Canadian Immigration Act," *Jewish Immigrant Aid Society Information Bulletin*, vol 347 (20 November 1973), 12, Canadian Jewish Congress Charities Committee National Archives.
20 Sharryn J Aiken, "Of Gods and Monsters: National Security and Canadian Refugee Policy" (2001) 14 Revue québécoise de droit international 1, 9.
21 *Ibid*, 9.
22 Mike Molloy, quoted in Laura Madokoro, "Remembering Uganda" (2012), online: *ActiveHistory.ca* <activehistory.ca/2012/03/remembering-uganda/>.
23 *Convention Relating to the Status of Refugees*, 28 July 1951, 189 UNTS 150 (entered into force 22 April 1954) [*Refugee Convention*].
24 Paul Weis, *The Refugee Convention, 1951: The Travaux Préparatoires Analysed with a Commentary by Dr Paul Weis*, International Documents Series (Cambridge, UK: Cambridge University Press, 1995), vol 7, 10.
25 In 1957, Canada became a member of the United Nations Refugee Fund Executive Committee. The Executive Committee of the High Commissioner's Programme was established in 1958 by Economic and Social Council Resolution E/RES/672 (XXV) (30 April 1958), and Canada continued on as a member. United Nations High Commissioner for Refugees (UNHCR), *Excom Membership by Date of Admission of Members* (30 June 2009).
26 "States Parties to the Convention and the Protocol," online: *UNHCR* <www.unhcr.org/pages/49da0e466.html> ["States Parties"]; *Protocol Relating to the Status of Refugees*, 31 January 1967, 606 UNTS 267 (entered into force 4 October 1967) [*1967 Protocol*].
27 Gerald E Dirks, *Canada's Refugee Policy: Indifference or Opportunism* (Montreal and Kingston: McGill-Queen's University Press, 1977), 180.

28 Christopher G Anderson, *Canadian Liberalism and the Politics of Border Control 1867–1967* (Vancouver: UBC Press, 2013), 147. Anderson provides a helpful review of the Canadian government's interest in, and then resistance to, signing the *Refugee Convention* (147–50).
29 "States Parties," *supra* note 26.
30 *Ibid.*
31 *Ibid.*
32 Department of Manpower and Immigration, *Annual Report: Department of Manpower and Immigration Canada* (Ottawa: Department of Manpower and Immigration, 1969), 11.
33 Office of the Minister of Manpower and Immigration, Press Release, "Statement by the Honourable Robert Andras, Minister of Manpower and Immigration" (17 September 1973). Prior to this announcement, a rudimentary system for dealing with both resettlement and refugee claims in Canada was implemented through Cabinet documents that were released on 27 July 1970 and 16 September 1970 and through an operations memorandum released on 17 January 1971, which was amended on 19 June 1972. It was this scheme that shaped Canada's response to the Indochinese refugees from May 1975 to December 1978. With thanks to Mike Molloy, former director of Refugee Policy Division, for this point.
34 The sentence read: "We want also to take into account our well-established tradition of receiving political refugees." Office of the Minister of Manpower and Immigration, *supra* note 33, 4.
35 Department of Manpower and Immigration, *A Report of the Canadian Immigration and Population Study* (Ottawa: Information Canada, 1974).
36 Allan Gotlieb, "Canada and the Refugee Question in International Law" (1975) 13 Canadian Yearbook of International Law 3, 15.
37 *Ibid*, 22.
38 Jennifer Hyndman, William Payne, & Shauna Jimenez, "The State of Private Refugee Sponsorship in Canada: Trends, Issues, and Impacts," Refugee Research Network/Centre for Refugee Studies Policy Brief, submitted to the Government of Canada (2 December 2016), online: *Refugee Research Network* <refugeeresearch.net/wp-content/uploads/2017/02/hyndman_feb%E2%80%9917.pdf>.
39 SC 1976–77, c 52 [*Immigration Act, 1976*]. The *Immigration Act, 1976* passed in 1976 and came into effect in 1978. While the act was brought into the *Revised Statutes of Canada* in 1985 (*Immigration Act*, RSC 1985, c I-2), all references in this chapter are to the original 1976 act.
40 Convention refugees were defined in subsection 2(1).
41 Dirks, "Policy within a Policy," *supra* note 18, 290.
42 Dirks, *Controversy and Complexity*, *supra* note 13, 25 [emphasis added].

43 Lorne Waldman, *Immigration Law and Practice*, 2nd ed (Markham, ON: LexisNexis Butterworths, 2005) (looseleaf), 13.1.
44 *Immigration Act, 1976, supra* note 39, s 47(3): "Where an adjudicator determines that a Convention refugee is a Convention refugee described in subsection 4(2), he shall, notwithstanding any other provision of this Act or the regulations, allow that person to remain in Canada."
45 *Ibid*, para 3(g).
46 *Ibid*, subsection 6(2).
47 Dirks, "Policy within a Policy," *supra* note 18, 306.
48 I take the contrast between generosity and humanitarianism from Matthew Gibney's critique of the American resettlement program. Matthew J Gibney, *The Ethics and Politics of Asylum: Liberal Democracy and the Response to Refugees* (Cambridge, UK: Cambridge University Press, 2004), 156.
49 Employment and Immigration Canada (EIC), *Indochinese Refugees: The Canadian Response, 1979 and 1980* (Ottawa: Minister of Supply and Services Canada, 1982), 14. The *Indochinese Designated Class Regulations*, SOR/78-931, applied to citizens of Kampuchea, Laos, and Vietnam who had left their countries as of 30 April 1975, had not settled elsewhere, and had Canadian citizens willing to sponsor their resettlement.
50 "Archive of Past Nansen Winners," online: *UNHCR* <www.unhcr.org/previous-nansen-winners.html>.
51 Aiken, *supra* note 20, 12.
52 Canada Employment and Immigration Advisory Council, *Perspectives on Immigration in Canada: Final Report* (Ottawa: Ministry of Supply and Services Canada, 1988), 1–2.
53 Robert Holten & Michael Lanphier, "Public Opinion, Immigration and Refugees" in Howard Adelman et al, eds, *Immigration and Refugee Policy: Australia and Canada Compared* (Toronto: University of Toronto Press, 1994), vol 1, 3, 132.
54 Michael Casasola, "Current Trends and New Challenges for Canada's Resettlement Program" (2001) 19 Refuge 76, 77.
55 Gary Troeller, "UNHCR Resettlement: Evolution and Future Direction" (2002) 14 International Journal of Refugee Law 85, 85.
56 EIC, *Annual Report to Parliament: Immigration Plan for 1991–1995: Year Two* (1991), 7 [EIC, *Annual Report to Parliament* (1991)].
57 EIC, *Annual Report to Parliament on Future Immigration Levels* (1986), 8; EIC, *Annual Report to Parliament on Future Immigration Levels* (1987), 10.
58 EIC, *Annual Report to Parliament: Immigration Plan for 1991–1995* (1990), 5 [EIC, *Annual Report to Parliament* (1990)].
59 *Ibid*, 5, 11. Amendments to the Immigration Appeal Board in 1973 had established the first statutory basis for the recognition of refugees in Canada by allowing the

board to quash deportation orders of those found to be refugees under the *Refugee Convention*. *An Act to Amend the Immigration Appeal Board Act*, SC 1973-74, c 27, ss 1, 5.

60 *Singh v Canada (Minister of Employment and Immigration)*, [1985] 1 SCR 177. See Christopher G Anderson, "Restricting Rights, Losing Control: The Politics of Control over Asylum Seekers in Liberal-Democratic States – Lessons from the Canadian Case, 1951–1989" (2010) 43:4 Canadian Journal of Political Science 937, for a summary of efforts towards oral hearings prior to *Singh*.

61 EIC, *Annual Report to Parliament* (1991), *supra* note 56, 10.
62 *Ibid*, 7.
63 Davis et al, *supra* note 9.
64 *Ibid*, 1.
65 *Ibid*, 82–83.
66 SC 2001, c 27 [*IRPA*].
67 Frank N Marrocco & Henry M Goslett, *The 2002 Annotated Immigration Act of Canada* (Toronto: Carswell, 2001), vii.
68 *Ibid*.
69 Catherine Dauvergne, "Evaluating Canada's New Immigration and Refugee Protection Act in Its Global Context" (2003) 41 Alberta Law Review 725, 731. Section 3 of the *IRPA*, *supra* note 66, contains eleven objectives with respect to immigration, eight objectives with respect to refugees, and five paragraphs on the application of the act.
70 Davis et al, *supra* note 9, 13.
71 Dauvergne, *Humanitarianism*, *supra* note 11, 174.
72 Questioning the legitimacy of this compassion is indeed central to the arguments of this book, and, undoubtedly, international relations, burden sharing, and foreign policy are also at play.
73 It does seem unlikely, however, that Western states would readily recommit themselves to the same obligations today that they did more than half a century ago. See Statsministeriet, Press Release, "Statement of Danish Prime Minister Lars Løkke Rasmussen at Press Briefing Concerning the Current Migration Situation in Denmark January 4, 2016" (4 January 2016), online: <www.stm.dk/_p_14281.html>; Ministry of Immigration, Integration and Housing (Denmark), News Release, "New Bill Presented before the Danish Parliament" (13 January 2016), online: <uibm.dk/nyheder/2016-01/new-bill-presented-before-the-danish-parliament>; Government Offices of Sweden, News Release, "Government Decides to Temporarily Reintroduce Internal Border Controls" (12 November 2015), online: <www.government.se/articles/2015/11/government-decides-to-temporarily-reintroduce-internal-border-controls/>. The soft law, non-binding commitments in the *Global Compact for Refugees* suggest that this is the limit of current state positions on refugee

protection. UNHCR, *Global Compact for Refugees: Final Draft* (26 June 2018), online: <www.unhcr.org/events/conferences/5b3295167/official-version-final-draft-global-compact-refugees.html>.

74 Department of Foreign Affairs and International Trade, *Canada's Actions since the September 11 Attacks Fighting Terrorism – A Top Priority*, cited in Erin Kruger, Marlene Mulder, & Bojan Korenic, "Canada after 11 September: Security Measures and 'Preferred' Immigrants" (2004) 15:4 Mediterranean Quarterly 72, 77.

75 Bill C-31 was first tabled in April 2000 but died when Parliament was dissolved later that year. Amended, Bill C-11 was introduced and passed in November 2001.

76 Jane Armstrong, "The Boat People's Big Gamble," *Globe and Mail* (22 July 2000), A7.

77 Terry Glavin, "Why Such Loopiness over a Few Rusty Boats?" *Globe and Mail* (10 September 1999), A11.

78 Casasola, *supra* note 54, 79. When tabling Bill C-31 on 6 April 2001, the minister of citizenship and immigration, Elinor Caplan, stated: "Closing the back door to those who would abuse the system allows us to ensure that the front door will remain open." CIC, News Release, 2000-09, "Caplan Tables New Immigration and Refugee Protection Act" (6 April 2000), online: <www.cic.gc.ca/english/press/00/0009-pre.html>.

79 Erika Feller et al, *Refugee Protection in International Law: UNHCR's Global Consultations on International Protection* (Cambridge, UK: Cambridge University Press, 2003), 5.

80 For examples of renewed discussion, see Casasola, *supra* note 54; Troeller, *supra* note 55; John Fredriksson, "Reinvigorating Resettlement: Changing Realities Demand Changed Approaches" (2002) 13 Forced Migration Review 28; Gregor Noll & Joanne van Selm, "Rediscovering Resettlement: A Transatlantic Comparison of Refugee Protection" (2003) 3 Migration Policy Institute Insight 1; David Steinbock, "The Qualities of Mercy: Maximizing the Impact of US Refugee Resettlement" (2003) 36 University of Michigan Journal of Law Reform 951.

81 Fredriksson, *supra* note 80, 28.

82 Joanne van Selm, "Refugee Protection in Europe and the U.S. after 9/11" in Niklaus Steiner, Mark Gibney, & Gil Loescher, eds, *Problems of Protection: The UNHCR, Refugees and Human Rights* (London: Routledge, 2003) 237.

83 James Hathaway, *The Rights of Refugees under International Law* (Cambridge, UK: Cambridge University Press, 2005), 964.

84 UNHCR, "The Strategic Use of Resettlement," Working Group on Resettlement Discussion Paper WGR/03/04.Rev4 (2003), online: <www.unhcr.org/protect/PROTECTION/3ee6dc6f4.pdf>.

85 Jennifer Hyndman, "Second-Class Immigrants or First Class Protection? Resettling Refugees to Canada" in Pieter Bevelander et al, eds, *Resettled and Included? The Employment Integration of Resettled Refugees in Sweden* (Malmö: Holmbergs, 2009) 247, 255.

86 In the 1990 annual report, the introduction of the in-Canada refugee determination system was premised on the changed reality that "Canada, like most Western countries, has become a country of first asylum for thousands of people." EIC, *Annual Report to Parliament* (1990), *supra* note 58, 7. Ironically, in 1984, the annual report justified the need for continued resettlement in Canada because, elsewhere, large waves of asylum seekers "alienate public support for refugee programs in host countries because they are perceived as movements of illegal migrants motivated by economic concerns." EIC, *Annual Report to Parliament on Future Immigration Levels* (1984), 12.

87 Andrew Schoenholtz, "Refugee Protection in the United States Post-September 11" (2005) 36 Columbia Human Rights Law Review 323, 324.

88 Since 1980, on average, the United States has admitted 98,000 people annually with a high of 207,000 in 1980 and a low of 27,110 in 2002. In 2018, the US administration announced that only 30,000 refugees would be admitted in the 2019 fiscal year, which will again constitute one of the lowest numbers of admissions in the history of the refugee admissions program. "History of the US Refugee Resettlement Program," online: *Refugee Council USA* <www.rcusa.org/history>; Refugee Council USA, Press Release, "RCUSA Responds to the Presidential Determination Announcement for 2019" (17 September 2018), online: <www.rcusa.org/blog/rcusa-responds-to-the-presidential-determination-announcement-for-2019>.

89 See *Executive Order Protecting the Nation from Foreign Terrorist Entry into the United States*, Executive Order 13769 (27 January 2017); *Executive Order Protecting the Nation from Foreign Terrorist Entry into the United States*, Executive Order 13780 (6 March 2017); as well as the various legal challenges to these orders.

90 See Alex Neve & Tiisetso Russell, "Hysteria and Discrimination: Canada's Harsh Response to Refugees and Migrants Who Arrive by Sea" (2011) 62:1 University of New Brunswick Law Journal 37.

91 Jason Kenney, quoted in Jane Armstrong & John Ibbitson, "Seeking a Safe Haven, Finding a Closed Door," *Globe and Mail* (20 October 2009), A1.

92 *Refugee Convention*, *supra* note 23, art 31(1).

93 Audrey Macklin, "Disappearing Refugees: Reflections on the Canada-US Safe Third Country Agreement" (2005) 36:2 Columbia Human Rights Law Review 365, 365–66.

94 *Agreement between the Government of Canada and the Government of the United States of America for Cooperation in the Examination of Refugee Status Claims from Nationals of Third Countries* (2004), online: <www.cic.gc.ca/english/department/laws-policy/safe-third.asp> [*Safe Third Country Agreement*].

95 Efrat Arbel, "Gendered Border Crossings" in Efrat Arbel, Catherine Dauvergne, & Jenni Millbank, eds, *Gender in Refugee Law: From the Margins to the Centre* (London: Routledge, 2014) 243.

96 Efrat Arbel & Alletta Brenner, *Bordering on Failure: Canada-U.S. Border Policy and the Politics of Refugee Exclusion* (Cambridge, MA: Harvard Immigration and Refugee Law Clinic, 2013), 100.

97 Claude Castonguay, quoted in Stephen Smith & Kalina Laframboise, "RCMP Says It Has Intercepted 3,800 Asylum Seekers Crossing Illegally into Quebec since Aug. 1," *CBC News* (17 August 2017), online: <www.cbc.ca/news/canada/montreal/rcmp-says-it-has-intercepted-3-800-asylum-seekers-crossing-illegally-into-quebec-since-aug-1-1.4250806>.

98 *IRPA*, *supra* note 66. See Shauna Labman & Jamie Chai Yun Liew, "Law and Moral Licensing in Canada: The Making of Illegality and Illegitimacy along the Border," International Journal of Migration and Border Studies [forthcoming].

99 *Immigration and Refugee Protection Regulations*, SOR/2002-227, s 229(2) [*IRPR*].

100 My thanks to Audrey Macklin, in her 2018 Ivan C Rand Memorial Lecture (15 February 2018), for highlighting this point.

101 Quoted in Nicholas Keung, "New Data Show 69% of Illegal Border-Crossers Are Being Granted Asylum," *Toronto Star* (19 October 2017), online: <www.thestar.com/news/canada/2017/10/19/new-data-show-69-of-illegal-border-crossers-are-being-granted-asylum.html>.

102 *BRRA*, *supra* note 3.

103 Canadian Bar Association, *supra* note 6.

104 Campbell Clark, "Tories 'Let's-Make-a-Deal' Approach Good Politics," *Globe and Mail* (11 June 2010), A10.

105 Celyeste Power, quoted in Stewart Bell, "Canada Monitors Suspicious Vessel," *National Post* (16 July 2010), A1.

106 John Ibbitson, Steven Chase, & Marten Youssef, "Ottawa Plans New Rules for Boat Migrants," *Globe and Mail* (13 August 2010), A1.

107 "On the Lookout for Tigers," editorial, *Globe and Mail* (12 August 2010), A16.

108 Even among refugee populations, who are now permanent residents and Canadian citizens, there is an increasing perception of the illegitimacy of in-Canada asylum claimants. A report on Colombian refugees in Ontario noted: "The dichotomy between the 'real' and the 'not real' refugee is a topic of constant tension, especially in London [Ontario] where ... most of the refugees are refugee claimants. The fact that many of these refugees have arrived through the United States, in contrast with the refugees from abroad by the government or privately, has created an important fracture within the Colombian community." Pilar Riaño Alcalá et al, *Forced Migration of Colombians: Colombia, Ecuador, Canada* (Colombia and Vancouver: Corporación Región (Spanish) and School of Social Work, University of British Columbia (English), 2008), 125.

109 Formerly Bill C-49, reintroduced as Bill C-4 on 16 June 2011.

110 SC 2012, c 17 (introduced on 16 February 2012, assented to 28 June 2012) (formerly Bill C-31) [*PCISA*].
111 Stephanie Silverman, "In the Wake of Irregular Arrivals: Changes to the Canadian Immigration Detention System" (2014) 30:2 Refuge 27.
112 *IRPA, supra* note 66, s 109.1. Section 12 of the *BRRA, supra* note 3, gave the minister authority to identify designated countries of origin (DCOs), and s 58 of the *PCISA, supra* note 110, provided more flexibility in determining which countries to designate. The quantitative threshold is at least thirty finalized claims within a twelve-month period. The designation is not automatic and requires consultation with other government departments. Immigration, Refugees and Citizenship Canada (IRCC), "Backgrounder: Designated Countries of Origin" (2013), online: *Government of Canada* <www.cic.gc.ca/english/department/media/backgrounders/2012/2012-11-30.asp>.
113 *PCISA, supra* note 110, s 10, adding *IRPA, supra* note 66, s 20.1(1), that designates a group as an "irregular arrival" when the minister is of the opinion that investigations of the group's identity or inadmissibility cannot be done in a timely manner or that human smuggling was involved in the group's arrival.
114 Silverman, *supra* note 111; "Protect Refugees from Bill C-31: Joint Statement" (March 2012), online: *Canadian Council for Refugees* <ccrweb.ca/en/protect-refugees-c31-statement>.
115 See Petra Molnar Diop, "The 'Bogus' Refugee: Roma Asylum Claimants and Discourses of Fraud in Bill C-31" (2014) 30:1 Refuge 67, 68–70.
116 Silverman, *supra* note 111, 28; Audrey Macklin & Lorne Waldman, "Ottawa's Bogus Refugee Bill," editorial, *Toronto Star* (26 December 2012), online: <www.thestar.com/opinion/editorialopinion/2012/02/22/ottawas_bogus_refugee_bill.html>; "Sun Sea: Five Years Later" (August 2015), online: *Canadian Council for Refugees* <ccrweb.ca/sites/ccrweb.ca/files/sun-sea-five-years-later.pdf>.
117 See Silverman, *supra* note 111; Stephanie Levitz, "New Canadian Immigration Rules: 'Safe' Countries List Aimed at Bogus Refugees," *Huffington Post* (14 December 2012), online: <www.huffingtonpost.ca/2012/12/14/new-canadian-immigration-rules_n_2301019.html>. Despite many withdrawn/abandoned and rejected claims between 2008 and 2012, 660 Hungarians were recognized as refugees. Julianna Beaudoin, Jennifer Danch, & Sean Rehaag, "No Refuge: Hungarian Romani Refugee Claimants in Canada" (2015) Osgoode Legal Studies Research Paper Series No 94, 25.
118 *IRPR, supra* note 99, s 159(9); *IRPA, supra* note 66, s 112(2)(b.1).
119 Rejected refugee claimants are given an additional fifteen days to submit written evidence after submitting their pre-removal risk assessment (PRRA) request. Certain countries, including Egypt, Somalia, and Syria, are exempt from the twelve-month bar on subsequent PRRA applications depending on the time the refugee status

determination decision was made. IRCC, "Processing Pre-Removal Risk Assessment Applications: Intake" (2015), online: *Government of Canada* <www.cic.gc.ca/english/resources/tools/refugees/prra/intake.asp>.
120 The new timelines create serious disadvantages for some of the most vulnerable refugee claimants who may require more time to prepare for their hearings and retain legal counsel. Refugee advocates are concerned that the shorter timelines may lead to errors in adjudication, which can determine the ultimate fate of claimants. Sean Rehaag, "Judicial Review of Refugee Determinations: The Luck of the Draw?" (2012) 38:1 Queen's Law Journal 1.
121 Jennifer Bond & David Wiseman, "Shortchanging Justice: The Arbitrary Refugee System Reform and Federal Legal Aid Funding" (2014) University of Ottawa Faculty of Law Working Paper No 2014-24, 604.
122 *Ibid*, 587.
123 *IRPA*, *supra* note 66, ss 20, 24(5), 25(1.01).
124 Julie Béchard & Sandra Elgersma, *Legislative Summary of Bill C-31: An Act to Amend the Immigration and Refugee Protection Act, the Balanced Refugee Reform Act, the Marine Transportation Security Act and the Department of Citizenship and Immigration Act*, Publication No 41-1-C31E (Ottawa: Library of Parliament Research Publications, 2012).
125 *IRPA*, *supra* note 66, s 55(3.1).
126 *Ibid*, s 56(2).
127 Bond & Wiseman, *supra* note 121, 605. There has also been substantial criticism of the mandatory detention of designated foreign nationals (DFNs), given the mental health consequences and unique impacts on detainees sixteen to eighteen years of age. "A Brief Concerning Bill C-31 Protecting Canada's Immigration System Act" (2012), online: *Centre de santé et de services sociaux de la Montagne* <www.csssdelamontagne.qc.ca/fileadmin/csss_dlm/Publications/MEMOIRE_SUR_C-31.ENG.CSSDLM_PRAIDA.mai_2012.pdf>.
128 *IRPA*, *supra* note 66, ss 57–58. For a detailed breakdown of the differences between detention reviews of each category of refugee claimants, see Béchard & Elgersma, *supra* note 124.
129 *IRPA*, *supra* note 66, s 110(2)(a); *IRPR*, *supra* note 99, s 231(2).
130 Amnesty International Canada and Amnistie international Canada francophone, "Unbalanced Reforms: Recommendations with Respect to Bill C-31," Brief to the House of Commons Standing Committee on Citizenship and Immigration (17 April 2012), 5, online: *Amnesty International Canada* <www.amnesty.ca/sites/amnesty/files/ai_brief_bill_c_31_to_parliamentary_committee_0.pdf>.
131 *IRPA*, *supra* note 66, s 98.1; *IRPR*, *supra* note 99, ss 174.1(1)–174.2.
132 *IRPR*, *supra* note 99, s 174.3; see also s 174.4, which states that, once a DFN acquires permanent residency, there is a cessation of reporting requirements.

133 Art 28 of the *Refugee Convention* requires that states provide travel documents for all those "lawfully staying" within their borders; see also *IRPA, supra* note 66, s 31.1.
134 UNHCR, Branch Office for Canada, *UNHCR Submission of Bill C-31* (May 2012), 8.
135 Department of Public Safety, Media Release, "Minister of Public Safety Makes First Designation of Irregular Arrivals under Protecting Canada's Immigration System's Act" (5 December 2012), online: *Government of Canada* <www.publicsafety.gc.ca/cnt/nws/nws-rlss/2012/20121205-eng.aspx>.
136 "Romanian Human Smuggling Ring Busted in Ontario," *CBC News* (5 December 2012), online: <www.cbc.ca/news/politics/romanian-human-smuggling-ring-busted-in-ontario-1.1292783>.
137 Silverman, *supra* note 111.
138 *Canadian Doctors for Refugee Care v Canada (AG)*, 2014 FC 651 [*Canadian Doctors*].
139 "The Issue," online: *Canadian Doctors for Refugee Health Care* <www.doctorsforrefugeecare.ca/the-issue.html>; Beaudoin, Danch, & Rehaag, *supra* note 117, 19; see also "Canadian Doctors for Refugee Care et al v Canada [Refugee Health Care]," online: *Justice for Children and Youth* <jfcy.org/en/cases-decisions/fc-refugee-health-care/>.
140 "Order Respecting the Interim Federal Health Program, 2012," 146:9 Canada Gazette (25 April 2012).
141 *Canadian Doctors, supra* note 138, para 840.
142 In February 2016, the Liberal government announced it would be reinstating Interim Federal Health Program (IFHP) benefits to all eligible persons. The minister further announced that, by April 2017, IFHP would be expanded. The program would offer certain health-care services to refugees approved for resettlement before they arrive, such as medical examinations and pre-departure vaccinations.
143 *IRPA, supra* note 66, para 110(2)(d.1), denying Refugee Appeal Division (RAD) access, became effective on the same day the RAD became operational.
144 *Canadian Charter of Rights and Freedoms*, Part 1 of the *Constitution Act, 1982*, being Schedule B to the *Canada Act 1982* (UK), 1982, c 11.
145 *YZ v Canada (Citizenship and Immigration)*, 2015 FC 892, para 130 [*YZ*]. Although a question was certified to enable review at the Federal Court of Appeal, the newly elected Liberal government announced in January 2016 that it would not pursue the challenge. "Liberals Drop Legal Appeal of Unconstitutional Conservative Refugee Measure," *CBC News* (4 January 2016), online: <www.cbc.ca/news/politics/liberals-drop-legal-appeal-of-unconstitutional-conservative-refugee-measure-1.3389336>.
146 Diop, *supra* note 115; Beaudoin, Danch, & Rehaag, *supra* note 117; Justice Boswell also noted that the provisions excluding DCO claimants from appealing RPD

decisions "serves to further marginalize, prejudice, and stereotype refugee claimants from DCO countries." *YZ, supra* note 145, para 124. Human rights groups have spoken out against the negative impact of DCO distinction. Amnesty International Canada, *supra* note 130, 6.

147 "Designated Countries of Origin" (2016), online: *Government of Canada* <www.cic.gc.ca/english/refugees/reform-safe.asp>.

148 See Prime Minister Justin Trudeau, "Minister of Immigration, Refugees and Citizenship Mandate Letter," online: *Office of the Prime Minister* <pm.gc.ca/eng/archived-minister-immigration-refugees-and-citizenship-mandate-letter>.

149 *Ibid.*

150 Silverman, *supra* note 111, 27.

151 See Chelsea Bin Han, "Smuggled Migrant or Migrant Smuggler: Erosion of Sea-Borne Asylum Seekers' Access to Refugee Protection in Canada" (MSc Thesis, Department of International Development, University of Oxford, 2014), 23, online: <www.rsc.ox.ac.uk/files/publications/working-paper-series/wp106-smuggled-migrant-or-migrant-smuggler.pdf/>.

152 *IRPA, supra* note 66, s 81(2), sets out one exception protecting those who are retroactively classified as a DFN from mandatory detention, who were not in detention at the time the DFN order was given. Béchard & Elgersma, *supra* note 124. On 15 December 2012, the minister declared five groups of Romani refugee claimants, arriving over the course of several months, as DFNs. Those individuals located were detained. "Romanian Human Smuggling Ring," *supra* note 136; see also "Sun Sea," *supra* note 116.

153 The CCR obtained the internal memo through an access to information request. See Peter D Hill, "Marine Migrants: Program Strategy for the Next Arrival," 3, online: *Canada Border Services Agency* <ccrweb.ca/sites/ccrweb.ca/files/atip-cbsa-sun-sea-strategy-next-arrival.pdf>.

154 "2017–18 Departmental Plan" (2017), online: *Canada Border Services Agency* <www.cbsa-asfc.gc.ca/agency-agence/reports-rapports/rpp/2017-2018/report-rapport-eng.pdf>.

155 Efrat Arbel, "Bordering the Constitution, Constituting the Border" (2016) 53 Osgoode Hall Law Journal 824.

156 *Ibid.* Johanna Reynolds & Jennifer Hyndman, "A Turn in Canadian Refugee Policy and Practice" (2015) 16 Journal of Diplomacy and International Relations 41; Pauline Maillet, Alison Mountz, & Kira Williams, "Exclusion through *Imperio*: Entanglements of Law and Geography in the Waiting Zone, Excised Territory and Search and Rescue Region" (2018) 27:2 Social and Legal Studies 142.

157 Reynolds & Hyndman, *supra* note 156, 45.

158 Arbel, *supra* note 155, 838.

159 See e.g. Anthea Vogl, "Over the Borderline: A Critical Inquiry into the Geography of Territorial Excision and the Securitisation of the Australian Border" (2015) 38 University of New South Wales Law Journal 114; Monique Failla, "Outsourcing Obligations to Developing Nations: Australia's Refugee Resettlement Agreement with Cambodia" (2016) 42 Monash University Law Review 638.

160 See e.g. Laura Bacon, "To What Extent Can the Right to Asylum Be Limited by a State's Sovereign Right to Control Its Borders? A Comparative Assessment of the Lawfulness of European Asylum Law and Procedure" (2016) 22 Auckland University Law Review 69.

161 See Ray Silvius et al, "What Does It Take to House a Syrian Refugee?" (January 2017), online: *Canadian Centre for Policy Alternatives* <www.policyalternatives.ca/publications/reports/what-does-it-take-house-syrian-refugee>.

162 "Statement from the Minister of Immigration, Refugees and Citizenship and the Minister of Justice and Attorney General of Canada" (16 December 2015), online: *Government of Canada* <www.canada.ca/en/immigration-refugees-citizenship/news/2015/12/statement-from-the-minister-of-immigration-refugees-and-citizenship-and-the-minister-of-justice-and-attorney-general-of-canada.html>.

163 YZ, *supra* note 145.

164 IRCC, News Release, "Changes to Regulations Will See Age Increased for Dependent Child" (3 May 2017), online: *Government of Canada* <www.canada.ca/en/immigration-refugees-citizenship/news/2017/05/changes_to_regulationswillseeageincreasedfordependentchild.html>.

165 New rules in December 2012 required all refugee claims to be heard within sixty days. This left almost 32,000 older "legacy" claims unheard. Immigration and Refugee Board of Canada, News Release, "Refugee Claimants Asked to Update Contact Information" (20 June 2017), online: *Government of Canada* <www.canada.ca/en/immigration-refugee/news/2017/06/refugee_claimantsaskedtoupdatecontactinformation.html>. Between January and June 2018, there were just over 1,500 legacy claims determined and a remaining 1,925 legacy claims pending as of June 2018. As of 30 June 2018, there were 55,567 claims pending. "Refugee Protection Claims (Legacy) by Country of Alleged Persecution – 2018," online: *Immigration and Refugee Board of Canada* <irb-cisr.gc.ca/en/statistics/protection/Pages/RPDLegStat2018.aspx>; "Refugee Protection Claims (New System) by Country of Alleged Persecution – 2018," online: *Immigration and Refugee Board of Canada* <irb-cisr.gc.ca/en/statistics/protection/Pages/RPDStat2018.aspx>.

166 "Reduced Capacity at the Immigration Appeal Division, Western Region: Latest News" (2017), online: *Immigration and Refugee Board of Canada* <www.irb-cisr.gc.ca/en/news/2017/Pages/redu_capac.aspx>; see also "The Trudeau Government Is Failing Refugee Claimants, and Canadians," editorial, *Globe and Mail* (3 July 2017),

online: <www.theglobeandmail.com/opinion/editorials/globe-editorial-the-trudeau-government-is-failing-refugee-claimants/article35522884/>.

167 Anneke Smit, "Canadians Have Turned a Blind Eye to the Liberals' Refugee Failures," *Maclean's* (1 May 2017), online: <www.macleans.ca/news/canada/canadians-have-turned-a-blind-eye-to-the-liberals-refugee-failures/>.

168 Hanna Gros, *Invisible Citizens: Canadian Children in Immigration Detention* (Toronto: International Human Rights Program, University of Toronto Faculty of Law, 2017), online: <ihrp.law.utoronto.ca/utfl_file/count/PUBLICATIONS/Report-InvisibleCitizens.pdf>.

169 Harvard Immigration & Refugee Clinical Program, *The Impact of President Trump's Executive Orders on Asylum Seekers* (8 February 2017), online: <today.law.harvard.edu/wp-content/uploads/2017/02/Report-Impact-of-Trump-Executive-Orders-on-Asylum-Seekers.pdf>. In response to changes in the United States, the prime minister of Canada responded on *Twitter*: "To those fleeing persecution, terror & war, Canadians will welcome you, regardless of your faith. Diversity is our strength. #Welcome to Canada." Justin Trudeau, "To Those Fleeing Persecution, Terror and War, Canadians Will Welcome You, Regardless of Your Faith. Diversity Is Our Strength #WelcomeToCanada" (28 January 2017), online: *Twitter* <twitter.com/justintrudeau/status/825438460265762816?lang=en>.

170 Letter to Honourable Ahmed D Hussen, Minister of Immigration, Refugees and Citizenship, "Re: Suspending the Safe Third Country Agreement" (31 January 2007), online: *Osgoode Hall* <www.osgoode.yorku.ca/wp-content/uploads/2017/01/Lettre-Letter.pdf>. It was signed by over 200 law professors; Amnesty International & Canadian Council for Refugees, "Contesting the Designation of the US as a Safe Third Country" (19 May 2017), online: <ccrweb.ca/sites/ccrweb.ca/files/stca-submission-2017.pdf>; *Canadian Council for Refugees v Canada (Minister of Immigration, Refugees and Citizenship)*, Court File No IMM-2977-17 (2017).

171 IRCC, News Release, "Canada to Welcome 1200 Yazidi and Other Survivors of Daesh" (21 February 2017), online: *Government of Canada* <www.canada.ca/en/immigration-refugees-citizenship/news/2017/02/canada_to_welcome1200yazidiandothersurvivorsofdaesh.html?_ga=2.193754349.1714855667.1499720794-1560752352.1474473562>.

172 Stephanie Levitz, "Liberals Pressured to Hold True to Refugee Rhetoric, Reform System" (20 June 2017), online: *Global News* <globalnews.ca/news/3543398/liberal-refugee-reform/>.

173 Immigration, Refugees and Citizenship Canada (IRCC), News Release, "Canada Ends the Designated Country of Origin Practice" (17 May 2019).

174 *An Act to Implement Certain Provisions of the Budget Tabled in Parliament on March 19, 2019 and Other Measures*, 1st Sess, 42nd Parl, 2019, cl 306.

Chapter 4: Numbers, Access, and Rights

1 "2012 Federal Budget" (29 March 2012), Table 5.1, online: *Government of Canada*, www.budget.gc.ca/2012/home-accueil-eng.html, which shows the planned reduction in Citizenship and Immigration Canada spending.
2 United Nations High Commissioner for Refugees (UNHCR), *Resettlement Handbook* (November 2004), "Country Chapter: Canada," 3, online: <www.unhcr.org/protect/3d4545984.html> [*UNHCR Handbook*].
3 Citizenship and Immigration Canada (CIC), *2009 Annual Report to Parliament on Immigration* (2009), s 2, online: <www.publications.gc.ca/collections/collection_2010/cic/Ci1-2009-eng.pdf>.
4 Standing Committee on Immigration and Citizenship, Member of Parliament Norman Doyle, Chair, *Safeguarding Asylum – Sustaining Canada's Commitments to Refugees*, 39-1 (Ottawa: House of Commons, 2007), 4, 8, online: <www.ourcommons.ca/Content/Committee/391/CIMM/Reports/RP2969755/cimmrp15/cimmrp15-e.pdf>.
5 UNHCR, Executive Committee of the High Commissioner's Programme, *Agenda for Protection*, Doc A/AC. 96/965/Add. 1, 3rd ed (October 2003), 6 [UNHCR, *Agenda for Protection*].
6 *Convention Relating to the Status of Refugees*, 28 July 1951, 189 UNTS 150 (entered into force 22 April 1954) [*Refugee Convention*].
7 UNHCR, *Agenda for Protection*, *supra* note 5.
8 High Commissioner's Forum, *Multilateral Framework of Understandings on Resettlement*, Doc FORUM/2004/6 (16 September 2004), online: <https://www.unhcr.org/en-lk/protection/convention/414aa7e54/multilateral-framework-understandings-resettlement-emforum20046em.html>.
9 *Ibid*, 8.
10 Calculation based on data from "Quarterly Administrative Data Release," 2011–15, now available through the Government of Canada's Open Data Portal, online: *Open Data Portal* <www.canada.ca/en/immigration-refugees-citizenship/corporate/reports-statistics/statistics-open-data.html>.
11 Canadian Council for Refugees (CCR), Media Release, "CCR Welcomes Opening of Door to More Privately Sponsored Refugees" (21 July 2010).
12 Jennifer Hyndman, "Second-Class Immigrants or First Class Protection? Resettling Refugees to Canada" in Pieter Bevelander et al, eds, *Resettled and Included? The Employment Integration of Resettled Refugees in Sweden* (Malmö: Holmbergs, 2009) 247, 262–63; *Immigration and Refugee Protection Act*, SC 2001, c 27 [*IRPA*].
13 "Global Trends: Forced Displacement in 2015," 26, online: *UNHCR* <www.unhcr.org/statistics/country/576408cd7/unhcr-global-trends-2015.html>.
14 *IRPA*, *supra* note 12, subsection 99(1)–(2).

15 *Ibid*, s 96.
16 *Ibid*, subsection 97(1). Note that the definition of a "person in need of protection" only applies to a "person in Canada" and is not considered in resettlement applications.
17 *Immigration and Refugee Protection Regulations*, SOR/2002-227, ss 145, 147, 148 [*IRPR*] (s 148 was repealed in the *Regulations Amending the Immigration and Refugee Protection Regulations*, SOR/2011-222, s 6) [*Regulations Amending the IRPR*].
18 *IRPR*, *supra* note 17, s 146.
19 *Regulations Amending the IRPR*, *supra* note 17. Chapter 7 reviews this class and its repeal in detail.
20 The *IRPR* do set out one exception: s 150(2): "A foreign national may submit a permanent resident visa application without a referral or an undertaking if the foreign national resides in a geographic area that the Minister has determined under subsection (3) to be a geographic area in which circumstances justify the submission of permanent resident visa applications not accompanied by a referral or an undertaking." *IRPR*, *supra* note 17.
21 *Ibid*, s 150(1).
22 *Ibid*, s 143.
23 The resettlement registration form (RRF) was introduced by the UNHCR in 1997 to harmonize resettlement referrals. "Workshop on the Resettlement Registration Form" (Annual Tripartite Consultations on Resettlement, Geneva, 15–16 June 2004) [on file with author].
24 CIC, *OP 5: Overseas Selection and Processing of Convention Refugees Abroad Class and Members of the Humanitarian-Protected Persons Abroad Classes*, manual (2006), 8, online: <www.canada.ca/content/dam/ircc/migration/ircc/english/resources/manuals/op/op05-eng.pdf> [*CIC, OP 5*].
25 *IRPR*, *supra* note 17.
26 The Quebec exception here and in subsequently cited legislation results from the *Canada-Québec Accord Relating to Immigration and Temporary Admission of Aliens* (5 February 1991), online: <www.micc.gouv.qc.ca/publications/pdf/Accord_canada_quebec_immigration_anglais.pdf>. The accord grants Quebec greater independence in the selection of immigrants.
27 Catherine Dauvergne, *Humanitarianism, Identity, and Nation: Migration Laws of Australia and Canada* (Vancouver: UBC Press, 2005), 93; Debra Pressé & Jessie Thomson, "The Resettlement Challenge: Integration of Refugees from Protracted Refugee Situations" (2007) 24 Refuge 48, 49; Judith Kumin, "New Approaches to Asylum: Reconciling Individual Rights and State Interests" (2004) 22 Refuge 3, 4.
28 *Immigration Regulations*, SOR/78-172.

29 Davies Bagambiire, *Canadian Immigration and Refugee Law* (Aurora, ON: Canada Law Book, 1996), 244.
30 Employment and Immigration Canada, *Annual Report to Parliament: Immigration Plan for 1991–1995* (1990), 10.
31 Susan Davis et al, *Not Just Numbers: A Canadian Framework for Future Immigration* (Ottawa: Minister of Public Works and Government Services Canada, 1997), 81.
32 *UNHCR Handbook*, *supra* note 2, "Country Chapter: Canada," 1.
33 Pressé & Thomson, *supra* note 27, 50.
34 CIC, *OP 5*, *supra* note 24, 29; "Guide to the Private Sponsorship of Refugees Program: 3.3 Urgent Protection Program," online: *Government of Canada* <www.cic.gc.ca/english/resources/publications/ref-sponsor/section-3-03.asp>.
35 UNHCR, *Resettlement Handbook* (July 2011), "Country Chapter: Canada" (2018 Revision) 8–9, online: <www.unhcr.org/3c5e55594.html>.
36 Michael Casasola, "Current Trends and New Challenges for Canada's Resettlement Program" (2001) 19 Refuge 76, 77.
37 *Ibid*.
38 Pressé & Thomson, *supra* note 27, 50.
39 Chris Friesen, Director of Settlement Services, Immigrant Services Society of British Columbia, interview with author, 26 February 2010; Marta Kalita, Co-Manager, Settlement Services, Manitoba Interfaith Immigration Council, interview with author, 17 March 2010; John Peters, Manager Sponsorship Services, Manitoba Interfaith Immigration Council, interview with author, 17 March 2010.
40 Lisa Ruth Brunner & Chris Friesen, "Changing Faces, Changing Neigbourhoods: Government-Assisted Refugee Resettlement Patterns in Metro Vancouver 2005–2009" (2011) 8 Our Diverse Cities 93, 94.
41 Friesen, interview, *supra* note 39.
42 The acronym AWR for women at risk is imported from the UNHCR's program "Assistance for Women at Risk." CIC, *OP 5*, *supra* note 24, 30.
43 *Ibid*.
44 *Ibid* [emphasis added].
45 *UNHCR Handbook*, *supra* note 2, "Country Chapter: Canada," 9.
46 *Ibid*.
47 In 2003, the CCR stated that "[m]ost refugees seeking resettlement in Canada still need to meet the 'successful establishment' requirement." CCR, *First Annual Report Card on Canada's Refugee and Immigration Programs* (November 2003), online: <www.ccrweb.ca/sites/ccrweb.ca/files/static-files/reportcard2003.htm>.
48 "A Year of Crises: UNHCR Global Trends 2011," 11, online: *UNHCR* <www.unhcr.org/4fd6f87f9.html>.

49 "Global Trends: Forced Displacement in 2017," 2, online: *UNHCR* <www.unhcr.org/5b27be547.pdf>.
50 Immigration, Refugees and Citizenship Canada (IRCC), "Table 3: Permanent Resident Admitted in 2017, by Destination and Immigration Category" (31 October 2018), online: *Government of Canada* <www.canada.ca/en/immigration-refugees-citizenship/corporate/publications-manuals/annual-report-parliament-immigration-2018/permanent-residents-admitted-destination.html>; IRCC, "Notice: Supplementary Information 2019–2021 Immigration Levels Plan" (31 October 2018), online: *Government of Canada* <www.canada.ca/en/immigration-refugees-citizenship/news/notices/supplementary-immigration-levels-2019.html>.
51 *IRPA, supra* note 12, s 72.
52 The *Federal Courts Act*, RSC 1985, c F-7, s 18.1(4), sets out the reasons for judicial intervention.
53 *Ibid*, s 18.1(3).
54 *IRPA, supra* note 12, s 74(4)(d).
55 *Chiarelli v Canada (Minister of Employment and Immigration)*, [1992] 1 SCR 711, 733, 90 DLR (4th) 289.
56 High Commissioner's Forum, *Resettlement and Convention Plus Initiatives*, discussion paper, Doc FORUM/2003/02 (18 June 2003), para 13.
57 *Singh v Canada (Minister of Employment and Immigration)*, [1985] 1 SCR 177, 17 DLR (4th) 422 [*Singh*].
58 *Canadian Charter of Rights and Freedoms*, Part I of the *Constitution Act, 1982*, being Schedule B to the *Canada Act 1982* (UK), 1982, c 11.
59 *Canadian Bill of Rights*, SC 1960, c 44.
60 Following the 1985 decision in *Singh, supra* note 57, the government introduced in 1988 the concept that refugee claimants would have access to an oral hearing before a quasi-judicial tribunal in Bill C-55.
61 *Jallow v Canada (Minister of Citizenship and Immigration)*, [1996] FCJ No 1452, 122 FTR 40 [*Jallow*].
62 *Ibid*, para 17.
63 *Singh, supra* note 57, paras 14, 35; *Jallow, supra* note 61, para 17.
64 *Oraha v Canada (Minister of Citizenship and Immigration)*, [1997] FCJ No 788, 39 Imm LR (2d) 39 [*Oraha*].
65 *Ibid*, para 11. This position is consistent with the UNHCR's direction that, while a person sheltered in a foreign embassy "may be considered to be outside his country's jurisdiction, he is not outside its territory and cannot therefore be considered under the terms of the 1951 Convention." The note addresses the situation of a person

claiming refugee status in a foreign embassy in his or her home country. UNHCR, *Handbook on Procedures and Criteria for Determining Refugee Status under the 1951 Convention and the 1967 Protocol Relating to the Status of Refugees*, Doc HCR/IP/4/Eng/Rev.1 (Geneva: UNHCR, 1992), n 11.

66 *Qarizada v Canada (Minister of Citizenship and Immigration)*, [2008] FCJ No 1662, para 27 [*Qarizada*].

67 *Chiau v Canada (Minister of Citizenship and Immigration)*, [2001] 2 FC 297, (2000), 195 DLR (4th) 422 (FCA), para 38, leave to appeal to SCC dismissed, [2001] SCCA No 71.

68 *UNHCR Handbook*, supra note 2, "Country Chapter: Canada," 5.4.

69 *Baker v Canada (Minister of Citizenship and Immigration)*, [1999] 2 SCR 817, para 26, 174 DLR (4th) 193.

70 See *Jallow*, supra note 61; *Oraha*, supra note 64; *Smajic et al v Canada (Minister of Citizenship and Immigration)*, [1999] FCJ No 1904, 94 ACWS (3d) 340.

71 *Kamara v Canada (Minister of Citizenship and Immigration)*, 2008 FC 785, para 19; *Qarizada*, supra note 66, paras 15–18.

72 *Oraha*, supra note 64, para 9.

73 *Ha v Canada (Minister of Citizenship and Immigration)*, [2004] FCJ No 174, para 61, [2004] 3 FCR 195 [*Ha*].

74 *Ibid*, para 55.

75 *Muhazi v Canada (Minister of Citizenship and Immigration)*, [2004] FCJ No 1670, 2004 FC 1392.

76 *Ibid*, para 36.

77 *Mohamed v Canada (Minister of Citizenship and Immigration)*, [1999] FCJ No 1230, para 23, 173 FTR 261.

78 "Statistics," online: *Federal Court* <http://www.fct-cf.gc.ca/fc_cf_en/Statistics.html>.

79 CCR, *The Refugee Appeal: Is No One Listening?* (31 March 2005), 4.

80 Sean Rehaag, "Judicial Review of Refugee Determinations: The Luck of the Draw?" (2012) 38:1 Queen's Law Journal 1.

81 See Appendix: Federal Court of Canada Resettlement Cases at the end of this book.

82 *Ha*, supra note 73.

83 For a more detailed analysis of this point, see Pierre-André Thériault, "Quality of Decision-Making and Access to Judicial Review in Canada's Refugee Resettlement Program" (PhD Thesis, York University, forthcoming).

84 CCR, Media Release, "Disturbing Upsurge in Rejection of Eritrean Refugees in Cairo by Canada" (30 November 2009).

85 Janet Dench, Executive Director, CCR, email correspondence with author, 7 February 2011. The original lead cases were IMM-6000-09, IMM 6005-09, and IMM-6009-09. Ultimately, four lead cases were heard.

86 "Concerns with Refugee Decision-Making at Cairo" (31 January 2010), 4, online: *Canada Council for Refugees* <www.ccrweb.ca/en/concerns-refugee-decision-making-cairo-0>.
87 *Ghirmatsion v Canada (Minister of Citizenship and Immigration)*, 2011 FC 519 [*Ghirmatsion*]; *Kidane v Canada (Minister of Citizenship and Immigration)*, 2011 FC 520; *Weldesilassie v Canada (Minister of Citizenship and Immigration)*, 2011 FC 521; *Woldesellasie v Canada (Minister of Citizenship and Immigration)*, 2011 FC 522.
88 *Ghirmatsion*, supra note 87, para 2; *Ghirmatsion v Canada (Minister of Citizenship and Immigration)*, 2011 FC 773, para 4 [*Ghirmatsion* (costs)].
89 *Ghirmatsion*, supra note 87.
90 *Ibid*, para 34.
91 *Ibid*, para 54.
92 *Ibid*, para 30.
93 CIC, *OP 5*, supra note 24, 57.
94 *Ghirmatsion*, supra note 87, paras 57–58.
95 *Ibid*.
96 *Federal Courts Rules*, SOR/98-106, s 400; *Federal Court Immigration and Refugee Protection Rules*, SOR/93-22, rule 22.
97 *Ghirmatsion* (costs), supra note 88, paras 3, 10.
98 *Ibid*, paras 9, 10.
99 *Ibid*, para 6.
100 *Ibid*, para 10. My thanks to Donald Galloway for directing me to this point.
101 *Regulations Amending the Immigration and Refugee Protection Regulations*, SOR/2012-225 [*Regulations Amending the IRPR*]; Citizenship and Immigration Canada, "Regulatory Impact Analysis Statement" 146:23 Canada Gazette Part 1 (9 July 2012) [CIC, "Regulatory Impact"]. The change is to para 153(1)(b) of the *IRPR*, supra note 17.
102 The sponsorship agreement holders (SAHs) account for approximately 60 percent of private sponsorship applications and groups of five 40 percent. Community sponsorship is minimal. CIC, "Regulatory Impact," supra note 101.
103 "Comments on Notice of Intent: Changes to the Private Sponsorship of Refugees Program" (9 January 2012), online: *Canada Council for Refugees* <ccrweb.ca/files/g5_comments_jan2012.pdf>. Canadian law goes beyond the strict refugee definition for both inland claims (*IRPA*, supra note 12, s 97) and resettlement (*IRPR*, supra note 17, s 147).
104 In 2010, 42 percent of sponsorship admissions were by groups of five, and 54 percent were SAHs. By 2014, SAH sponsorships had jumped to 79 percent of admissions, while group-of-five sponsorships plummeted to 17 percent. IRCC, "Evaluation of the Resettlement Programs" (7 July 2016), 5.7, online: *Government of Canada* <www.

cic.gc.ca/english/resources/evaluation/resettlement.asp#toc4> [IRCC, "Evaluation of Resettlement Programs"].

105 From 2006 to 2010, private sponsorship approval rates averaged 57 percent compared to a government assisted refugee (GAR) approval rating, which was closer to 90 percent. At the close of 2011, the private sponsorship backlog sat at 29,125 persons. *Regulations Amending the IRPR, supra* note 101, ii. The government's program evaluation for 2010–15 noted: "Between 2010 and 2014, PSRs had lower approval rates and longer processing time compared to GARs." However, the report also sets out that the private sponsorship of refugees (PSR) inventory was reduced by 13 percent, while the GAR inventory increased by 35 percent. IRCC, "Evaluation of Resettlement Programs," *supra* note 104.

106 CIC, *OP 5, supra* note 24, 13.3.

107 CIC, "Regulatory Impact," *supra* note 101. The Centralized Processing Offices in Winnipeg as well as in Vancouver were merged with the Matching Centre in Ottawa to create a Resettlement Operations Centre in Ottawa on 1 April 2017.

108 IRCC, "Evaluation of the Resettlement Programs," *supra* note 104, 4.1.1.

109 Jennifer Hyndman, William Payne, & Shauna Jimenez, *The State of Private Refugee Sponsorship in Canada: Trends, Issues, and Impacts*, Refugee Research Network/ Centre for Refugee Studies Policy Brief (2 December 2016), online: <refugeeresearch.net/wp-content/uploads/2017/02/hyndman_feb%E2%80%9917.pdf>. It is important to note that pre-2012 there were no limits on sponsorship applications, a reality that led to a significant backlog.

110 See David Steinbock, "The Qualities of Mercy: Maximizing the Impact of US Refugee Resettlement" (2003) 36 University of Michigan Journal of Law Reform 951, 961.

111 Davis et al, *supra* note 31, 13.

112 James C Hathaway, *The Law of Refugee Status* (Toronto: Butterworths, 1991), 231, 233.

113 CIC, News Release, "Canada's Resettlement Programs" (18 March 2011), online: <www.cic.gc.ca/english/department/media/backgrounders/2011/2011-03-18b.asp>.

114 *IRPA, supra* note 12, s 11(1).

115 Celyeste Power, quoted in Stewart Bell, "Canada Monitors Suspicious Vessel," *National Post* (16 July 2010), A1.

116 Jason Kenney, quoted in Jane Armstrong & John Ibbitson, "Seeking a Safe Haven, Finding a Closed Door," *Globe and Mail* (20 October 2009), A1.

117 Public Safety Canada, News Release, "Canada's Generous Program for Refugee Resettlement Is Undermined by Human Smugglers Who Abuse Canada's Immigration System" (21 October 2010), online: <www.publicsafety.gc.ca/cnt/nws/nws-rlss/2011/20110616-3-en.aspx?wbdisable=true> [emphasis added].

118 *Refugee Convention, supra* note 6, art 31(1).

119 *IRPA, supra* note 12, s 3(2)(b).
120 *Ibid,* s 106.

Chapter 5: Privatized Protection

1 "Canada, UNHCR and the Open Society Foundations Seek to Increase Refugee Resettlement through Private Sponsorship: News Release" (19 September 2016), online: *Government of Canada* <www.canada.ca/en/immigration-refugees-citizenship/news/2016/09/canada-unhcr-open-society-foundations-seek-increase-refugee-resettlement-through-private-sponsorship.html>.
2 "Permanent Resident Admissions by Category," online: *Government of Canada* <open.canada.ca/data/en/dataset/ad975a26-df23-456a-8ada-756191a23695>.
3 Barbara Treviranus & Michael Casasola, "Canada's Private Sponsorship of Refugees Program: A Practitioner's Perspective of Its Past and Future" (2003) 4 Journal of International Migration and Integration 177, 180.
4 Citizenship and Immigration Canada (CIC), *Guide to the Private Sponsorship of Refugees Program* (Ottawa: Minister of Public Works and Government Services Canada, 2011), 2.7, online: *Government of Canada* <www.cic.gc.ca/english/resources/publications/ref-sponsor/index.asp> [CIC, *Guide to Private Sponsorship*].
5 Canadian Council for Refugees (CCR), *The Private Sponsorship of Refugees Program: Current Challenges and Opportunities* (April 2006), 2.
6 Immigration, Refugees and Citizenship Canada (IRCC), "Guide for Groups of Five to Privately Sponsor Refugees (IMM 2200)" (5 October 2018), online: *Government of Canada* <www.canada.ca/en/immigration-refugees-citizenship/services/application/application-forms-guides/guide-sponsor-refugee-groups-five.html#costtables>.
7 CIC, *Guide to Private Sponsorship, supra* note 4.
8 See Shauna Labman, "Private Sponsorship: Complementary or Conflicting Interests?" (2016) 32:2 Refuge 67.
9 *Immigration Act, 1976,* SC 1976–77, c 52.
10 Howard Adelman, *Private Sponsorship Consultation* (1991), cited in Employment and Immigration Canada (EIC), "Private Sponsorship of Refugee Program" (1992) 12:3 Refuge 2, 2 [Adelman, *Private Sponsorship*; EIC, "Private Sponsorship"].
11 Howard Adelman, *Canada and the Indochinese Refugees* (Regina: LA Weigl Educational Associates, 1982), 85; see also 110 [Adelman, *Canada and the Indochinese Refugees*]. The Jewish Immigrant Aid Services of Canada (JIAS) was widely regarded in this period as a stand-out organization with effective and successful lobbying techniques. Freda Hawkins, *Canada and Immigration: Public Policy and Public Concern* (Montreal and Kingston: McGill-Queen's University Press, 1972), 350 [Hawkins, *Canada and Immigration*].

12 Joseph Kage, *Re-Appraising the Canadian Immigration Policy: An Analysis and Comments on the White Paper on Immigration* (January 1967), 18, Canadian Jewish Congress Charities Committee National Archives.
13 Joseph Kage, "Stepping Stones towards the New Canadian Immigration Act," *Jewish Immigrant Aid Society Information Bulletin*, vol 347 (20 November 1973), 12, Canadian Jewish Congress Charities Committee National Archives.
14 In the full quote from the excerpt above, Joseph Kage suggested to the JIAS Board of Directors: "We hope that the legislation in the forthcoming revisions of the Immigration Act will show sufficient understanding and flexibility by giving consideration to those who are refugees de jure *as well as de facto*. We also suggest that consideration be given to provisions which would *enable individuals or responsible voluntary social agencies to offer sponsorship or co-sponsorship* in deserving cases of refugees or other immigrants, which would come under the category of 'humanitarian immigration'. This may apply to individual cases or *sponsorship of groups*." Ibid, 12 [emphasis added].
15 Adelman, *Canada and the Indochinese Refugees*, supra note 11, 107.
16 William Janzen, "The 1979 MCC Canada Master Agreement for the Sponsorship of Refugees in Historical Perspective" (2006) 24 Journal of Mennonite Studies 211, 212.
17 Adelman, *Canada and the Indochinese Refugees*, supra note 11, 107.
18 Hawkins, *Canada and Immigration*, supra note 11, 304.
19 Hugh Keenleyside, Deputy Minister of Mines and Resources (Speech at Dalhousie University, November 1948), quoted in *ibid*, 239.
20 Adelman, *Canada and the Indochinese Refugees*, supra note 11, 107–8.
21 Hawkins, *Canada and Immigration*, supra note 11, 305. A thorough examination of this period can be found in Geoffrey Cameron, "Religion and Refugees: The Evolution of Refugee Resettlement in the United States and Canada" (PhD Thesis, University of Toronto, 2018).
22 Letter from Joseph Kage to RB Curry, 29 May 1969, 2, Canadian Jewish Congress Charities Committee National Archives.
23 Jewish Immigrant Aid Society, *1972 in Review: Highlights – JIAS Activities and Pending Issues* (1972), 1, Canadian Jewish Congress Charities Committee National Archives.
24 Letter from Joseph Kage to Robert M Adams, 18 December 1972, 1–2, Canadian Jewish Congress Charities Committee National Archives.
25 Treviranus & Casasola, *supra* note 3, 184.
26 Mike Molloy, Former Director of Refugee Policy Division, interview with author, 24 March 2011; Janzen, *supra* note 16, 212.
27 Janzen, *supra* note 16, 212.
28 Citizenship and Immigration Canada, "Regulatory Impact Analysis Statement" 146:23 Canada Gazette Part1 (9 June 2012) [CIC, "Regulatory Impact"].

29 "Private Sponsorship of Refugees Program: Sponsorship Agreement Holders," online: *Government of Canada* <www.cic.gc.ca/english/refugees/sponsor/list-sponsors.asp>.
30 CCR and Elected Sponsorship Agreement Holder Representatives, *Comments on Private Sponsorship Evaluation* (Montreal: CCR, 2007), 8.
31 CIC, *Guide to Private Sponsorship, supra* note 4, 2.3; *Immigration and Refugee Protection Act*, SC 2001, c 27 [*IRPA*].
32 *Immigration and Refugee Protection Regulations*, SOR/2002-227, s 157 [*IRPR*].
33 CIC, *Guide to Private Sponsorship, supra* note 4, 3.1.
34 Ibid.
35 Treviranus & Casasola, *supra* note 3, 182.
36 CIC, *Guide to Private Sponsorship, supra* note 4, 3.1.
37 Rivka Augenfeld, former JIAS employee, telephone interview with author, 9 July 2010; interview with author, 23 August 2010.
38 CIC, *Guide to Private Sponsorship, supra* note 4, 2.9.
39 CIC, "Summative Evaluation of the Private Sponsorship of Refugees Program" (2007), 3.2.4 ["Summative Evaluation"]; see also "Selection" section of Tom Denton, "Unintended Consequences of Canada's Private Sponsorship of Refugees Program" (9 September 2013), online: *Hospitality House* <www.hhrmwpg.org/opinion/unintended-consequences-of-canada-s-private-sponsorship-of-refugees-program_102>.
40 CIC, *Blended Visa Office–Referred Program: Sponsoring Refugees* (30 April 2014) [CIC, *Blended Visa Office–Referred Program*]. The blended visa office–referred (BVOR) program will be discussed in more detail in Chapter 6.
41 A point acknowledged by IRCC in 2016 when it committed to "review the VOR program in order to assess its continued relevance in light of the BVOR program." IRCC, "Evaluation of the Resettlement Programs" (7 July 2016), Action No 2a, online: *Government of Canada* <www.cic.gc.ca/english/resources/evaluation/resettlement.asp#toc-eval> [IRCC, "Evaluation of Resettlement Programs"].
42 CIC, "Undertaking/Application to Sponsor (IMM 5373)" (October 2013), s E(i).
43 CIC, *Guide to Private Sponsorship, supra* note 4, 2.8.
44 "Resettlement Assistance Program," online: *Government of Canada* <www.cic.gc.ca/english/refugees/outside/resettle-assist.asp>.
45 Navjot K Lamba & Harvey Krahn, "Social Capital and Refugee Resettlement: The Social Networks of Refugees in Canada" (2003) 4 Journal of International Migration and Integration 335, 339.
46 Treviranus & Casasola, *supra* note 3, 182. Lamba and Krahn's survey, for example, consisted of data collected from only 525 adult refugees resettled in Alberta in the 1990s on their formal and informal social networks. Lamba & Krahn, *supra* note 45; see also Jennifer Hyndman, William Payne, & Shauna Jimenez, "The State of Private Refugee Sponsorship in Canada: Trends, Issues, and Impacts," policy brief (20 January

2017), 2, 3, 8, online: *Refugee Research Network/Centre for Refugee Studies* <jhyndman.info.yorku.ca/files/2017/05/hyndman_et-al.-RRN-brief-Jan-2017-best.pdf>.
47 EIC, "Private Sponsorship," *supra* note 10, 8.
48 CIC, *Guide to Private Sponsorship*, *supra* note 4.
49 EIC, "Private Sponsorship," *supra* note 10, 2.
50 CIC, *PSRP: Results-Based Management and Accountability Framework (RMAF)*, final report (November 2004), 4.
51 "Important Changes in Canada's Private Sponsorship of Refugees Program" (January 2013), online: *Canadian Council for Refugees* <ccrweb.ca/en/changes-private-sponsorship-refugees>.
52 IRCC, "Evaluation of Resettlement Programs," *supra* note 41, 4.2.2.
53 Adelman, *Canada and the Indochinese Refugees*, *supra* note 11, 85, 109; see also Janzen, *supra* note 16, 219.
54 Janzen, *supra* note 16, 211.
55 Augenfeld, interviews, *supra* note 37.
56 *Immigration Act, 1976*, *supra* note 9.
57 EIC, *Indochinese Refugees: The Canadian Response, 1979 and 1980* (Ottawa: Minister of Supply and Services Canada, 1982), 8 [EIC, *Indochinese Refugees*]; see also Mike Molloy et al, *Running on Empty: Canada and the Indochinese Refugees 1975–1980* (Montreal and Kingston: McGill-Queen's University Press, 2017).
58 EIC, *Indochinese Refugees*, *supra* note 57.
59 *Ibid*.
60 *Ibid*.
61 David Humphreys, "Two Ministers Condemn Vietnam, Canada Will Take 3,000 More Asian Refugees," *Globe and Mail* (22 June 1979), P9.
62 Molloy, interview, *supra* note 26. Mike Molloy, email correspondence with author, 12 November 2018.
63 Janzen, *supra* note 16, 217.
64 Molloy, interview, *supra* note 26; Molloy, email correspondence, *supra* note 62.
65 Howard Adelman, "The Policy Maker and the Advocate: Case Studies in Refugee Policy" in Peter Harries-Jones, ed, *Making Knowledge Count: Advocacy and Social Science* (Montreal and Kingston: McGill-Queen's University Press, 1991) 54, 62 [Adelman, "The Policy Maker"]; Howard Adelman, telephone interview with author, 8 July 2010. The meeting resulted in the creation of "Operation Lifeline," a name given by Dick Beddoes in a newspaper article on the sponsorship that credited Adelman with its genesis. Dick Beddoes, "A Rush of Aid," *Globe and Mail* (27 June 1979), P8. Operation Lifeline became a leader in organizing and promoting the Indochinese sponsorship.

66 Robert Sheppard, "Ottawa's Challenge: Triple Flow of Refugees to 50,000," *Globe and Mail* (19 July 1979), P1.
67 Adelman, "The Policy Maker," *supra* note 65, 60.
68 Treviranus & Casasola, *supra* note 3, 184.
69 Gertrude Neuwirth & JR Rogge, "Canada and the Indochinese Refugees" in Supang Chantavanich and E Bruce Reynolds, eds, *Indochinese Refugees: Asylum and Resettlement* (Bangkok: Institute of Asian Studies, Chulalongkorn University, 1988) 249, 254.
70 James C Hathaway, "Selective Concern: An Overview of Refugee Law in Canada" (1987–88) 33 McGill Law Journal 676, 685 [emphasis added].
71 Canada Employment and Immigration Commission, Refugee Policy Division, *Refugee and Humanitarian Plans* (1980), 3.
72 Rosie DiManno, "Refugee Burden Is Too Heavy, Private Sponsorship Head Says," *Globe and Mail* (25 July 1979), P4.
73 *Immigration Act, 1976*, *supra* note 9.
74 EIC, *Indochinese Refugees*, *supra* note 57, 18.
75 Robert Kaplan, "A Critique of Government Policy on Refugees" in Howard Adelman, ed, *The Indochinese Refugee Movement: The Canadian Experience* (Toronto: Operation Lifeline, 1979) 17, 18 [Adelman, *Indochinese Refugee Movement*].
76 Neuwirth & Rogge, *supra* note 69, 255.
77 EIC, *Indochinese Refugees*, *supra* note 57, 8.
78 *Ibid*, 14.
79 Ninette Kelley & Michael J Trebilcock, *The Making of the Mosaic: A History of Canadian Immigration Policy* (Toronto: University of Toronto Press, 1998), 407.
80 Freda Hawkins, *Critical Years in Immigration: Canada and Australia Compared*, 2nd ed (Montreal and Kingston: McGill-Queen's University Press, 1991), 184.
81 Adelman, telephone interview, *supra* note 65.
82 *Ibid*.
83 Adelman, "The Policy Maker," *supra* note 65, 62; Howard Adelman, "Changes in Policy: Background on the Federal Government Decision to Alter Its Position with Respect to the Indochinese Refugees" in Adelman, *Indochinese Refugee Movement*, *supra* note 75, 23, 23 [Adelman, "Changes in Policy"].
84 Adelman, "Changes in Policy," *supra* note 83, 23.
85 Canadian Press, "Onus Put on Public Groups, Ottawa Won't Sponsor More Refugees," *Globe and Mail* (6 December 1979), P1.
86 Formed in 1978, the Standing Conference of Organizations Concerned for Refugees was the original name of the Canadian Council for Refugees. "Canada Refugee History," online: *Canadian Council on Refugees* <ccrweb.ca/canadarefugeeshistory5.htm>.

87 Quoted in Adelman, "Changes in Policy," *supra* note 83, 25.
88 "Ottawa Revamps Refugee Program, Increases 1980 Quota by 10,000," *Globe and Mail* (3 April 1980), P1.
89 Gerald E Dirks, "A Policy within a Policy: The Identification and Admission of Refugees to Canada" (1984) 17 Canadian Journal of Political Science 279, 299.
90 *Ibid*, 295–96.
91 Canada Employment and Immigration Commission, *supra* note 71, s 3.
92 Dirks, *supra* note 89, 296.
93 *Ibid*, 299.
94 *Ibid*.
95 Thomas Walkom, "No Bias in Shuffled Border Quotas, Axworthy," *Globe and Mail* (4 November 1981), P8.
96 It was in 1986 that the United Nations High Commissioner for Refugees (UNHCR) awarded the people of Canada the Nansen Medal for their resettlement of the Indochinese. "Archive of Past Nansen Winners," online: *UNHCR* <www.unhcr.org/previous-nansen-winners.html>. While recipients have included private citizens, politicians, royalty, and organizations, the award to the Canadian people is the only instance in which the entire population of a country has been recognized.
97 See Table 4: Private sponsorship ranges and landings, 1979–2021, in this chapter.
98 Treviranus & Casasola, *supra* note 3, 186.
99 Robert Holten & Michael Lanphier, "Public Opinion, Immigration and Refugees" in Howard Adelman et al, eds, *Immigration and Refugee Policy: Australia and Canada Compared* (Toronto: University of Toronto Press, 1994), vol 1, 125, 132.
100 EIC, "Private Sponsorship," *supra* note 10, 5; Adelman, *Private Sponsorship*, *supra* note 10.
101 EIC, "Private Sponsorship," *supra* note 10, 3.
102 *Ibid*, 4.
103 Treviranus & Casasola, *supra* note 3, 190.
104 Thomas R Denton, "Understanding Private Refugee Sponsorship in Manitoba" (2003) 4 Journal of International Migration and Integration 257, 264 [Denton, "Understanding"].
105 Rivka Augenfeld, "Giving Refugees a Second Chance: A Personal Reflection on Refugee Sponorship," *JIAS Canada Newsletter* (April 2004), 2.
106 Treviranus & Casasola, *supra* note 3, 178.
107 EIC, *Indochinese Refugees*, *supra* note 57, 12.
108 "Summative Evaluation," *supra* note 39, 3.2.4.
109 Denton, "Understanding," *supra* note 104, 258.
110 Thomas R Denton, "Relational Migration and Refugee Policy" (paper presented at 2011 National Metropolis Conference, Vancouver, BC, 25 March 2011) [Denton, "Relational Migration"].

111 *IRPA, supra* note 31, s 12.
112 Denton, "Relational Migration," *supra* note 110, 4.
113 EIC, "Private Sponsorship," *supra* note 10, 4.
114 *Ibid.*
115 UNHCR, "Standing Committee 15th Meeting – Family Protection Issues EC/49/Sc/Crp.14" (1999) 18:4 Refugee Survey Quarterly 155, 159. The UNHCR considers family reunification as a criterion in its resettlement referrals. UNHCR Resettlement Service, *UNHCR-NGO Toolkit for Practical Cooperation on Resettlement: 1. Operational Activities – Identification and Referral of Refugees in Need of Resettlement: Definitions and FAQs* (June 2015), 245, online: <www.unhcr.org/protection/resettlement/4cd416d79/unhcr-ngo-toolkit-practical-cooperation-resettlement-1-operational-activities.html>.
116 Treviranus & Casasola, *supra* note 3, 187.
117 In 2005, a non-governmental organization (NGO)–government sub-committee was created as a sub-set of the NGO-Government Committee and meets more frequently with a greater focus on operational and policy issues. "Summative Evaluation," *supra* note 39, 1.2.1.
118 Kelley & Trebilcock, *supra* note 79, 406.
119 CIC, *A Broader Vision: Immigration and Citizenship Plan 1995–2000* (1994), 21.
120 CIC, "Speaking Notes for the Honourable Jason Kenney, P.C., M.P. Minister of Citizenship, Immigration and Multiculturalism" (29 June 2010) [on file with author].
121 "2012 Federal Budget" (29 March 2012), online: *Government of Canada* <www.budget.gc.ca//2012/home-accueil-eng.html>, shows the planned reduction in Citizenship and Immigration Canada's spending in Table 5.1 resulting from this shift; see also CIC, "Departmental Performance Report for the period ending March 31, 2012," online: *Government of Canada* <www.cic.gc.ca/english/resources/publications/dpr/2012/dpr.asp#strategic2-5>.
122 Debra Pressé, Director of Refugee Resettlement at Citizenship and Immigration Canada, interview with author, 18 November 2009.
123 "Summative Evaluation," *supra* note 39, 1.2.1.
124 CIC, *A Broader Vision: Immigration Plan (1996 Annual Report to Parliament)* (Canada: Minister of Supply and Services Canada, 1995), 14.
125 CIC, *Guide to Private Sponsorship, supra* note 4, 3.1.
126 Denton, "Relational Migration," *supra* note 110, 3.
127 CIC, News Release, "Government of Canada and the Anglican Church of Canada Encourage Canadians to Sponsor Refugees" (16 April 2009), online: <www.cic.gc.ca/english/department/media/releases/2009/2009-04-16.asp>; Suzanne Rumsey, Public Engagement Program Coordinator, Primate's World Relief and Development Fund, Anglican Church of Canada, email correspondence with author, 13 December 2010.

128 CIC, News Release, "Canada and Anglican Church Give 50 Refugee Families New Hope" (13 Febraury 2012).
129 CIC, News Release, "Canada's Commitment to Iraqi Refugees Remains Strong" (18 March 2011) [CIC, "Canada's Commitment"].
130 Citizenship and Immigration Canada (CIC), *2009 Annual Report to Parliament on Immigration* (2009), online: <www.publications.gc.ca/collections/collection_2010/cic/Ci1-2009-eng.pdf> ["2009 Annual Report"].
131 Significant Iraqi resettlement had already been achieved. In 2009, more than 1,400 Iraqi refugees were resettled as government-assisted refugees (GARs), and 2,500 were privately sponsored. In 2010, 1,700 Iraqi refugees were resettled through the GAR program, and 2,300 were privately sponsored. CIC, News Release, "Canada's Resettlement Programs" (18 March 2011), online: <www.cic.gc.ca/english/department/media/backgrounders/2011/2011-03-18b.asp>.
132 CIC, "Canada's Commitment," *supra* note 129.
133 *Ibid.*
134 CIC, News Release, "Government of Canada to Help Gay and Lesbian Refugees Fleeing Persecution" (24 March 2011) [CIC, "Government of Canada"].
135 *Ibid.* Sharalyn Jordan, Rainbow Refugee Committee, email correspondence with author, 1 April 2011.
136 CIC, "Government of Canada," *supra* note 134; Jordan, email correspondence, *supra* note 135.
137 CIC, *Blended Visa Office–Referred Program*, *supra* note 40.
138 "Summative Evaluation," *supra* note 39, 1.2.1.
139 Jackie Halliburton, City of Winnipeg, Wellness and Diversity Coordinator, interview with author, 11 March 2011.
140 S West, Corporate Support Services and Community Services, *Syrian Humanitarian Crises: Refugee Resettlement Assistance* (Winnipeg: Executive Policy Committee, 14 October 2015), 5 [on file with author].
141 Winnipeg Private Refugee Assurance Program, *Report of the Executive Policy Committee*, File G-8 (18 September 2002), vol 6, 199.38.
142 *Agreement to Establish the Winnipeg Private Refugee Sponsorship Assurance Program between the City of Winnipeg and Manitoba Refugee Sponsors Group* (October 2002) [*Agreement on Winnipeg Private Refugee Program*]; Tom Carter et al, *Privately Sponsored Refugees Phase One Report*, prepared for Manitoba Labour and Immigration (Winnipeg: University of Winnipeg, 2008), 57.
143 *Agreement on Winnipeg Private Refugee Program*, *supra* note 142. The yearly $30,000 was initially renewed for two years by Mayor Katz and was then subject to annual renewal.
144 Winnipeg Private Refugee Assurance Program, *supra* note 141, 199.37.

145 *Ibid*, 199.38.
146 Corporate Support Services and Community Services, *supra* note 140, 6; City of Winnipeg, Executive Policy Committee, *Reports* "Winnipeg Private Refugee Sponsorship Assurance Program" (17 January 2018).
147 Manitoba Interfaith Immigration Council, *2010 Annual Report: Summarized Financial Statements* (31 March 2010); *Agreement on Winnipeg Private Refugee Program*, *supra* note 142.
148 Halliburton, interview, *supra* note 139.
149 *Ibid*.
150 Corporate Support Services and Community Services, *supra* note 140, 6.
151 *Ibid*.
152 Denton, "Relational Migration," *supra* note 110.
153 Halliburton, interview, *supra* note 139.
154 Evelyn Jones, Immigrant Settlement and Integration Services Refugee Sponsorship Coordinator, email correspondence with author, 18 June 2012; Immigrant Settlement and Integration Services, *ISIS Annual Report 2012* (2012), 6 [on file with author].
155 Samantha Power, *"A Problem from Hell": America and the Age of Genocide* (New York: Perennial, 2003), 444–50.
156 CIC, News Release, 99-24, "Appeal to Canadians to Sponsor the Kosovar Refugees" (10 May 1999) [on file with author].
157 Treviranus & Casasola, *supra* note 3, 192; see also Pressé, interview, *supra* note 122.
158 CIC, *Planning Now for Canada's Future: Introducing a Multi-Year Planning Process and the Immigration Plan for 2001 and 2002* (2001), 19.
159 "Facts and Figures 2005" (2005), online: *Government of Canada* <web.archive.org/web/20061231004748/www.cic.gc.ca/english/pub/facts2005/overview/01.html>.
160 UNHCR, *Protection Framework Guidance: Kosovo Situation – Revision 1* (30 April 1999), online: <www.unhcr.org/refworld/docid/3ae6b33414.html>.
161 Treviranus & Casasola, *supra* note 3, 194.
162 Jane Armstrong, "The Boat People's Big Gamble," *Globe and Mail* (22 July 2000), A7.
163 See Kathy Sherrell, Jennifer Hyndman, & Preniqi Fisnik, "Sharing the Wealth, Spreading the 'Burden'? The Settlement of Kosovar Refugees in Smaller British Columbia Cities" (2005) 37 Canadian Ethnic Studies 76.
164 Treviranus & Casasola, *supra* note 3, 194.
165 "#WelcomeRefugees: Canada Resettled Syrian Refugees," online: *Government of Canada* <www.cic.gc.ca/english/refugees/welcome/index.asp>; Danielle da Silva, "Operation Ezra Welcomes More Yazidi Newcomers," *Winnipeg Free Press* (24 February 2017), online: <www.winnipegfreepress.com/our-communities/souwester/Operation-Ezra-welcomes-more-Yazidi-newcomers-414744693.html>; IRCC, News Release, "Canada to Welcome 1200 Yazidi and Other Survivors of Daesh"

(21 February 2017), online: <www.canada.ca/en/immigration-refugees-citizenship/news/2017/02/canada_to_welcome1200yazidiandothersurvivorsofdaesh.html>.
166 Pressé, interview, *supra* note 122; "Summative Evaluation," *supra* note 39, 3.2.3.
167 "Summative Evaluation," *supra* note 39, 4.0.
168 CIC, "Regulatory Impact," *supra* note 28.
169 Standing Committee on Immigration and Citizenship, MP Norman Doyle, Chair, "Safeguarding Asylum – Sustaining Canada's Commitments to Refugees," 39-1 (Ottawa: House of Commons, 2007), "Introduction."
170 *Ibid*. Ed Wiebe, Coordinator, National Refugee Program, Mennonite Central Committee Canada, noted to the committee: "Last spring, I and six of my colleagues from Canada and two based in Africa spent several weeks exploring refugee protection issues in Kenya and South Africa, including many NGO visits, visits with UNHCR hubs and branch offices, and also visits with the respective Canadian High Commissions in each of those countries. Something that stands out was a comment we heard several times from NGOs involved in resettlement. They noted how difficult it must be for Canadian SAHs to assess refugee cases exclusively from within Canada when they find it incredibly difficult to do that right at the source."
171 CCR and Elected Sponsorship Agreement Holder Representatives, *supra* note 30, 4.
172 *Ibid*, 6.
173 *Ibid*, 4.
174 CIC, *Departmental Performance Report for the Period Ending March 31, 2003* (Ottawa: Minister of Public Works and Government Services, 2003).
175 "About the RSTP," online: *Refugee Sponsorship Training Program* <www.rstp.ca/index.php>.
176 "Community Sponsorship of Refugees Guidebook and Planning Tools" (2017), online: *Global Refugee Sponsorship Initiative* <www.refugeesponsorship.org/guidebook>.
177 IRCC, "Evaluation of Resettlement Programs," *supra* note 41, 5.4.2.
178 CIC, *Departmental Performance Report for the Period Ending March 31, 2002* (Ottawa: Minister of Public Works and Government Services, 2002), 23 [CIC, *Departmental Performance Report 2002*].
179 Pressé, interview, *supra* note 122.
180 Treviranus & Casasola, *supra* note 3, 195.
181 CIC, *Departmental Performance Report 2002*, *supra* note 178, 23.
182 "2009 Annual Report," *supra* note 130.
183 CIC, News Release, "Expanding Canada's Refugee Resettlement Programs" (29 March 2010).
184 "2012 Federal Budget," *supra* note 121.
185 Catherine Dauvergne, *Humanitarianism, Identity, and Nation: Migration Laws of Australia and Canada* (Vancouver: UBC Press, 2005), 93.

186 CIC, "Canada's Commitment," *supra* note 129.
187 "2009 Annual Report," *supra* note 130.
188 "Annual Report to Parliament on Immigration 2011: Supplementary Information for the 2012 Immigration Levels Plan" (4 November 2011) online: *Government of Canada* <www.cic.gc.ca/english/department/media/notices/notice-levels2012.asp>.
189 "2009 Annual Report," *supra* note 130.
190 "2012 Federal Budget," *supra* note 121.
191 See Table 4, pp. 96–97.
192 CIC, "Regulatory Impact," *supra* note 28.
193 Hyndman, Payne & Jimenez, *supra* note 46, 3.
194 Tom Denton, "Refugee Program Good in Theory, Flawed in Practice," *Winnipeg Free Press* (21 September 2016), A7.
195 Tom Denton, Executive Director, Hospitality House Refugee Ministry, email correspondence with author, 21 July 2017.
196 "Providing Timely Protection for Privately Sponsored Refugees," online: *Government of Canada* <www.cic.gc.ca/english/department/laws-policy/protect-psr.asp>.

Chapter 6: The State of Sponsorship

1 Barbara Treviranus & Michael Casasola, "Canada's Private Sponsorship of Refugees Program: A Practitioner's Perspective of Its Past and Future" (2003) 4 Journal of International Migration and Integration 177, 178; United Nations High Commissioner for Refugees (UNHCR), *Resettlement Handbook* (November 2004), 220.
2 Treviranus & Casasola, *supra* note 1, 183.
3 Canadian Council for Refugees (CCR) & Elected Sponsorship Agreement Holder Representatives, *Comments on Private Sponsorship Evaluation* (Montreal: CCR, 2007), 5.
4 James C Hathaway, "Selective Concern: An Overview of Refugee Law in Canada" (1987–88) 33 McGill Law Journal 676, 700.
5 Employment and Immigration Canada (EIC), "Private Sponsorship of Refugee Program" (1992) 12 Refuge 2, 3.
6 Donald Galloway, "Liberalism, Globalism, and Immigration" (1993) 18 Queen's Law Journal 266, 295.
7 Howard Adelman, "The Policy Maker and the Advocate: Case Studies in Refugee Policy" in Peter Harries-Jones, ed, *Making Knowledge Count: Advocacy and Social Science* (Montreal and Kingston: McGill-Queen's University Press, 1991) 54, 56.
8 Components of this section are developed in Shauna Labman & Madison Pearlman, "Blending, Bargaining, and Burden-Sharing: Canada's Resettlement Programs" (2018) 19:2 Journal of International Migration and Integration 439.

9 Mennonite Central Committee, *Blended VOR Initiative: 2014 Update* (2014); Citizenship and Immigration Canada (CIC), *Guide to the Private Sponsorship of Refugees Program* (Ottawa: Minister of Public Works and Government Services Canada, 2011), 11, online: <www.cic.gc.ca/english/resources/publications/refsponsor/index.asp>.
10 "Facts and Figures 2014," online: *Government of Canada* <www.cic.gc.ca/english/pdf/2014-Facts-Permanent.pdf>.
11 The government's own evaluation noted "less engagement" with the blended visa office–referred (BVOR) program than with either the sponsorship agreement holders (SAHs) or the groups of five. Immigration, Refugees and Citizenship Canada (IRCC), "Evaluation of the Resettlement Programs" (7 July 2016), 5.4.1, online: *Government of Canada* <www.cic.gc.ca/english/resources/evaluation/resettlement.asp#toc-eval> [IRCC, "Evaluation of Resettlement Programs"].
12 "2012 Federal Budget" (29 March 2012), Table 5.1, online: *Government of Canada* <budget.gc.ca/2012/home-accueil-eng.html>. Table 5.1 shows the planned reduction in the CIC's spending, resulting from this shift; see also CIC, "Departmental Performance Report for the period ending March 31, 2012," online: *Government of Canada* <www.cic.gc.ca/english/resources/publications/dpr/2012/dpr.asp#strategic2-5>.
13 "Statement on Blended Visa Office Referred Refugees" (21 July 2016), online: *Canada Council for Refugees* <ccrweb.ca/en/BVOR-statement>.
14 IRCC, "Evaluation of Resettlement Programs," *supra* note 11, 5.2.1.
15 Carol Sanders, "More Refugees Approved, Sponsors Needed," *Winnipeg Free Press* (21 April 2012), A14.
16 Ratna Omidvar, "Private Sponsors Build a Nation – and Leave a Legacy," *Globe and Mail* (16 November 2015); Caroline Barghout, "Image of Alan Kurdi Dead on a Beach Moves Winnipeg Woman to Help Syrian Refugees," *CBC News* (25 November 2015).
17 CIC, "2016 Annual Report to Parliament on Immigration," online: *Government of Canada* <www.cic.gc.ca/english/resources/publications/annual-report-2016/index.asp>.
18 The IRCC tracked Syrian resettlement numbers from 4 November 2015 to 29 January 2017 on "#Welcome Refugees: Key Figures," online: *Government of Canada* <www.cic.gc.ca/english/refugees/welcome/milestones.asp>.
19 IRCC, "Notice – Supplementary Information for the 2017 Immigration Levels Plan," online: *Government of Canada* <www.cic.gc.ca/english/department/media/notices/2016-10-31.asp>.
20 IRCC, "Notice: Supplementary Information 2019–2021" (31 October 2018), online: *Government of Canada* <www.canada.ca/content/dam/ircc/migration/ircc/english/pdf/pub/annual-report-2018.pdf>.

21 Ibid.
22 Sheena Goodyear, "Syrian Refugees Not Always Available for Sponsorship, Canadians Learn," *CBC News* (23 December 2015); Judy Aldous, "Sponsoring Syrian Refugees Easier Said than Done, Calgary Group Finds," *CBC News* (8 October 2015).
23 Wendy Lai, "A Balance of Excitement and Apprehension" (15 July 2015), online: *Ripple Refugee Project* <ripplerefugee.blogspot.ca/search?updated-max=2015-09-05T11:44:00-07:00&max-results=7>. My thanks to Elizabeth Coffin-Karlin, 2017 summer fellow, Spanish Commission for Refugees, Madrid, for directing me to this passage.
24 Stephanie Levitz, "Syrian Refugee Sponsors Upset with Slowing Pace of Arrivals," *CBC News* (29 March 2016).
25 "Syrian BVOR Info Sheet" (2016), 2, online: *Refugee Sponsorship Training Program* <www.rstp.ca/wp-content/uploads/2014/03/Syrian-BVOR-Info-Sheet_May-2016.pdf>.
26 Letter from David Manicom, Associate Assistant Deputy Minister, Strategic and Program Policy Sector, and Dawn Edlund, Associate Assistant Deputy Minister, Operations Sector, to SAH Council, August 2016 [on file with author].
27 Ibid.
28 Nicholas Keung, "Ottawa Offers Trade-In for Refugee Sponsors Caught in Delays," *Toronto Star* (31 August 2016), online: <www.thestar.com/news/immigration/2016/08/31/ottawa-offers-trade-in-for-refugee-sponsors-caught-in-delays.html>.
29 Eric Andrew-Gee, "Sponsors of Refugees Awaiting Security Clearance Offered 'Replacement' Families," *Globe and Mail* (2 September 2016), online: <www.theglobeandmail.com/news/national/sponsors-of-refugees-awaiting-security-clearance-offered-replacement-families/article31699220/>.
30 Ibid.
31 Thomas R Denton, "Relational Migration and Refugee Policy" (paper presented at 2011 National Metropolis Conference, Vancouver, British Columbia, 25 March 2011).
32 See Jodi Kantor & Catrin Einhorn, "What Does It Mean to Help One Family?" *New York Times* (22 October 2016), online: <www.nytimes.com/interactive/2016/10/22/world/americas/canada-refugees-syria.html?mcubz=1>.
33 See Ashley Chapman, *Private Sponsorship and Public Policy: Political Barriers to Church-Connected Refugee Resettlement in Canada* (Ottawa: Citizens for Public Justice, September 2014), online: <www.cpj.ca/sites/default/files/docs/files/PrivateSponsorshipandPublicPolicyReport.pdf>; "Letter from Rick Cober Bauman, Executive Director, Mennonite Central Committee Ontario, to Member of Parliament," 4 April 2016, online: *Mennonite Central Committee* <mcccanada.ca/sites/mcccanada.ca/files/media/common/documents/mpsrefugeerightsdayletter-signedapril42016.pdf>.

34 IRCC, "Evaluation of Resettlement Programs," *supra* note 11, Recommendation No 2.
35 *Ibid*, Response No 2.
36 Power and Politics, "Canada Has Taken the Mantle of Humanitarian Leadership in the World," *CBC News* (21 March 2016), online: <https://www.cbc.ca/player/play/2685680470>.
37 Stephanie Levitz, "Canada's Refugee Effort Hailed as Model for World by Head of UN Agency," *CBC News* (21 March 2016), online: <www.cbc.ca/news/politics/un-refugee-private-government-sponsor-1.3501400>.
38 "High-Level Meetings of the 71st Session (2016)," online: *United Nations General Assembly* <www.un.org/en/ga/71/meetings/>.
39 "Canada, UNHCR and the Open Society Foundations Seek to Increase Refugee Resettlement through Private Sponsorship: News Release" (19 September 2016), online: *Government of Canada* <www.canada.ca/en/immigration-refugees-citizenship/news/2016/09/canada-unhcr-open-society-foundations-seek-increase-refugee-resettlement-through-private-sponsorship.html>. The University of Ottawa and the Radcliffe Foundation later formalized partnerships as well.
40 "Global Refugee Sponsorship Initiative Promotes Canada's Private Refugee Sponsorship Model: News Release" (15 December 2016), online: *Government of Canada* <www.canada.ca/en/immigration-refugees-citizenship/news/2016/12/global-refugee-sponsorship-initiative-promotes-canada-private-refugee-sponsorship-model.html?=undefined&wbdisable=true>.
41 "About GRSI," online: *Global Refugee Sponsorship Initiative* <www.refugeesponsorship.org/who-we-are>.
42 Kathleen Harris, "'Extraordinary Initiative': Canada's Private Refugee Sponsorship System Exported as Model for the World," *CBC News* (14 December 2016), online: <www.cbc.ca/news/politics/canada-refugees-privately-sponsored-global-initiative-1.3895704>.
43 Kristen Shane, "Exporting a Canadian Success Story," *Hill Times* (8 February 2017), online: <www.hilltimes.com/2017/02/08/exporting-canadian-success-story/94736>.
44 "Global Initiative Brings Canada's Refugee Sponsorship Model to the World" (27 June 2017), online: *Global Refugee Sponsorship Initiative* <docs.wixstatic.com/ugd/7b79e6_ea40ad5508304e2da7378a8b6cbb5d90.pdf>.
45 Judith Kumin, *Welcoming Engagement: How Private Sponsorship Can Strengthen Refugee Resettlement in the European Union* (Brussels: Migration Policy Institute Europe, 2015), 4, online: <www.migrationpolicy.org/research/welcoming-engagement-how-private-sponsorship-can-strengthen-refugee-resettlement-european>.

46 Theresa May, address delivered at the Conservative Party Conference, Manchester, reprinted in "Theresa May's Speech to the Conservative Party Conference – in Full," *Independent* (6 October 2015), online: <www.independent.co.uk/news/uk/politics/theresa-may-s-speech-to-the-conservative-party-conference-in-full-a6681901.html>.
47 Kumin, *supra* note 45, 4.
48 Refugee Council of Australia, *Australia's Refugee and Humanitarian Program: Community Views on Current Challenges and Future Directions*, 2010 Intake Submission (2010), 3.
49 Department of Immigration and Border Protection, "Community Support Program Consultation," online: *Refugee Council of Australia* <www.refugeecouncil.org.au/wp-content/uploads/2015/07/1507-CSP.pdf>.
50 Kumin, *supra* note 45.
51 Daniel Hiebert, *What's So Special about Canada? Understanding the Resilience of Immigration and Multiculturalism* (Washington, DC: Migration Policy Institute, 2016), 13.
52 Bolu Coker, "Canada's Refugee Policy Must Be Improved before Export" (28 September 2016), online: *Citizens for Public Justice* <www.cpj.ca/canada-s-refugee-policy-must-be-improved-export>.
53 Jennifer Hyndman, William Payne, & Shauna Jimenez, "The State of Private Refugee Sponsorship in Canada: Trends, Issues, and Impacts," policy brief (2 December 2016), 9–12, online: *Refugee Research Network/Centre for Refugee Studies* <http://refugeeresearch.net/wp-content/uploads/2017/02/hyndman_feb%E2%80%9917.pdf>.
54 Shauna Labman, "Private Sponsorship: Complementary or Conflicting Interests?" (2016) 32:2 Refuge 67.
55 Stuart Scheingold, *The Politics of Rights: Lawyers, Public Policy and Political Change* (Ann Arbor: University of Michigan Press, 2004), 39.
56 *Ibid*, 58.
57 See Matthew J Gibney, *The Ethics and Politics of Asylum: Liberal Democracy and the Response to Refugees* (Cambridge, UK: Cambridge University Press, 2004); Catherine Dauvergne, *Humanitarianism, Identity, and Nation: Migration Laws of Australia and Canada* (Vancouver: UBC Press, 2005).
58 Dauvergne, *supra* note 57, 174.
59 Hathaway, *supra* note 4, 700.
60 The Nordic countries provide the UNHCR with an emergency quota that permits the quick transfer of refugees in certain circumstances, usually for medical reasons. "Resettlement in the Nordics and the Role of UNHCR," online: *UNHCR* <www.unhcr.se/en/what-we-do/durable-solutions/resettlement-in-the-region.html>.

61 Gregor Noll & Joanne van Selm, "Rediscovering Resettlement: A Transatlantic Comparison of Refugee Protection" (2003) 3 Migration Policy Institute Insight 1; Joanne van Selm, "Public-Private Partnerships in Refugee Resettlement: Europe and the US" (2003) 4:2 Journal of International Migration and Integration 157.
62 Van Selm, *supra* note 61, 159.
63 See Stephen Castles, "The Factors that Make and Unmake Migration Policies" (2004) 38 International Migration Review 852, 870.
64 *Immigration Act, 1976*, SC 1976-77, c 52, s 3(G).
65 Hathaway, *supra* note 4, 700.
66 Between the spring of 1975 and the spring of 1980, Canada's five-year resettlement total was 74,000. With a population of twenty-four million, this meant a ratio of refugees to population of 1 to 324. Australia's ratio during the same period was 1 to 332, and the United States was 1 to 374. EIC, *Indochinese Refugees: The Canadian Response, 1979 and 1980* (Ottawa: Minister of Supply and Services Canada, 1982), 33.
67 "Canada, UNHCR and the Open Society Foundations," *supra* note 39.
68 "Nairobi: Protection Delayed, Protection Denied" (2009), online: *Canada Council for Refugees* <www.ccrweb.ca/documents/Nairobireport.pdf>; CCR, Media Release, "Disturbing Upsurge in Rejections of Eritrean Refugees in Cairo by Canada" (30 November 2009).
69 Pilar Riaño Alcalá et al, *Forced Migration of Colombians: Colombia, Ecuador, Canada* (Colombia and Vancouver: Corporación Región School of Social Work (Spanish) and University of British Columbia (English), 2008), 125.
70 African resettlement jumped from 1,473 (14 percent of the offshore program) in 1997–98 to 8,486 (70 percent of the offshore program) in 2004–05. Mary Crock, Ben Saul, & Azadeh Dastyari, *Future Seekers II: Refugees and Irregular Migration in Australia* (Sydney: Federation Press, 2006), 15–16.
71 CIC, "#WelcomeRefugees: Canada Resettled Syrian Refugees," online: *Government of Canada* <www.cic.gc.ca/english/refugees/welcome/index.asp>; Jodi Kantor & Catrin Einhorn, "Refugees Welcome," *New York Times* (series), online: <www.nytimes.com/interactive/2016/world/americas/canada-syrian-refugees.html>; Terry Pedwell, "Canada to Give Asylum to 1,200 Primarily Yazidi Refugees by End of 2017," *Globe and Mail* (21 February 2017), online: <www.theglobeandmail.com/news/politics/canada-to-give-asylum-to-1200-primarily-yazidi-refugees-by-end-of-2017/article34099645/>; Danielle Da Silva, "Operation Ezra Welcomes More Yazidi Newcomers," *Winnipeg Free Press* (24 February 2017), online: <www.winnipegfreepress.com/our-communities/souwester/Operation-Ezra-welcomes-more-Yazidi-newcomers-414744693.html>.
72 Paul Wells, "A New Survey Explores What Makes Us Canadian," *Maclean's* (1 June 2017), online: <www.macleans.ca/news/canada/a-new-survey-for-canada-150-explores

-what-makes-us-canadian/>. Arrivals have also brought forward the generosity and compassion of many Canadians. See e.g. Morgan Lowrie, "Border Towns Mobilizing to Help Asylum-Seekers Coming to Canada," *Toronto Star* (23 April 2017), online: <www.thestar.com/news/canada/2017/04/23/border-towns-mobilizing-to-help-asylum-seekers-coming-to-canada.html>; Laura Glowacki, "Emerson Reeve Says Military at Border Would Be Overkill," *CBC News* (28 March 2017), online: <www.cbc.ca/news/canada/manitoba/emerson-reeve-border-security-1.4044730>; Thomson Reuters, "RCMP Help Asylum-Seeking Family through Snow after Run-In with U.S. Border Patrol," *CBC News* (18 February 2017), online: <www.cbc.ca/news/canada/montreal/rcmp-help-asylum-seeking-family-through-snow-after-run-in-with-u-s-border-patrol-1.3989830>.

73 Quoted in Tasha Kheiriddin, "Commentary: Close Canada's Loophole for Border-Hoppers to Even the Field for Refugees," *Global News* (21 March 2017), online: <globalnews.ca/news/3322405/commentary-close-canadas-loophole-for-border-hoppers-to-even-the-field-for-refugees/>.

74 *Ibid.*

75 See Shauna Labman & Jamie Chai Yun Liew, "Law and Moral Licensing in Canada: The Making of Illegality and Illegitimacy along the Border" International Journal of Migration and Border Studies [forthcoming].

76 Gertrude Neuwirth & JR Rogge, "Canada and the Indochinese Refugees" in Supang Chantavanich and E Bruce Reynolds, eds, *Indochinese Refugees: Asylum and Resettlement* (Bangkok: Institute of Asian Studies, Chulalongkorn University, 1988) 249, 254.

77 David Steinbock, "The Qualities of Mercy: Maximizing the Impact of US Refugee Resettlement" (2003) 36 University of Michigan Journal of Law Reform 951, 990.

78 EIC, *Annual Report to Parliament: Immigration Plan for 1991–1995 Year Two* (1991), 22.

79 *Immigration and Refugee Protection Act*, SC 2001, c 27.

80 Hathaway, *supra* note 4, 685.

81 "Statement on Blended Visa Office Referred Refugees," *supra* note 13. To the Trudeau government's credit, this was at least acknowledged.

Chapter 7: Beyond the Convention

1 Citizenship and Immigration Canada (CIC), *Repeal of the Source Country Class of Humanitarian-Protected Persons Abroad*, Operational Bulletin 346 (7 October 2011) [CIC, *Repeal of the Source Country Class*]; *Immigration and Refugee Protection Regulations*, SOR/2002-227.

2 SC 1976–77, c 52.

3 *Ibid*, s 6(3).

4 Employment and Immigration Canada, Policy and Program Development Immigration, *Future Immigration Levels: 1988 Consultation Issues* (1988), 12.
5 *Indochinese Designated Class Regulations*, SOR/78-931, s 6; *Self-Exiled Persons Designated Class Regulations*, SOR/78-933, s 6; *Political Prisoners and Oppressed Persons Designated Class Regulations*, SOR/82-977, s 6 [*Political Prisoner Regulations*].
6 *Political Prisoner Regulations*, supra note 5, s 2.
7 James C Hathaway, "Selective Concern: An Overview of Refugee Law in Canada" (1987–88) 33 McGill Law Journal 676, 694.
8 Letter from Robert M Adams to Joseph Kage, 9 January 1973, 1–2, Canadian Jewish Congress Charities Committee National Archives.
9 David Matas, "Political Prisoners and Oppressed Persons Class and the Soviet Union" (1991) 10 Refuge 3, 8.
10 Hathaway, *supra* note 7, 697.
11 *Ibid*.
12 Bill Frelick, "In-Country Refugee Processing of Haitians" (2003) 21 Refuge 66, 69.
13 *Immigration and Refugee Protection Regulations*, SOR/2002-227, s 146 [*IRPR*], previously read: "(1) For the purposes of subsection 12(3) of the Act, a person in similar circumstances to those of a Convention refugee is a member of one of the following humanitarian-protected persons abroad classes: (*a*) the country of asylum class; or (*b*) the source country class. (2) The country of asylum class and the source country class are prescribed as classes of persons who may be issued permanent resident visas on the basis of the requirements of this Division." See also *Regulations Amending the Immigration and Refugee Protection Regulations*, SOR/2011-222, s 5 [*Regulations Amending the IRPR*].
14 CIC, *Repeal of the Source Country Class, supra* note 1.
15 *IRPR*, supra note 13, s 148: "(1) A foreign national is a member of the source country class if they have been determined by an officer to be in need of resettlement because (*a*) they are residing in their country of nationality or habitual residence and that country is a source country within the meaning of subsection (2) at the time their permanent resident visa application is made as well as at the time a visa is issued; and (*b*) they (i) are being seriously and personally affected by civil war or armed conflict in that country, (ii) have been or are being detained or imprisoned with or without charges, or subjected to some other form of penal control, as a direct result of an act committed outside Canada that would, in Canada, be a legitimate expression of freedom of thought or a legitimate exercise of civil rights pertaining to dissent or trade union activity, or (iii) by reason of a well-founded fear of persecution for reasons of race, religion, nationality, political opinion or membership in a particular social group, are unable or, by reason of such fear, unwilling to avail themself of the protection of any of their countries of nationality or habitual residence. (2) A source country is a country (*a*) where persons are in refugee-like situations

as a result of civil war or armed conflict or because their fundamental human rights are not respected; (*b*) where an officer works or makes routine working visits and is able to process visa applications without endangering their own safety, the safety of applicants or the safety of Canadian embassy staff; (*c*) where circumstances warrant humanitarian intervention by the Department in order to implement the overall humanitarian strategies of the Government of Canada, that intervention being in keeping with the work of the United Nations High Commissioner for Refugees; and (*d*) that is set out in Schedule 2." *Regulations Amending the IRPR, supra* note 13, s 6.

16 A self-supporting refugee is a refugee who has enough money for basic necessities. Self-supporting refugees still require a referral or private sponsorship undertaking. They are eligible for government language and orientation programs but do not receive the financial assistance provided to government-assisted refugees (GARs). CIC, "Guide 6000 – Convention Refugees Abroad and Humanitarian-Protected Persons Abroad" (2012), online: *Government of Canada* <www.cic.gc.ca/english/information/applications/guides/E16000TOC.asp>.

17 *IRPR, supra* note 13, Schedule 2; *Regulations Amending the IRPR, supra* note 13, s 12.
18 *IRPR, supra* note 13, s 148(1)(a); *Regulations Amending the IRPR, supra* note 13, s 6.
19 The list was last reviewed in 2003, but no change to the listed countries was made. Debra Pressé, Subcommittee on International Human Rights of the Standing Committee on Foreign Affairs and International Development, *Evidence*, 40-3 (9 December 2010) [Pressé, *Evidence*].
20 *Ibid.*
21 *IRPR, supra* note 13, s 148(1)(b); *Regulations Amending the IRPR, supra* note 13, s 6.
22 *IRPR, supra* note 13, s 148(2)(b); *Regulations Amending the IRPR, supra* note 13, s 6.
23 Pressé, *Evidence, supra* note 19.
24 *Ibid.*
25 Citizenship and Immigration Canada, "Regulatory Impact Analysis Statement" 145:12 Canada Gazette Part 1 (19 March 2011) 1003 [CIC, "Regulatory Impact"].
26 *Ibid.*
27 CIC, News Release, "Government to Refocus Resettlement Efforts" (18 March 2011) [CIC, "Government to Refocus"].
28 CIC, "Regulatory Impact," *supra* note 25, 1002.
29 *Ibid.*
30 CIC, "Government to Refocus," *supra* note 27.
31 CIC, "Proposed Regulatory Text," 145:12 Canada Gazette Part 1 (19 March 2011) 1007.
32 CIC, News Release, "Canada's Commitment to Iraqi Refugees Remains Strong" (18 March 2011).
33 CIC, "Government to Refocus," *supra* note 27. The Bhutanese resettlement is addressed in detail in the group processing section of this chapter.

34 CIC, "Regulatory Impact," *supra* note 25.
35 *Ibid*.
36 *Ibid*, 1005.
37 *Ibid*, 1007.
38 Refugee Council USA, *Living on the Edge: Colombian Refugees in Panama and Ecuador* (2011), 1. In response to expressed concern from the Canadian Council for Refugees (CCR) on the fate of Colombians who benefited from the source country class, the CIC indicated that, "once the class is repealed, CIC can increase the number of resettlement spaces for UNHCR-referred refugees, some of which may go to Colombian refugees in need of protection in Ecuador." CIC, "Regulatory Impact," *supra* note 25.
39 Formerly Bill C-49, reintroduced as Bill C-4 on 16 June 2011 and then brought into the omnibus Bill C-31, *Protecting Canada's Immigration System Act*, SC 2012, c 17 (introduced on 16 February 2012, assented to 28 June 2012).
40 Jim Creskey, "Jason Kenney's Troubling Refugee Legacy," *Embassy* (30 March 2011).
41 CIC, "Regulatory Impact," *supra* note 25, 1004; *Immigration and Refugee Protection Act*, SC 2001, c 27 [*IRPA*].
42 *Balanced Refugee Reform Act*, SC 2010, c 8, s 4 (assented to 29 June 2010) (formerly Bill C-11).
43 *Protecting Canada's Immigration System Act*, *supra* note 39.
44 The previous section read: "25 The Minister must, on request of a foreign national in Canada who is inadmissible or who does not meet the requirements of this Act, and may, on request of a foreign national outside Canada, examine the circumstances concerning the foreign national and may grant the foreign national permanent resident status or an exemption from any applicable criteria or obligations of this Act if the Minister is of the opinion that it is justified by humanitarian and compassionate considerations relating to the foreign national, taking into account the best interests of a child directly affected ... 25.1 (1) The Minister may, on the Minister's own initiative, examine the circumstances concerning a foreign national who is inadmissible or who does not meet the requirements of this Act and may grant the foreign national permanent resident status or an exemption from any applicable criteria or obligations of this Act if the Minister is of the opinion that it is justified by humanitarian and compassionate considerations relating to the foreign national, taking into account the best interests of a child directly affected ... 25.2 (1) The Minister may, in examining the circumstances concerning a foreign national who is inadmissible or who does not meet the requirements of this Act, grant that person permanent resident status or an exemption from any applicable criteria or obligations of this Act if the Minister is of the opinion that it is justified by public policy considerations."

45 For example, the section is used in instances of family class sponsorship in which the sponsor does not meet the eligibility requirements. CIC, *OP 4: Processing of Applications under Section 25 of the IRPA*, manual (2008), 8.2 [on file with author].
46 CIC, "Regulatory Impact," *supra* note 25.
47 "(D) Proposal to End Source Country Class," *Canadian Council for Refugees E-Chronicle*, vol 6 (8 April 2011), online: <ccrweb.ca/en/bulletin/11/04/08#_Toc290021136>.
48 "Comments on Proposed Elimination of Source Country Class" (18 April 2011), online: *Canada Council for Refugees* <ccrweb.ca/en/comments-proposed-elimination-source-country-class> ["Comments on Proposed Elimination"].
49 Interested persons did have the opportunity to make representations concerning the proposed regulations within thirty days after the date of publication of the *Gazette* notice. I sent comments on 14 April 2011 regarding the interviews I participated in as part of the CCR delegation in Bogota and the interest expressed by organizations in Colombia to continue making referrals to the Canadian embassy.
50 Judith Kumin, "In-Country 'Refugee' Processing Arrangements: A Humanitarian Alternative?" in Michael Jandl, ed, *Innovative Concepts for Alternative Migration Policies* (Amsterdam: Amsterdam University Press, 2007) 79.
51 *Ibid*.
52 *Ibid*.
53 *Ibid*, 80.
54 *Ibid*, 85.
55 *Ibid*, 83.
56 Judith Kumin, *Welcoming Engagement: How Private Sponsorship Can Strengthen Refugee Resettlement in the European Union* (Brussels: Migration Policy Institute Europe, 2015), online: <www.migrationpolicy.org/research/welcoming-engagement-how-private-sponsorship-can-strengthen-refugee-resettlement-european>.
57 Francisco Rico Martinez & CCR, "The Future of Colombian Refugees in Canada: Are We Being Equitable?" (2011), 35–36, online: *Canada Council for Refugees* <ccrweb.ca/files/ccr_colombia_report_2011.pdf>. These targets include both government and private sponsorship.
58 The Colombian government commenced registering internally displaced persons (IDPs) in 1997, and, by the end of 2011, more than 3.8 million were registered. Other observers place the estimate much higher at 5.3 million. See "Global Overview 2011: People Internally Displaced by Conflict and Violence" (April 2012), 8, online: *Internal Displacement Monitoring Centre* <www.internal-displacement.org/publications/internal-displacement-global-overview-2011-people-internally-displaced-by-conflict-and>; UNHCR, "UNHCR Global Appeal 2010–2011," *UNHCR Fundraising Reports* (1 December 2009), 100 [UNHCR, "UNHCR Global Appeal"]; "A Year of Crisis: UNHCR Global Trends 2011," 19, online: *UNHCR* <www.unhcr.org/4fd6f87f9.html>.

59 "Colombia: Global Focus, 2018: People of Concern," online: *UNHCR* <reporting.unhcr.org/node/2542?y=2018#year>.
60 *Ibid.*
61 Debra Pressé, Director of Refugee Resettlement, CIC, interview with author, 18 November 2009.
62 Pilar Riaño Alcalá et al, *Forced Migration of Colombians: Colombia, Ecuador, Canada* (Colombia and Vancouver: Corporación Región, School of Social Work (Spanish), and University of British Columbia (English), 2008), 96, 103, 104.
63 Pressé, interview, *supra* note 61.
64 Colombia is the only country with more than one million IDPs in the western hemisphere. The other four countries at the time with more than one million IDPs were Iraq, Sudan, the Democratic Republic of the Congo, and Somalia. "Global Overview 2011," *supra* note 58, 8.
65 UNHCR, "UNHCR Global Appeal," *supra* note 58, 9, "Latin America."
66 Rico Martinez & CCR, *supra* note 57, 5. These targets include both government and private sponsorship.
67 *Ibid*, 5. Full resettlement targets for government and privately sponsored refugees for 2010 and 2011 are on file with author.
68 Alcalá et al, *supra* note 62, 141.
69 Rico Martinez & CCR, *supra* note 57, 27.
70 *Ibid*, 27.
71 *Ibid.*
72 *Ibid.*
73 *Ibid.*
74 *Ibid.*
75 CIC, "Regulatory Impact," *supra* note 25.
76 *Ibid.*
77 Peter Stucky, quoted in Nicholas Keung, "Ottawa Eyes Axing 'Life-Saving' Asylum Program," *Toronto Star* (12 April 2011).
78 Shauna Labman, "CCR Visit Finds Colombia Not Safe for Some" (2010) 69 Refugee Update 5 [Labman, "CCR Visit Finds"]; Rico Martinez & CCR, *supra* note 57, 7–11.
79 Rico Martinez & CCR, *supra* note 57, 11.
80 The CCR's fact-finding mission to Colombia found strong evidence to contradict this claim. *Ibid*; Labman, "CCR Visit Finds," *supra* note 78.
81 Rico Martinez & CCR, *supra* note 57, 28.
82 *Ibid*, 26.
83 Oakland Ross, "Canada Is Conned into Taking Rebels; Colombians Given Refugee Status; Bogota Arrests 3 Civil Servants," *Toronto Star* (8 September 2004), A1; Oakland Ross, "Colombian Immigrants Fear Fallout from Scam," *Toronto Star* (10 September 2004), A15.

84 CIC, "Regulatory Impact," *supra* note 25, 1003.
85 Joseph Kage, "Re-Appraising the Canadian Immigration Policy: An Analysis and Comments on the White Paper on Immigration" (January 1967), 18, Canadian Jewish Congress Charities Committee National Archives.
86 UNHCR, Executive Committee of the High Commissioner's Programme, *Agenda for Protection*, Doc A/AC. 96/965/Add. 1, 3rd ed (October 2003), Goal 5, Objective 6.
87 High Commissioner's Forum, *Multilateral Framework of Understandings on Resettlement*, Doc FORUM/2004/6 (16 September 2004), 17–19.
88 Michael Casasola, "The Indochinese Refugee Movement and the Subsequent Evolution of UNHCR and Canadian Resettlement Selection Policies and Practices" (2016) 32:2 Refuge 41, 44, online: <refuge.journals.yorku.ca/index.php/refuge/article/viewFile/40270/36409>; see also "Backgrounder: Group Resettlement to Canada: Karen Refugees in Mae La Oon Camp, Thailand" (2006), online: *Government of Canada* <www.cic.gc.ca/English/department/media/backgrounders/2006/2006-06-20.asp#tphp%20idtphp> ["Backgrounder: Group Resettlement"].
89 *IRPR, supra* note 13.
90 Pressé, *Evidence, supra* note 19.
91 Casasola, *supra* note 88, 44.
92 UNHCR, "Progress Report on Resettlement" (2007) 26:1 Refugee Survey Quarterly 150, 150.
93 UNHCR, *UNHCR Refugee Resettlement Trends 2015* (June 2015), 11.
94 Casasola, *supra* note 88, 44.
95 Monte Solberg, Minister of Citizenship and Immigration, "Speaking Notes" (Tenth Biennial Conference of the International Association for the Study of Forced Migration and the International Refugee Rights Conference of the Canadian Council for Refugees, Toronto, 18 June 2006).
96 CIC, *2005 Annual Report to Parliament on Immigration* (Ottawa: CIC, 2005), s 4.
97 One hundred and fifty-four Acehnese were strategically settled as a group in Metro Vancouver between 2004 and 2006, but they were individually processed and did not enter under the group processing methodology. See Jennifer Hyndman & James McLean, "Settling Like a State: Acehnese Refugees in Vancouver" (2006) 19:3 Journal of Refugee Studies 345; James McLean, Chris Friesen, & Jennifer Hyndman, "The First 365 Days: Acehnese Refugees in Vancouver, British Columbia" (2006) RIIM Working Paper Series 06-07; Lisa Ruth Brunner, Jennifer Hyndman, & Chris Friesen, "Post-IRPA GARs from Aceh: An Analysis of Refugee Integration Five Years On" (2011) 8 Our Diverse Cities 106.
98 Pressé, interview, *supra* note 61.
99 This is the same section, *IRPA, supra* note 41, s 25(1), mentioned above in the discussion of source country resettlement. Here though it is the minister's ability to exempt a foreign national from an aspect of the act rather than granting permanent

residence that is being applied. The revised s 25(1) still permits the minister to exempt a foreign national from any applicable criteria or obligations of the act.
100 Pressé, interview, *supra* note 61. The "successful establishment" requirement is set out in *IRPR, supra* note 13, s 139, and discussed in detail in Chapter 3.
101 Citizenship and Immigration Canada, "Backgrounder – Bill C-11: *The Balanced Refugee Reform Act*" (14 October 2010).
102 *Ibid.*
103 CIC, News Release, "Canada's Resettlement Programs" (18 March 2011), online: <www.cic.gc.ca/english/department/media/backgrounders/2011/2011-03-18b.asp>.
104 Steven O'Brien, "It's a Long Way from Myanmar for Karen Refugees," *UNHCR News Stories* (28 January 2008).
105 "Resettling Bhutanese Refugees: Update on Canada's Commitment" (2010), online: Government of Canada <www.cic.gc.ca/English/refugees/outside/bhutanese.asp#tphp%20idtphp>.
106 CIC, News Release, "Canada Announces Plan to Resettle More Bhutanese Refugees" (20 June 2012), online: <www.cic.gc.ca/english/department/media/releases/2012/2012-06-20a.asp>.
107 "Resettling Bhutanese Refugees – Update on Canada's Commitment" (2014), online: Government of Canada <www.cic.gc.ca/english/refugees/outside/bhutanese.asp> ["Resettling Bhutanese Refugees"].
108 *Ibid.*
109 *Ibid.*
110 "Backgrounder: Group Resettlement," *supra* note 88.
111 Pratibedan Baidya & Nini Gurung, "Resettlement Programme for Refugees in Nepal Passes 40,000 Mark" (13 December 2010), online: *UNHCR* <http://www.unhcr.org/refworld/docid/4d07286e2.html>.
112 Pressé, *Evidence, supra* note 19.
113 Baidya & Gurung, *supra* note 111. The majority of these refugees – 34,129 – have been resettled to the United States.
114 Pressé, *Evidence, supra* note 19.
115 Pressé, interview, *supra* note 61.
116 Canada, Australia, the United States, New Zealand, Denmark, Switzerland, and Finland participated in the démarche. Norway was initially also involved but pulled out. Pressé, interview, *supra* note 61.
117 Baidya & Gurung, *supra* note 111.
118 "Resettling Bhutanese Refugees," *supra* note 107.
119 *Ibid.*
120 *Ibid;* "Backgrounder: Group Resettlement," *supra* note 88; Citizenship and Immigration Canada, "Backgrounder: Karen Refugees" (2007); Citizenship and

Immigration Canada, "Refugee Resettlement in Canada Information Bulletin No 1 (Bhutan)," (2008); Citizenship and Immigration Canada, "Refugee Resettlement in Canada Information Bulletin No 2" (2010) [CIC, "Refugee Resettlement, Bulletin No 2"]; Citizenship and Immigration Canada, "Refugee Resettlement in Canada Information Bulletin No 3" (2010) [CIC, "Refugee Resettlement, Bulletin No 3"]; Citizenship and Immigration Canada, "Refugee Resettlement in Canada Information Bulletin No 4 (Bhutan)"; "Canada to Welcome 2,000 More Karen Refugees," online: *Government of Canada* <www.cic.gc.ca/english/department/media/releases/2007/2007-02-09.asp>; "Canada's New Government to Accept 5,000 Bhutanese Refugees," online: *Government of Canada* <www.cic.gc.ca/english/department/media/releases/2007/2007-05-22.asp>; CIC, News Release, "Government of Canada and the Anglican Church of Canada Encourage Canadians to Sponsor Refugees" (16 April 2009), online: *Government of Canada* <www.cic.gc.ca/english/department/media/releases/2009/2009-04-16.asp>.

121 A search of the terms "group resettlement," "group processing methodology," and "group processing" on 11 May 2012 resulted in no matches on the Australian government's Department of Immigration and Citizenship website (<www.immi.gov.au>) and no relevant matches on the US government's Bureau of Population, Refugees and Migration website (<www.state.gov/j/prm/>).

122 Personal email correspondence [on file with author].

123 "Resettling Bhutanese Refugees," *supra* note 107.

124 Citizens for Public Justice, "Group Processing of Refugees," Policy Notes (September 2006), online: *Citizens for Public Justice* <https://cpj.ca/wp-content/uploads/CPJ-Group-processing-of-Refugees.pdf>.

125 Dale Smith, "Queer Ugandans Ask Parliament for Refugee Assistance," *X-tra* (5 November 2010).

126 Sharalyn Jordan, Rainbow Refugee Committee, email correspondence with author, 1 April 2011.

127 Alcalá et al, *supra* note 62, 90.

128 Lisa Ruth Brunner & Chris Friesen, "Changing Faces, Changing Neigbourhoods: Government-Assisted Refugee Resettlement Patterns in Metro Vancouver 2005–2009" (2011) 8 Our Diverse Cities 93, 94; see also Kathy Sherrell et al, "From 'One Nation, One People' to 'Operation Swaagatem': Bhutanese Refugees in Coquitlam, BC" (2011) Metropolis British Columbia Working Paper 11-11, online: *Metropolis British Columbia* <mbc.metropolis.net/wp_2011.html>. Jennifer Hyndman and James McLean coined the term "new and few" in their article on the settlement of Acehnese refugees in Vancouver. Hyndman & McLean, *supra* note 97, 351.

129 Chris Friesen, Immigrant Services Society of British Columbia, Director of Settlement Services, interview with author, 26 February 2010.

130 *Ibid*.

131 Jane Armstrong, "From Refugees to Pioneers," *Globe and Mail* (18 July 2009), A1; Matthew Kruchak, "Family's Journey to Canada Started Years Ago," *Globe and Mail* (18 July 2009), A5; see also Jane Armstrong, "A New Set of Challenges," *Globe and Mail* (17 October 2009), A15.
132 "Mexicans, Czechs Will Need Visas to Visit Canada" (13 July 2009), online: *CBC News* <www.cbc.ca/news/canada/mexicans-czechs-will-need-visas-to-visit-canada-1.817998>; see also Shauna Labman, "Refocus Concern for Refugees," *Winnipeg Free Press* (12 August 2009), A11.
133 Jason Kenney, quoted in Campbell Clark, "Minister Calls for Overhaul of Canada's Refugee System," *Globe and Mail* (15 July 2009), A1.
134 Pressé, *Evidence, supra* note 19.
135 Pressé, interview, *supra* note 61.
136 Internal UNHCR report (5 July 1998), quoted in Jeff Crisp, "A State of Insecurity: The Political Economy of Violence in Refugee-Populated Areas of Kenya," New Issues in Refugee Research (Geneva: Evaluation and Policy Analysis Unit, UNHCR, 1999), 27.
137 Internal UNHCR report (March 1998), quoted in Crisp, *supra* note 136, 27.
138 Pressé, interview, *supra* note 61.
139 "Resettling Bhutanese Refugees," *supra* note 107.
140 Integrated Regional Information Networks, "Nepal: Repatriation or Resettlement for Bhutanese Refugees?" (22 June 2009), online: *UNHCR* <www.unhcr.org/refworld/docid/4a433cf5c.html>.
141 "Bhutan PM Coming: Nepal to Seek Dialogue on Refugees' Return," *Katmandu Post* (11 April 2011).
142 CIC, "Refugee Resettlement, Bulletin No 2," *supra* note 120.
143 CIC, "Refugee Resettlement, Bulletin No 3," *supra* note 120.
144 *Ibid.*
145 Casasola, *supra* note 88, 48.
146 IRCC, "Evaluation of Resettlement Programs," 4.2.3, online: *Government of Canada* <www.cic.gc.ca/english/resources/evaluation/resettlement.asp#toc4>.
147 *Ibid.*
148 Matas, *supra* note 9, 5.
149 Emily F Carasco et al, *Immigration and Refugee Law: Cases, Materials and Commentary* (Toronto: Emond Montgomery, 2007), 177. For more recent case law on section 25, see *Toussaint v Canada (Citizenship and Immigration)*, 2011 FCA 146; *Kanthasamy v Canada*, 2015 SCC 61.
150 Carasco et al, *supra* note 149.
151 CIC, *IP 5 Immigrant Applications in Canada Made on Humanitarian or Compassionate Grounds*, manual (1 April 2011), 7.
152 "Comments on Proposed Elimination," *supra* note 48.

153 *IRPA, supra* note 41, ss 25(1.1), 25.1(2).
154 Keung, *supra* note 77; Elizabeth Thompson, "Finding Refuge in Canada Could Get Tougher," *Vancouver Sun* (22 March 2011), B3.
155 Peter Stucky, quoted in Keung, *supra* note 77.

Chapter 8: Unsettling Refugee Resettlement

1 High Commissioner's Forum, *Multilateral Framework of Understandings on Resettlement*, Doc FORUM/2004/6 (16 September 2004).
2 See Debra Pressé & Jessie Thomson, "The Resettlement Challenge: Integration of Refugees from Protracted Refugee Situations" (2007) 24 Refuge 48; Alexander Betts & Jean-François Durieux, *Convention Plus as a Norm-Setting Exercise* (Oxford: Oxford University Press, 2007). Jennifer Hyndman, William Payne, & Shauna Jimenez, *The State of Private Refugee Sponsorship in Canada: Trends, Issues, and Impacts*, Refugee Research Network/Centre for Refugee Studies Policy Brief (20 January 2017), 2, 3, 8, online: <jhyndman.info.yorku.ca/files/2017/05/hyndman_et-al.-RRN-brief-Jan-2017-best.pdf>.
3 Claudena M Skran, *Refugees in Inter-War Europe: The Emergence of a Regime* (Oxford: Clarendon Press, 1995), 4.
4 BS Chimni, *The Geopolitics of Refugee Studies and the Practice of International Institutions: A View from the South* (Oxford: Refugee Studies Programme, 1998), 351.
5 *Immigration and Refugee Protection Act*, SC 2001, c 27 [*IRPA*].
6 Margaret Davies, *Asking the Law Question*, 2nd ed (Sydney: Law Book Company, 2002), 5.
7 Robert Mnookin & Lewis Kornhauser, "Bargaining in the Shadow of the Law: The Case of Divorce" (1978–79) 88 Yale Law Journal 950, 997.
8 Howard Erlanger et al, "New Legal Realism Symposium: Is It Time for a New Legal Realism?" (2005) 2 Wisconsin Law Review 335, 339.
9 See Catherine Dauvergne, *Humanitarianism, Identity, and Nation: Migration Laws of Australia and Canada* (Vancouver: UBC Press, 2005).
10 This image of legal worship comes from Dauvergne's work on the rule of law in which she argues that "law is becoming an act of faith. When law is held up in this way, it becomes an object of secular idolatry." Catherine Dauvergne, *Making People Illegal: What Globalization Means for Migration and Law* (Cambridge, UK: Cambridge University Press, 2008), 188.
11 Citizenship and Immigration Canada, News Release, "Canada's Resettlement Programs" (18 March 2011), online: <www.cic.gc.ca/english/department/media/backgrounders/2011/2011-03-18b.asp> [emphasis added].
12 Davies, *supra* note 6, 7.

13 While I support, in concept, significant increases in resettlement numbers in Canada, and globally, I have not made any recommendation to this effect. My reasoning for this is twofold. First, the misuse and manipulation of resettlement outlined in this work must be brought under control before such increases would be advisable. Second, the integration of resettlement refugees is beyond the scope of this book, but it is an essential aspect of a successful plan to resettle more refugees.

14 *Agreement between the Government of Canada and the Government of the United States of America for Cooperation in the Examination of Refugee Status Claims from Nationals of Third Countries* (2004), online: <www.cic.gc.ca/english/department/laws-policy/safe-third.asp>.

15 Erin Patrick, "The US Refugee Resettlement Program," *Migration Information Source* (1 June 2004); Asher Hirsch, Khanh Hoang, & Anthea Vogl, "Australia's Private Refugee Sponsorship Program: Creating Complementary Pathways or Privatising Humanitarianism?" (2019) 35:2 *Refuge* [forthcoming].

16 *IRPA, supra* note 5, s 12.

17 "Community Sponsorship of Refugees Guidebook and Planning Tools" (2017), online: *Global Refugee Sponsorship Initiative* <www.refugeesponsorship.org/guidebook>.

18 WH Auden, "Refugee Blues," *Collected Shorter Poems 1927–1957* (New York: Random House, 1967).

19 Social Science and Humanities Research Council, "Targeted Research: Syrian Refugee Arrival, Resettlement and Integration," online: *Government of Canada* <www.sshrc-crsh.gc.ca/funding-financement/programs-programmes/syrian_refugee-refugie_syrien-eng.aspx>.

20 United Nations High Commissioner for Refugees (UNHCR), *Global Compact for Refugees: Final Draft* (26 June 2018), online: <www.unhcr.org/events/conferences/5b3295167/official-version-final-draft-global-compact-refugees.html>.

21 *Ibid*, 18.

22 Franz Kafka, "Before the Law" in Nahum N Glazer, ed, *Kafka: The Complete Stories and Parables*, translated by Willa Muir & Edwin Muir (New York: Schocken Books, 1971) 3.

23 *Convention Relating to the Status of Refugees*, 28 July 1951, 189 UNTS 150 (entered into force 22 April 1954). In 2017, 16.2 million people were forced to flee their countries and become refugees. By the end of 2017, 68.5 million people were forcibly displaced worldwide. This is 2.9 million more than in 2016 (65.6 million). The past decade has seen a 50 percent increase in the global population of forcibly displaced people with 1 out of every 110 people in the world being displaced. "Global Trends: Forced Displacement in 2017," 2, 4, online: *UNHCR* <www.unhcr.org/5b27be547.pdf>.

Index

Note: "(t)" after a page number indicates a table. For abbreviations used in subentries, please see the list on pages xii–xiii.

Adams, Robert, 84, 126
Adelman, Howard, 89
Afghanistan, Ismaili refugees from, 98, 99
Agenda for Protection (2003), 58, 140
Aleinikoff, Alexander, 24–25, 26
Amin, Idi, 35
Andras, Robert, 38
Armenian Community Centre of Toronto, 99–100
Asmaro Chaldean Society (Windsor, ON), 99–100
asylum: access to, 18; "back door" of, 45, 46–47, 163; Canada as country of, 5, 6, 39–42, 80, 117; geography and, 5, 6, 18, 39, 77, 117, 120–21; importance of, 169; and legal obligations of protection/*non-refoulement*, 4–6, 22, 29–30, 36, 39, 42–44, 77–80, 154, 157; in non-Convention states, 3–4, 19; numbers of applications for, 6, 29–30; as protraction, 4, 19, 26, 28–29, 30, 76, 167. *See also entries below;* resettlement, *and entries following*
asylum and resettlement, problematic relationship of, 2–3, 9, 16, 32–55, 154–62; as bound together in legislation, 42–44; during crises of mass movement, 22–23, 40–41, 54–55; and legal/popular privileging of resettlement, 9–10, 16, 33, 39, 77–80, 107–9, 154–62; as one of unpredictability vs control/order, 27, 39–40, 104; in post-9/11 era, 45–47; recommendations to rebalance, 162–67
asylum seekers: vs camp-based refugees, 32, 119, 145–48, 159–62; detention/criminalization of, 25, 53–54; in Europe, 115; Harper government and, 44–54, 65–66, 145–46; illegal/irregular entry by, 27, 46–49, 79, 120, 161, 163–64; perceived illegitimacy/problem of, 18, 41, 44–55, 119, 145–46, 156–57,

163, 188n68, 197n86, 198n108; refugee status of, 29–30, 163–64. *See also* refugee claimants
Atkey, Ronald, 91
Australia, 30, 54, 142, 143; and camp refugees, 119, 141; family reunification in, 166; private sponsorship in, 115–16; resettlement history/trends in, 6, 22, 34, 36, 82
Axworthy, Lloyd, 92

Baker v. Canada (Minister of Citizenship and Immigration), 69–70, 71
Balanced Refugee Reform Act (BRRA), 48, 49–50, 199n112
Bernier, Maxime, 120
Betts, Alexander, 28
Bhutanese refugees, group resettlement of, 130, 141, 142–44, 149; media coverage of, 145; misinformation issues of, 147–48; and repatriation campaign, 147
blended pilot projects, 98–104, 125; Iraqi refugees and, 99–100, 105, 107, 130, 219n131; LGBTQ refugees and, 100
blended visa office–referred (BVOR) program, 111–14, 121–24, 152, 158, 163–64; introduction of, 56, 86, 100, 111–12; Syrian refugees and, 112–14, 122
"boat people." *See* Indochinese refugees (1970s–90s); Sri Lankan refugees (2000s)
border(s), 2, 11, 80, 168–69; refugee camps near, 26. *See also entries below*
border(s), of law, "unsettling" of resettlement at, 9, 13, 154–62; recommendations to correct/rebalance, 162–67

border control, 24, 154; by Canada, 18, 32, 36, 41; DCO/DFN claimants and, 49–55; *Safe Third Country Agreement* and, 47–48, 54–55, 119–20; source country resettlement and, 125, 127–28, 129, 131, 151, 166
border crossing: Canada-US tensions over, 47–48, 54, 119–20; dangers of, after repeal of source country resettlement, 131, 151, 166; interdiction strategies to deny, 54–55; perceived illegality of, 47–48
Boswell, Justice Keith, 52, 201n146
Brunnée, Jutta, 12
burden sharing, of resettlement, 20, 40–41, 58, 59, 65, 148; by private sponsors, 82, 83, 99, 118, 121, 131, 158; and refugee protection, 2, 4, 5–6, 8, 28, 59, 77, 80, 137, 154; by source countries' neighbours, 131, 135
Burma/Myanmar. *See* Karen refugees, group resettlement of

camps, 15, 16, 18, 41, 88, 103, 119, 137, 180n8; containment in, 24–26; group resettlement in, 140, 141, 142–43, 145, 146–48, 151; refugees in, vs asylum seekers, 32, 119, 145–48, 159–62; security in, 135
Canada Employment and Immigration Commission, 92
Canadian Bar Association, 48
Canadian Bill of Rights, 67
Canadian Border Services Agency (CBSA), 50, 53
Canadian Charter of Rights and Freedoms, 52, 67

Canadian Christian Council for the Resettlement of Refugees (CCCRR), 83–84
Canadian Council for Refugees (CCR), 32, 59, 71–72, 73, 82; author's work with, 14–15, 136–40; history of, 183n56; on importance of sponsors, 105, 111–12; and Indochinese refugees, 91; on repeal of source country class, 134, 231n38
Canadian Employment and Immigration Advisory Council, 41
Canadian Jewish Congress, 14, 84
Casasola, Michael, 44–45, 64
Centralized Processing Office (CPO-W), in Winnipeg, 76
Chance, Leslie, 35, 36
Chiarelli v. Canada (Minister of Employment and Immigration), 67
Chiau v. Canada (Minister of Citizenship and Immigration), 69
Chile, 115; refugees from, 35, 126
Chimni, B.S., 25, 156
Citizens for Public Justice (CPJ), 116, 144
Citizenship and Immigration Canada (CIC), 13–14, 32, 64, 75, 78, 86, 106, 107, 183n54; and blended pilot projects, 98, 99–100, 101, 103; and group resettlement, 141, 143, 147; and Refugee Sponsorship Training Program, 105; and source country class, 128, 134, 137, 139, 150, 151; and Sri Lankan refugees, 46, 48. *See also* Immigration, Refugees and Citizenship Canada (IRCC)
Clark, Joe, 90, 91
Coles, Gervase, 23, 26
Colombia, refugees from, 99, 128, 129–31, 149, 151, 198n108, 231n38; as "desirable," 137, 143; as IDPs, 15, 137, 232n58, 233n64; at Immigration and Refugee Board, 14–15, 136–40
Colombian Mennonite Church (Bogota), 139
containment, 24–26. *See also* camps
Convention Concerning the Status of Refugees Coming from Germany (1938), 20–21
"Convention Plus" initiative (UNHCR), 27, 58–59, 156
convention refugee abroad class, 59–60, 61, 64, 74, 80, 129
Convention Relating to the International Status of Refugees (1933), 20, 186n23
Convention Relating to the Status of Refugees (Refugee Convention, 1951), 13, 45, 58, 169; Canada and, 33, 38, 40–42, 47–48, 59, 77, 79–80; Canada's delayed signing of, 35–36; exilic bias of, 23; *non-refoulement* principle in, 2–4, 5, 22, 23, 29–30, 36, 40, 43–44, 59, 77, 79; *Protocol* of 1967 and, 17, 35–36, 184n9; state parties to, 36, 37–38(t), 184n9; states not party to, 2, 3, 18, 19
Corbett, David, 34–35
country of asylum class, 60, 64, 94, 128, 129, 229n13
Crock, Mary, 119
Curry, R.B., 84

Dadaab refugee camps (Kenya), 141, 142, 146–47
Dastyari, Azadeh, 119
Dauvergne, Catherine, 12, 107, 117
Davies, Margaret, 11, 12, 161

designated countries of origin (DCOs), 49–55, 119n112, 201n146
designated foreign nationals (DFNs), 49–55, 200n127, 200n132, 202n152
Dirks, Gerald, 33–34, 39, 92
discourse, 9, 13, 24–25; as divisive, 47, 53, 145–46, 163
discretionary decision-making, 63, 66–80, 121–22, 164; judicial review of, 66–76, 157; vs legal obligations, 66, 75, 77–80; of source country class/group resettlement, 125–52, 158–59
durable solutions, to plight of refugees, 2–5, 19, 23, 27, 61, 180n12; resettlement as, 7, 19, 23, 27, 45, 148. *See also* integration, local; repatriation, voluntary; resettlement, *and entries following*
Durieux, Jean-François, 28

Emerson, Sir Herbert, 21
encampment, 24. *See also* camps
Eritrean refugee applicants in Cairo, rejection of, 73
European Union (EU): Conclusions on Resettlement (2017) by, 7; private sponsorship in, 116, 136; resettlement policy of, 7
exile: of protracted asylum, 4, 19, 26, 28–29, 30, 76, 167; self-, as designated class, 126
exilic bias/orientation, of UNHCR/resettlement, 22, 23–26

family reunification, 65, 93–98, 103–6, 168; Kosovar refugees and, 103–4; private sponsorship as used for, 9, 93–95, 105–6, 109, 120, 158, 164, 165–66; recommendation on, 165–66; UNHCR and, 27, 95, 109, 218n115
Federal Court of Canada, 51–52, 54, 80; judicial review at, 66–76, 157; list of resettlement cases at (1994–2016), 170–78
FOCUS Humanitarian Canada, 98
Foster, Michelle, 30
Fredriksson, John, 45
Frelick, Bill, 127

Galloway, Donald, 110
Germany, 7, 72, 83, 116; refugees escaping Nazism in, 20–21
Ghirmatsion v. Canada (Minister of Citizenship and Immigration), 73–75
Gibney, Matthew, 18, 26
Gibson, Justice Frederick, 68, 70
Global Compact for Refugees (2018), 27, 168
Global Refugee Sponsorship Initiative (GRSI), 105, 115–17, 158, 167
Gotlieb, Allan, 39
government-assisted ranges and landings, compared to PSR program (2001–21), 56–58, 57(t), 59
government-assisted refugee (GAR) program, 1, 55–80, 85, 92, 106, 128, 157, 162, 168, 219n131, 230n16; compared to PSR program, 56–58, 59, 82, 87, 90–91, 98, 111–12, 211n105; as complemented by PSR program, 87, 92, 106, 107–9, 120, 122, 123–24, 157–58, 164–66; discretionary aspects of, 77–80, 157; as "humanitarianism," 87, 107, 110, 115, 158; judicial reviews of decisions made under, 66–76, 157;

legislative/policy framework of, 59–66; numeric ranges/landings under, 56–58, 57(t), 59; and resettlement vs asylum, 107–9, 157, 158
Grandi, Filipo, 115
group resettlement, 125–26, 140–52; of Bhutanese refugees, 130, 141, 142–44, 145, 147–48, 149; discretionary nature of, 140–41, 148–52, 158–59; of Karen refugees, 141–42, 143; of Somali-Sudanese refugees, 141, 142, 146–47; of Ugandan LGBTQ refugees, 144

Ha v. Canada (Minister of Citizenship and Immigration), 70
Hamlin, Rebecca, 30
Harvard Immigration and Refugee Law Clinical Program, 47
Harvard Law Review, 12–13
Hathaway, James, 26, 30, 45, 89, 110, 118
Hibbitts, Bernard, 12–13
Hiebert, Daniel, 116
Hospitality House Refugee Ministry (Winnipeg), 108–9
human smuggling, 16, 47, 49, 52; Conservative bill on, 49, 79, 131, 160; as exacerbated by repeal of source country class, 131, 151, 166
humanitarian and compassionate applications (*IRPA*, s. 25), 132–36, 141, 149–50, 164, 231*n*44; outside Canada (2002–10), 134, 135(t)
humanitarian protected persons abroad class, 60, 127–28, 229*n*13. *See also* country of asylum class; source country class, *and entry following*

humanitarianism, 1, 18; of Canada's refugee policy, 32–36, 38–46, 50–51, 60, 65, 77, 80, 87, 94, 115; containment/encampment and, 24–26; interwar refugee crisis and, 21, 25; of private sponsorship, 83, 94, 101, 107, 110, 112–13, 115, 117–18, 121, 158; of *Refugee Convention*/UNHCR, as "Eurocentric," 23
Hungary, 7; early refugees from, 35; Romani people, as unprotected minority group in, 50
Hussen, Ahmed, 53
Hyndman, Jennifer, 26, 27, 39

Immigrant Services Society of British Columbia (ISSBC), 14, 145
Immigrant Settlement and Integration Services (Nova Scotia), 14, 102
Immigration Act (1906), 191*n*13
Immigration Act (1952), 34
Immigration Act (1976), 42, 43, 71, 118, 140, 193*n*39, 213*n*14; designated classes in, 126; inclusion of refugees in, 38, 39–40, 82–83, 121, 194*n*44; Indochinese refugees and, 88, 90, 103–4, 126
Immigration and Refugee Board of Canada, 50, 51, 54, 71–72, 108; Colombian refugees at, 14–15, 136–40; Refugee Appeal Division of, 51, 52
Immigration and Refugee Protection Act (IRPA), 13–14, 42–48, 59–60, 63–66, 78–79, 85, 156, 166; and "humanitarian and compassionate application," 132–36, 141, 149–50, 164, 231*n*44; humanitarian/security focus of, 44–46; introduction of, 42–43; judicial review under, 69, 71;

protection aspect of, 63–65, 104; referral system of, 60; shared goals of, as problematic, 42–44; UNHCR and, 44–45, 60, 64; women at risk program of, 65

Immigration and Refugee Protection Regulations (IRPR), 13; and permanent resident visas, 61–62, 63–64; and resettlement applications, 62–63, 75–76; and source country class, 125, 127–36

Immigration, Refugees and Citizenship Canada (IRCC), 13, 86, 113–14, 183n54; and multi-year resettlement commitments, 148; on refugee sponsorship cost, 82. *See also* Citizenship and Immigration Canada (CIC)

Indochinese refugees (1970s–90s), 22, 40–41, 119, 144, 156; as designated class, 126; *Immigration Act* and, 88, 90, 103–4, 126; private sponsorship of, 88–93, 94

integration, local, 2, 4, 5, 19, 23, 27, 28; in *IRPR*, 62, 63

Inter-Church Committee for Refugees, 92, 97

Intergovernmental Committee on Refugees (IGCR), 21, 22

Interim Federal Health Program (IFHP), 52–53, 54, 201n142

internally displaced persons (IDPs): in Colombia, 15, 137, 232n58, 233n64; recommendation to protect, 166

International Committee of the Red Cross (ICRC), 19; in Colombia, 138, 139

International Labour Organization (ILO), 20, 24

International Refugee Organization (IRO), 21–22, 23, 34, 83

Iraqi refugees, 99–100, 105, 107, 130, 219n131

Ismaili Council for Canada, 98, 99

Jallow v. Canada (Minister of Citizenship and Immigration), 67–68

Jesuit Refugee Service, 137

Jewish Immigrant Aid Services (JIAS), 83, 84, 87–88, 100, 126, 140

Jimenez, Shauna, 39

joint assistance sponsorship (JAS) program, 85, 98, 102, 165–66

judicial review, of visa officers' resettlement decisions, 66–76, 157; and application of *Singh* case, 67–68; in *Ghirmatsion* case, 73–75; in rejection of Eritrean refugees at Cairo office, 73; as sole route of legal challenge, 71

Kafka, Franz, 169

Kage, Joseph, 83, 84, 126, 140, 213n14

Kaplan, Robert, 90

Karen refugees, group resettlement of, 141–42, 143

Kenney, Jason, 18, 46, 98, 122, 130, 145, 191n4

Kenya, 72; refugee camps in, 26, 141, 142, 146–47, 180n8

Kornhauser, Lewis, 11

Kosovars, resettlement of, 102–4; UNHCR guidance on, 103

Kumin, Judith, 116, 135–36

Kurdi, Alan, 1, 112

Latin American designated class, 126, 127

law, 1–16; as examined beyond traditional/doctrinal concepts, 10–16;

and judicial review of visa officers' decisions, 66–76, 157; and legal obligation of *non-refoulement*, 3–6, 29–30, 31, 36, 42–44, 77–80, 117, 123, 154, 157, 160–61; and role in/relevance to resettlement, 1–16, 154–55, 159–62; and voluntary/non-legal nature of resettlement, 2–6, 9–10, 42–44, 59, 79, 108, 123, 132, 150, 154–55

law's border, "unsettling" of resettlement at, 9, 13, 154–62; recommendations to correct/rebalance, 162–67

League of Nations, 19–21

Legal Aid Toronto, 50

Lemieux, Justice François, 71

LGBTQ refugees, 100, 144

Lubbers, Ruud, 58

MacDonald, David, 91

MacDonald, Flora, 91

Macklin, Audrey, 47

Mactavish, Justice Anne, 52

mandate status, in non-*Convention* states, 3–4, 19

Manderson, Desmond, 10–11

Manitoba Interfaith Immigration Council (MIIC), 14, 100–2

Matas, David, 149

McAdam, Jane, 30

McCallum, John, 53

McDonald, James G., 20

Mennonite Central Committee of Canada, 83, 87–88, 221n70

Mnookin, Robert, 11

Mohamed v. Canada (Minister of Citizenship and Immigration), 71

Molloy, Mike, 35

Muhazi v. Canada (Minister of Citizenship and Immigration), 71

Multilateral Framework of Understandings on Resettlement (MFU, 2004), 59, 140, 155

multi-year resettlement commitments, 148

Nansen, Fridtjof, 19–20

Nansen International Office, 20–21

Nansen Medal (UNHCR), 40–41, 217n96

National Inter-Faith Immigration Committee, 84

Nepal. *See* Bhutanese refugees, group resettlement of

New York Declaration for Refugees and Migrants (2016), 27

NGO–Government Committee on the Private Sponsorship of Refugees, 97, 218n117

non-governmental organizations (NGOs), 56, 93, 98, 104, 105, 138, 183n49, 221n170

non-refoulement, 2–8, 29–31, 42–44, 77–79, 163, 185n17; as legal obligation, 3–6, 29–30, 31, 36, 42–44, 77–80, 117, 123, 154, 157, 160–61; as principle of *Refugee Convention* (1951), 2–4, 5, 22, 23, 29–30, 36, 40, 43–44, 59, 77, 79

Not Just Numbers: A Canadian Framework for Future Immigration (1997), 42–43, 78

Ocean Lady (ship), 46, 48, 53

Open Society Foundations, 81, 115

Oraha v. Canada (Minister of Citizenship and Immigration), 68, 70, 71 overseas refugee claimants, 33–34, 39–41, 42–43. *See also* discretionary decision-making; visa officers

Payne, William, 39
political prisoners and oppressed persons class, 126, 127
pre-removal risk assessments (PRRAs), 50, 52, 199*n*119
Pressé, Debra, 128, 129
Preventing Human Smugglers from Abusing Canada's Immigration System Act, 49, 79, 131, 160
private sponsorship of refugees (PSR) program, 56, 76, 81–109, 131, 157–58; background to/precursors of, 81–84; blended pilot projects under, 98–104, 125; compared to GAR program, 56–58, 59, 82, 87, 90–91, 98, 111–12, 211*n*105; as complement to GAR program, 87, 92, 106, 107–9, 120, 122, 123–24, 157–58, 164–66; family reunification and, 9, 93–95, 105–6, 109, 120, 158, 164, 165–66; generosity/goodwill of, 82, 84, 92, 117–21, 158; government reliance on, 91, 107–9, 117–21, 122, 158; groups permitted under, 84–85; joint assistance program under, 85, 98, 102, 165–66; as model to be exported/promoted, 81, 82, 111, 115–17, 122; numeric ranges/landings under, 56–58, 57(t), 59, 95, 96–97(t), 97; obligations under, 86; referrals under, 85–86; and refusal rates/protection concerns, 104–6; and resettlement of "boat people," 88–93, 94; and resettlement vs asylum, 107–9, 157, 158. *See also* *entry below;* blended pilot projects; blended visa office–referred (BVOR) program; Global Refugee Sponsorship Initiative (GRSI)
private sponsorship ranges and landings: (1979–2021), 95, 96–97(t), 97; compared to GAR program (2001–21), 56–58, 57(t), 59
privatized responsibility, for refugee sponsorship/resettlement, 81–85; blended projects and, 98–104; as policy shift away from government, 92–93, 97, 107–9, 117–18, 121–24, 131, 152, 158; recommendation on, 164–65
Project FOCUS Afghanistan, 98, 99
Protecting Canada's Immigration System Act (PCISA), 49–50, 51, 132
protection, refugee, 16, 17, 19, 32–33, 36, 39, 41, 46; *non-refoulement* and, 2–3, 42–44; as resettlement goal, 2, 4, 5–6, 8, 28, 59, 77, 80, 137, 154
Protocol Relating to the Status of Refugees (1967 Protocol), 17, 35–36, 184*n*9
protracted situations, refugees living in, 4, 19, 26, 28–29, 30, 76, 167; Canada and, 59, 141, 142, 146; definition of, 28

Qarizada v. Canada (Minister of Citizenship and Immigration), 68–69

Rainbow Refugee Committee, 100, 144
Red Cross. *See* International Committee of the Red Cross (ICRC)
refugee claimants, 29, 67–76, 79, 120; inland, 42–43, 47, 60, 69, 107–8, 127, 157, 160, 162–63, 168; illegal/

irregular entry by, 27, 46–49, 79, 120, 161, 163–64; overseas, 33–34, 39–41, 42–43; and right to oral hearings, 42, 67, 208n60. *See also* asylum seekers; visa officers

Refugee Council of Australia, 116

Refugee Research Network/Centre for Refugee Studies, policy brief by, 116–17

Refugee Sponsorship Training Program (RSTP), 105

refugees, 2–5, 17, 18; as "desirable," 137, 143; determining status of, 29–30; as "law-abiding"/"patient," 46, 78–79, 146, 159–60; mandate status of, 3–4, 19; as "normal," 25; political, 35, 126–27, 193n34; protection of, 2, 4, 5–6, 8, 28, 59, 77, 80, 137, 154; Third World, 23, 25–26. *See also entry below;* asylum, *and entries following*

refugees, durable solutions to plight of, 2–5, 19, 23, 27, 61, 180n12; resettlement as, 7, 19, 23, 27, 45, 148. *See also* integration, local; repatriation, voluntary; resettlement, *and entries following*

Rehaag, Sean, 30

repatriation, voluntary, 2, 4, 19, 23, 28, 30, 42, 135, 185n17; by Bhutanese refugees, 147; in *IRPR*, 61; as response to UN's exilic bias, 24–26; UNRRA's experience with, 21

resettlement, 2–5; around the world, 6(t), 6–8; vs containment, 24–26; definition of, 2; and dual purposes of burden sharing/protection, 2, 4, 5–6, 8, 28, 59, 77, 80, 137, 154; as durable solution, 7, 19, 23, 27, 45,

148; exilic nature of, 22, 23–25; history of, 19–23, 156; law's role in/relevance to, 1–16, 154–55, 159–62; realities/challenges of, 27–29; and rejection of traditional legal concepts, 10–16; resurgence of interest in, 23, 27; and status determination process, 29–30; as voluntary/non-legal solution, 2–6, 9–10, 42–44, 59, 79, 108, 123, 132, 150, 154–55. *See also entries below;* asylum, *and entries following;* burden sharing, of resettlement

resettlement, in Canada, 1, 6, 7–8, 156–57; background/history of, 32–55; blended program of, 111–14, 158, 163–64; global promotion of, 115–17, 158, 167; as government-assisted, 55–80, 157, 162; by groups, 125–26, 140–52, 158–59; law's role in/relevance to, 1–16, 155, 159–62; as privately sponsored, 81–124, 157–58; recommended restructuring of, 162–67. *See also* government-assisted refugee (GAR) program; private sponsorship of refugees (PSR) program

resettlement, in Canada, refugees considered for, 59–60; convention refugee abroad class, 59–60, 61, 64, 74, 80, 129; country of asylum class, 60, 64, 94, 128, 129, 229n13; source country class, 60, 125–40, 148–52, 158–59

Romani people, 50; as refugee claimants, 51–52, 202n152

Rouleau, Justice Paul, 68

Rural Settlement Society of Canada, 84

Safe Third Country Agreement
   (Canada–US), 47–48, 54, 163
Saul, Ben, 119
Scheingold, Stuart, 117
self-exiled designated persons
   class, 126
self-supporting refugees, 128, 230n16
Sharlow, Justice Karen, 71
Sierra Leone, refugees from, 128;
   blended sponsorship of, 99, 106,
   165–66
*Singh v. Canada (Minister of
   Employment and Immigration)*,
   67–68
Snider, Justice Judith, 73–75
Somali refugees, group resettlement of,
   141, 142, 146–47
source country class, 60, 125–40, 158–59;
   defined, 128; designated countries of,
   by year (1997–2011), 128, 128(t);
   discretionary nature of, 126–27,
   135–36, 148–52. See also entry below
source country class, repeal of, 15, 125,
   127, 128, 129–36, 158–59; and case
   of Colombia, 136–40; and
   "humanitarian and compassionate
   application" section of *IRPA*,
   132–34, 164; as leading to more
   human smuggling, 131, 151, 166;
   poor media coverage of, 150;
   regulatory impact analysis statement
   released with, 130–31, 134–35, 139
Soviet Union, refugees from, 19–20, 83
sponsorship agreement holders
   (SAHs), 75–76, 85, 112, 210n102
Sri Lankan refugees (2000s), 46, 48–49,
   53, 156
Standing Conference of Canadian
   Organizations Concerned for

Refugees, 91. *See also* Canadian
   Council for Refugees (CCR)
Stucky, Peter, 139, 151
Sudan, 37(t), 99; as source
   country, 128, 128(t); group
   resettlement of refugees from, 141,
   142, 146–47
Sun Sea (ship), 48–49, 53
Syrian refugees, 1, 41, 102, 104,
   112–14, 116, 121, 152, 162, 168;
   BVOR program and, 112–14, 122;
   change of government and, 54, 123;
   as compared to Canada-US border
   crossers, 119–20; numbers of, 1,
   112–13, 118, 155; plight of, as
   captured in photo of young drowning
   victim, 1, 112; Trudeau's welcoming
   of, 1, 54, 204n169

Tibet, refugees from, 35
Toews, Vic, 49
Toope, Stephen, 12
Trudeau, Justin, 1, 54, 122, 204n169
Trudeau, Pierre, 90, 92

Uganda, 26, 37(t); LGBTQ refugees
   from, 144; refugees from Amin
   regime in, 35
United Nations General Assembly
   (UNGA), 4, 17, 115
United Nations High Commissioner
   for Refugees (UNHCR), 14, 15, 17,
   19, 35, 56, 66, 75, 115, 155; author's
   work with, 16; and camp-based
   refugees, 119, 137; "Convention
   Plus" initiative of, 27, 58–59, 156;
   creation of, 22; and designated
   refugee classes, 126, 130–31, 134,
   136; exilic orientation of, 22, 23–26;

and family reunification, 27, 95, 109, 218n115; group resettlement by, 140–42, 144, 146–47, 148, 151–52; and *IRPA,* 44–45, 60, 64; and Kosovar refugees, 103; and *PCISA,* 51; and private sponsorship model, 81, 94–95, 105, 109, 115, 118, 163–64; recognition of Canada by, 40–41, 115, 217n96; refugee assessment/resettlement by, 27–29, 30; "resettlement" as defined by, 2; resettlement data from (2010–17), 6(t), 6–7; and shift to reduced/restricted resettlement (late 1980s–90s), 23–25, 41, 42; Statute of, 3, 4, 22, 23; and visa officers' decisions, 60, 69, 74–75, 76, 80, 157

United Nations Relief and Rehabilitation Agency (UNRRA), 21, 23

United Nations Summit for Refugees and Migrants, 115

United States, 7, 21, 30, 39, 51–52, 81, 88, 136; and Bhutanese refugees, 142–43; border issues of, 47–48, 54, 119–20; Canada's *Safe Third Country Agreement* with, 47–48, 54, 163; and Colombian refugees, 137; family reunification in, 166; global resettlement program in, 146; resettlement history/trends in, 6, 22, 34, 36, 45–46, 54, 82, 152; terrorist attacks of 9/11 in, 45–46

urgent protection program (UPP), 64, 65

Versailles, Treaty of, 19

visa officers, 60–80; and BVOR refugees, 56, 86, 100, 111–14, 121–24, 152, 158, 163–64; and global reach of group resettlement, 146; and joint assistance sponsorship, 85; judicial review of decisions by, 66–76, 157; overseas processing manual of, 33, 60, 65, 74, 76; and private sponsorship, 92, 93, 104, 107; regulations governing, 62–64; in source countries, 129, 138; traditional process of referrals by, 85–86, 104, 107, 111; UNHCR and, 60, 69, 74–75, 76, 80, 157; and women at risk, 65

#WelcomeRefugees, 54

Wilson, Justice Bertha, 67–68

Winnipeg, 14, 142; Central Processing Office in, 76; private sponsorship in, 100–2, 108–9

women at risk (AWR) program, 65

Yazidi refugees, 54–55, 104, 119, 152

Yugoslavia, former: pilot sponsorship of refugees from, 98, 99; resettlement of Kosovars from, 102–4